THEMES AND ISSUES IN MODERN
SOCIOLOGY

A Sociology of Work
in Industry

ALAN FOX

Lecturer in Industrial Sociology,
University of Oxford, England

COLLIER-MACMILLAN LIMITED LONDON
THE MACMILLAN COMPANY

To my mother, and in memory of my father

Collier-Macmillan Limited
10 South Audley Street, London W1

The Macmillan Company
Collier-Macmillan Canada Ltd, Toronto

Library of Congress Catalogue Card Number: 69–10537

Printed in England by C. Tinling & Co Ltd.
Prescot and London

CONTENTS

PREFACE

The primary purpose of this book is to suggest a theoretical framework for use in thinking about work relations and the social structures and mechanisms which govern and arise out of them. There is hardly need to stress the importance of theoretical frameworks in organizing and systematizing data, structuring perceptions and definitions of social situations and processes, and generating questions and hypotheses. Since we can scarcely think at all about a subject without some kind of framework, however crude, fragmented, and internally inconsistent, the choice is not between using a framework and not using one, but between using one that is implicit and unconsidered and one that has at least the virtue of being explicit and thus susceptible to conscious thought and challenge.

The sets of phenomena linked by the framework presented here are many and diverse, ranging from the individual's experience in work to propositions about the increasing similarities between the social structures of industrial societies. The hope is that the reader will be alerted to an extensive selection of themes and issues which between them cover a substantial part of the ground usually defined as industrial sociology. The phrase 'extensive selection' connotes further characteristics of this book. 'Selection' speaks for itself, and I have indicated at certain points the directions in which the framework needs to be extended to connect with other major fields of sociological study, such as class structure. The fact of this study being 'extensive' rather than 'intensive' also has consequences worth noting. An extensive examination of a wide-ranging field does not permit such a full delineation of the various viewpoints bearing upon a given controversy as is possible in an intensive study of a limited subject area. This fact has contributed towards making the book very much a personal interpretation, eclectic in its sources of building materials but possibly new in the way it assembles them. One of these sources is the field of study known as 'industrial relations'. This has its own inter-disciplinary practitioners who pursue what has become known in Britain as the 'institutional' approach, and who concern themselves with what are currently defined in public discourse as 'problems' which impede or threaten what they deem the orderly and 'rational' working of the industrial relations system. There is everything to be said, however, for the same phenomena being examined also within the context of a sociological framework which may, in the hands of its users, yield alternative perspectives and generate different kinds of questions. If the framework suggested here achieves no more than the encouragement of better ones it will have served a purpose. Even such usefulness as the present one may possess owes the customary debt to friends and colleagues. The editors of this series, Jean Floud and John Goldthorpe, made many valuable suggestions. Discussions over a long period with Allan Flanders have contributed to my approach to some of the themes and issues dealt with here, and he also read the whole draft and made many constructive comments. I owe a considerable debt, too, to my colleague, A. H. Halsey, who went through the manuscript with great care and at considerable cost in time. Neither he nor anyone else, however, must necessarily be identified with my way of structuring the framework of ideas to be found here.

Finally, I thank Mrs. Sylvia Boyce and Mrs. Jackie Evans for typing successive drafts with speed, accuracy, and great patience.

A.F.

Department of Social and
Administrative Studies,
University of Oxford
May, 1970

CHAPTER I

Orientations to Work

What is the significance and meaning of work in the lives of men and societies? There can hardly be any doubt about one aspect, at least, of its significance. Work is necessary for the production of goods and services. This accounts for the universal interest in the question of what work does *for* people. But it is also possible to be interested in the question of what work does *to* people. Can such a major part of a man's life fail to shape him in some way—to enlarge or diminish him? How does he himself regard work—what does he expect and want from it? How do these expectations and aspirations interact with the work organizations in which he finds himself? What new social processes and structures emerge out of these interactions? How do these affect, in turn, the work organization and the wider society of which it is a part? These are the themes and issues to which this essay will refer. Such is the massive scope of the field, however, that discussion will be confined, in this limited space, to industrial work and organizations.

The opportunity to engage in a widely-ranging discussion of meanings in work is one of the luxuries of technical advance and emancipation from social tradition. For most of man's history, and for many societies still today, the struggle for bare survival has imposed its own imperatives, leaving few choices. These compulsions have often been reinforced by a social fabric of tradition, upheld by a ruling group, which integrated work, status, and religious practices in a way which left little scope for independent speculation. Release from economic necessity and from the bonds of tradition has enabled a small minority in more fortunate societies to engage in philosophical debate about the nature of man and work and the part it should play in human life. As man's command over his physical environment increases, this debate may well grow.

It is a debate of profound significance. Men have no innate, genetically-given orientation towards work. As Wright Mills put it:

'Work may be a mere source of livelihood, or the most significant part of one's inner life; it may be experienced as expiation, or an exuberant expression of self; as bounden duty, or as the development of man's universal nature. Neither love nor hatred of work is inherent in man, or inherent in any given line of work. For work has no intrinsic meaning' (1956, p. 215). This means that attitudes to work are socially and culturally moulded. Men are taught what to expect and want from work—taught by a variety of socializing agencies. What they learn to want is a social fact of great importance and there will be a variety of institutions and groups eager to do the teaching. If war is too important to be left to the generals, work is too important to be left to the workers. Not only will the state itself implicitly or explicitly encourage certain attitudes to work and discourage others, but so also will social institutions such as industry, business and commerce, religion, and the educational system. Relevant strands in the cultural tradition will exert their influence through education and communications media. The local community, the family and the work group will also contribute their effect. Finally, interested parties such as professional associations, employers' associations and trade unions may seek to consolidate or change the prevailing orientations. Out of all these influences upon different social groups and classes, different orientations to work are created. Theoretically, perhaps, a society could be so monolithic that all the agencies of socialization disseminate one doctrine only and no rival philosophy is permitted. Orwell's *1984* offers a sketch of what such a society might be like. Thought control has not, however, reached this stage in practice. Nevertheless, societies differ considerably in the freedom with which they permit competing doctrines to vie for influence over men's orientations to work. Countries within the Soviet orbit use their control over communications to maintain an ideology of perpetual national emergency, 'anchored in the theory of a working-class state surrounded by imperialist powers of the capitalist West' (Bendix, 1956, p. 443). The ideology is then used to support an 'unremitting pressure for performance' in work. By contrast, societies which allow a large measure of freedom of association and expression of opinion are likely to contain a range of diverse philosophies. In the United States, for example, a gospel which values work as a means to maximizing consumption exists alongside a minority youth culture which urges the total rejection of these·values.

1 WORK IN HISTORICAL PERSPECTIVE

No adequate history of the meaning of work has been written, but Tilgher's study at least demonstrates how these meanings have shifted along with changes in the social order (1930). To the ancient Greeks, for example, work was simply a curse. Most Greek thinkers grudgingly accepted agriculture as not unworthy of a citizen since it brought livelihood and independence, but most deplored the mechanical arts as brutalizing the mind in a way that rendered it unfit for contemplation and the practice of virtue. Rome followed Greece in these respects. The Hebrews likewise saw work as painful drudgery, but also as a way of expiating sin and recovering lost spiritual dignity. For primitive Christianity, labour had no intrinsic value or importance, but was instrumental in promoting health of body and soul, making possible the virtue of charity and guarding against 'evil thoughts and habits'. Early Catholicism does something to dignify work, and the aristocratic Greek scorn of the labouring classes diminishes. But work is never exalted as having any value in itself, and remains simply an instrument of purification, charity and expiation.

With Luther is ushered in the Protestant Ethic. For Luther, as for medieval Catholicism, work is the natural affliction of 'fallen man'. But originality enters with the notion that work is a form of serving God. With this idea, Luther sweeps away all distinction between religious piety and worldly activity; profession becomes 'calling' and work is valued as a means towards spiritual salvation. To this, Calvin added the virtues of austerity. Men must not lust after the fruits of their labour—wealth, possessions, soft living. Their sweat and toil have value only as they help to establish the Kingdom of God on earth.

'All this', observes Tilgher, 'sounds like the beginning of modern business. And so it is ... With the new creed comes a new man, strong-willed, active, austere, hard-working from religious conviction ... Dislike of work is considered a sign that election is doubtful'. Moreover, intermittent work will not do: it must be methodical, disciplined and rational. 'To select a calling and follow it with all one's conscience is a religious duty. Calvinism thus lays the foundation of the tremendous discipline of the modern factory founded on the division of labour—very different from the easygoing ways of the independent artisan' (Tilgher, 1962, p. 19). The significance of these ideas for the growth of modern capitalism has of course been argued by Weber (1930). None of the religious reformers 'had any thought of promoting "the spirit of capitalism"', but Weber hoped to show that their doctrines nevertheless contained implicit incentives in this direction. . . .' (Bendix, 1966, p. 58).

Worldly success and the acquisition of possessions proved not long compatible, however, with ideas of austerity and asceticism. In the course of a massive process of secularization, the search for the kingdom of God through work was replaced by a utilitarian industriousness and a specifically bourgeois economic ethos. 'Since asceticism undertook to remodel the world. . . .', wrote Weber, 'material goods have gained an increasing and finally an inexorable power over the lives of men as at no previous period in history . . . Victorious capitalism, since it rests on mechanical foundations, needs its support no longer . . . The idea of duty in one's calling prowls about in our lives like the ghost of dead religious beliefs' (1930, pp. 181–2). Ideas and values generated within a specific social and religious order thus took on autonomous life for ideological use in a vastly different context. The nineteenth century was the Golden Age for the idea of work. Its leading thinkers exalted work to a position far above any it had hitherto held in religion or ethics, making it the cause of all human progress, material, intellectual, and spiritual. The essence of this gospel was that productivity and technical progress were the only justifications that work needed. It was not only the medium for individual advancement, offering 'opportunity' for 'self-help' and 'self-improvement', but also the major criterion by which societies were to be compared. In the words of Frederick Winslow Taylor, the pioneer of scientific management, 'In my judgment, the best possible measure of the height in the scale of civilization to which any people has arisen is its productivity' (Ward, 1964, p. 66). Only in modern Western civilization could that remark have been made. It remains today the most frequently adduced criterion of judgement between the countries of the world.

All the philosophies of work noted so far ascribe to it an extrinsic meaning. Work yields no value in and through itself, but is seen solely in terms of its instrumental character, as a means to some end. But other philosophies invest work with intrinsic meaning. Value is sought in and through the activities of work themselves, which are seen, not as a burden to be borne for the sake of their instrumental usefulness, but as enriching experiences through which men can meet challenges and overcome obstacles, develop their aptitudes and abilities, and enjoy the satisfactions of achievement. In the course of these experiences men undergo psychological growth, realise themselves, and reach due stature as full, mature and autonomous moral agents. Perhaps the central notion here can be expressed in the language of decision-making, choice and responsibility. Men make themselves through their own choices—by taking decisions and accepting responsibility for what they choose. This is the process of self-determination and growth. A work situation which offers no—or only the most trivial—opportunities for choice, decision, and the acceptance of responsibility is therefore one which offers no opportunities for growth.

This concept derives essentially from the Renaissance, but received passionate emphasis during the nineteenth century by minority critics convinced that capitalism was destroying these characteristics of work. In a powerful assertion of what was now becoming a secular humanism, Marx argued in his early philosophical writings that alienation, or the loss of a sense of self, was rooted primarily in the dehumanization of work. 'In what does this alienation of labour consist? First, that the work is *external* to the worker, that it is not a part of his nature, that consequently he does not fulfil himself in his work but denies himself, has a feeling of misery, not of well-being, does not develop freely a physical and mental energy, but is physically exhausted and mentally debased. The worker therefore feels himself at home only during his leisure, whereas at work he feels homeless. His work is not voluntary but imposed, *forced labour*. It is not the satisfaction of a need, but only a *means* for satisfying other needs' (Bottomore and Rubel, 1963, p. 177).

In the same tradition was William Morris who, along with others such as Ruskin and Carlyle, denounced the increasingly elaborate division of labour and fragmentation of work. One kind of work, argued Morris, was good—'not far removed from a blessing'—the other kind was bad—'a burden to life'. The difference was that good work contained hope—'hope of product, hope of pleasure in the work itself ... All other work but this is worthless; it is slaves' work—mere toiling to live, that we may live to toil' (1885, reprinted in Briggs, 1962, pp. 117–9). The Renaissance ideal had come forward to other spokesmen of modern liberalism who stressed the priceless value of the individual personality; asserted man to be the measure of all things; and urged that institutions and societies be judged in terms of what they meant to and for the individual human being. L. T. Hobhouse's classic statement of this position in *Liberalism* declares that the liberal's concept of the common good 'is founded on personality, and postulates free scope for the development of personality in each member of the community' (1911, p. 130).

The same conception is to be found in the writings of Maslow (1954, 1965), Argyris (1957, 1964), McGregor (1960), Herzberg (1957, 1968), and others. The individual is seen as having potentiality for meeting challenges, exercising responsibility, developing independence, and freely expressing a range of talents and aptitudes. Through these means he becomes an autonomous moral agent and achieves psychological growth in a process of 'self-actualization'. Argyris, for example, asserts that 'healthy adults will tend to obtain optimum personality expression while at work if they are provided with jobs which permit them to be more active than passive; more independent than dependent; to have longer rather than shorter time perspectives; . . . to have control over their world; and to express many of their deeper, more important abilities' (1957, p. 53). Modern industry often fails, however, in the opinion of this school, to provide the structural conditions for producing the mature, healthy, self-actualizing individual. Rather does it, in many cases, through its fragmentation and dehumanization of work and its bureaucratic, authoritarian forms of organization, stunt and impoverish his development.

Some of the most important spokesmen of this school present their definition of man's needs in work as a universal concept.[1] The assumption is that all men, everywhere, can and should achieve self-actualization within an organizational context structured to promote psychological growth along the dimensions described. Herzberg's model relates to 'the nature of man' not 'as imposed by any particular economic or social institution, but the nature of man as it is in reality, regardless of the needs of the controlling forces' (1968, p. 43). Other members of the school enter appropriate *caveats*. Maslow, more cautious than many of his disciples, stresses the 'shaky foundation' of his self-actualization propositions; suggests that their validity may well be limited to certain kinds of culture and certain types of personality structure; and emphasizes the need for more research (1965).

Most writers of this persuasion, however, have not hesitated to urge the re-designing, re-organizing and re-structuring of work to meet the supposed requirements of the 'natural man'. Some of the features they recommend derive from what Wright Mills calls the

---

[1] Etzioni, too, asserts the usefulness of the concept of a universal set of basic human needs which have attributes of their own that are not determined by social structure, cultural patterns, or socialization processes (1968). These go beyond the purely biological to include such needs as affection and recognition for achievement.

'craft ethic', which can of course apply to intellectual, artistic and other non-manual work as well as manual. First, the supreme concern is with the quality of the product and the skill of its making. Other motives and results—money, status, reputation or spiritual salvation—are subordinate. Second, although the producer (*pace* Marx) need not legally own the product, he must own it psychologically, 'in the sense that he knows what goes into it by way of skill, sweat, and material, and that his own skill and sweat are visible to him'. He sees the place of his contribution in the whole, and thus understands the meaning of his exertion in terms of that whole. Some of the work may be drudgery and some difficult, but the producer gains positive satisfaction from encountering a resistance and subduing it. Third, the producer is free to work according to his own plan, and bears the commensurate responsibility. He is thereby master of both the activity and of himself. Fourth, his work is therefore both a means of developing his skill and a means of developing himself as a man. Self-development is not an ulterior goal, but the cumulative result of devotion to, and practice of, his skills. As he gives to his work the quality of his own mind and skill, he is further developing his own nature and so lives in and through his work, 'which confesses and reveals him to the world'. Fifth, in the craft ethic there is no divorce of work and play, work and culture. 'Play is something you do to be happily occupied, but if work occupies you happily, it is also play, although it is also serious, just as play is to the child'. In the craft model of activity, 'consumption' and 'production' are blended in the same act, and there is no split between culture and work. Finally, the craftsman's work 'is the mainspring of the only life he knows; he does not flee from work into a separate sphere of leisure; he brings to his non-working hours the values and qualities developed and employed in his working time' (Mills, 1956, pp. 220–23).

As against the contention of the self-actualization school that work, as a central life interest, should be designed to provide these deeper, intrinsic meanings and values, there are modern re-statements of the alternative doctrine that is readier to accept that much work can be expected to yield only, or predominantly, extrinsic satisfactions. In the Protestant Ethic work is seen as a means to spiritual grace. In the new ethic of instrumentality work is seen largely as a means to a steadily-rising material standard of life and the pursuit of leisure activities of a wide variety of kinds outside work—as a means, in short, of expanding consumption generally.

Along with this view goes a repudiation of the contention that work ought to be a central, integrating principle crucial to the development of the individual's personality and social frame of reference. The same purposes can be served, it is said, by activities outside work (Dubin, 1956; Dubin, 1959). 'Many people find a full measure of challenge, creativity, and autonomy in raising a family, pursuing a hobby, or taking part in community affairs' (Strauss, 1963, pp. 47, 52). Writers of this persuasion are not simply recording facts. They also reveal their belief that there is nothing specially to regret or deplore in the fact that, 'for probably a majority of workers and even extending into the ranks of management', work does not offer experiences sufficiently meaningful to constitute a central life interest (Dubin, 1968, pp. 90–92). Any preoccupation with this as a social problem they dismiss as being inspired by academics and other intellectuals who merely seek to impose their own work ethic upon their fellows (Strauss, 1963).

Whatever validity is accorded to a purely or predominantly instrumental view of work, the extrinsic rewards are obviously of great importance. To those mentioned already must be added status, security, and satisfying social relationships. 'As a social role played in relation to other people, work may become a source of self-esteem, on the job, among co-workers, superiors, subordinates, and customers, if any; and off the job, among friends, family and community at large ... It is the status conferred on the exercise of given skills and on given income levels that is often the prime source of gratification or humiliation' (Mills, 1956, p. 231). Security may be of even greater significance. 'An undertow of anxiety about sickness, accident, or old age must support eagerness for work, and gratification may be based on the compulsion to relieve anxiety by working hard. Widespread unemployment, or fear of it, may even make an employee happily thankful for any job ...' (Mills, 1956, p. 231). Finally, the quality of social relationships with subordinates, fellow-employees or superiors may be sufficiently central for some to determine their choice of employment.

2 SUBSTANTIVE AND PROCEDURAL ORIENTATIONS

The orientations towards work that have been examined so far relate to the nature of the work and its accompanying social relations, how it is to be done, its rights and obligations, and its rewards and prospects. These quantitative and qualitative dimensions of work are determined, as we shall see, by decisions made both inside and outside the work organization. The orientations which the individual brings to bear upon these various dimensions of work may be called 'substantive' orientations. Insofar as he aspires to improve his position in respect of one or more of these dimensions—in the sense of wanting more money, for example, or greater security, or more challenging work—he may be said to have substantive aspirations. But besides having orientations towards the substantive outcome of the decision-making procedures which determine the nature and rewards of work, the individual may also be said to have orientations towards the nature of the decision-making procedures themselves. In other words, he has 'procedural' orientations. He may be prepared, for example, to see the decisions made wholly by others. If, on the other hand, he aspires to play some part, directly or indirectly, in decision-making procedures, he can be said to have procedural aspirations. The range of possible aspirations is wide. He may seek the right simply to be informed of proposed decisions in the hope that his reactions may be taken into account; or to protest against decisions when made; or to make suggestions before they are made; or to participate jointly, directly or indirectly through representatives, with management in actually making them, or to make them in concert with his fellows and impose them on management. Even these do not include all the possibilities. The range of substantive decisions in which the individual may seek to participate is equally wide, extending from the determination of a piece-rate to major policy decisions at the highest level.

Whether he prefers some sort of participation or none, he may see his choice as either instrumental (a means to an end) or terminal (an end in itself). An instrumental preference for non-participation may result from the individual's conviction (i) that to demand a role in decision-making would be construed by organizational leaders as evidence of disaffection or of lack of confidence in their ability or good faith, and (ii) that this reaction on their part would be harmful to his or his group's interests. A terminal preference for non-participation would indicate a situation in which he valued a dependency relationship for its own sake—as, for example, in the case of deference to a charismatic leader, or in a successful paternalistic system where the employer ranks as a father figure, or in an authoritarian culture where he has internalized a principle of submissiveness to the superior.

An instrumental preference for participation expresses a belief that only by being free from dependence on management's grace and favour can the individual be sure of the chance to pursue substantive aspirations and defend such gains as may have been made. His concern may be purely self-regarding or on behalf of his group or class. The terminal preference for participation arises in situations where the individual presents some degree of ideological challenge to managerial prerogative, or where he has internalized values linking participation with self-respect and human dignity for himself, his group or his class.

In this whole question of participation and non-participation we are concerned with attitudes towards relationships of superordination and subordination in which cultural and subcultural influences are of obvious importance. This presents us with contrasts such as those between Japanese and American management. The system of authority in the Japanese industrial enterprise is strikingly undifferentiated from that in the family, the related family clan, and other social groupings. The values of traditional Japanese feudalism appear to have been carried over, and with this heritage Japanese management has 'found it relatively easy to develop a subordinated and loyal work force, and . . . has encountered relatively little difficulty in the preservation and the exercise of its prerogatives' (Harbison and Myers, 1959, p. 254; Abegglen, 1958; Hagen, 1965).[2] In the United States, on the other hand, as political ideals of equality and the importance of the individual have gained wider acceptance there has developed a 'conflict between a deep-seated egalitarianism and the functional necessity for a certain degree of authoritarianism in relationships within the industrial organization' (Worthy, 1957, p. 18).

3 EXTRINSIC AND INTRINSIC VALUES IN WORK

Industrial societies thus offer conflicting doctrines of the meaning of work which vie for men's allegiance. The broadest division is between those doctrines which seek to persuade us that work ought to be a central integrating principle of man's individual and social being, offering opportunities of choice, decision, and responsibility, and those which find no ethical difficulty in seeing its major significance in terms of its extrinsic outcome. Those who accept the former have to endure moral unease, for it is clear not only that a

---

[2] Odaka (1963) adds some necessary qualifications to this view and argues that in any case the institutions and values of work and industry in Japan will increasingly resemble those of the West.

great deal of work is designed in ways which afford no opportunities for individual growth and development, but also that this is widely known and tolerated. Those who accept the latter view are rejecting, not the proposition that *some* men may find work a fulfilling and deeply satisfying life interest, but the proposition that work necessarily *ought* to play this role. If fulfilment can be found outside the work sphere, and if work is seen as having no special significance in man's individual and social life, we have a convenient way of avoiding an apparent moral dilemma.

But what if the quality of experience in work helps to determine the quality of experience outside work? How far does the former 'spill over' into the latter, as distinct from the latter 'compensating' for the former? The relationships between work and non-work cannot be pursued here, but research hardly supports the proposition that those whose personality is, in terms of the cultural definitions of most Western industrial societies, stunted and impoverished by their work situation are easily able and likely to find fulfilment and enrichment outside it (Clarke, 1956; Parker, 1965; Kornhauser, 1965). There is persuasive evidence that work is a major formative experience which can either promote or limit a man's growth in ways which affect the whole man and which therefore shape his life outside the job as well as within it.[3]

Should we, then, as Friedmann suggests (1961), set ourselves the long-term goal of re-designing work in directions which lead towards self-actualization for everyone? (See also Davis, 1966). There are arguments on two different levels which must caution us in this apparently admirable aim. Those whose life experience and cultural values have created neither the expectation of, nor the aspiration for, self-actualization may prove remarkably resistant to this treatment, as may also those whose authoritarian personality structure disposes

---

[3] New considerations may apply, however, if technology brings the advanced countries to a point where they can and do choose to make leisure the decisively predominant part of each day. When work can no longer be, for good or ill, a major formative experience, those who attach value to what they define as 'psychological growth' will no doubt hope to shape leisure behaviour along lines which provide an adequate substitute. We may thus see an accelerated growth of leisure activities which involve challenge, skill, knowledge and judgement. We may also expect a growing anxious debate on the relationship between work and leisure (Greenberg, 1958; Riesman, 1958; Dumazedier, 1967; Ross, 1966; Wilensky, *et al.,* 1962), and on the moral nature of a society whose members experience self-actualization, if at all, not as the by-product of efforts towards some independently-valued social objective, but as the central aim of activities specifically designed to absorb the energies and talents of the individual.

them to prefer a situation of dependence on, and domination by, others. On a more fundamental level we are faced with a structural dilemma deriving from the fact that work, besides being a major force in shaping us as persons, is also an instrumental necessity. Whether or not men are concerned with its effects upon their personality growth and development—with the effects work has upon them as producers—they can hardly be indifferent to the instrumental effectiveness with which work serves their needs and desires for goods and services—to its efficiency in meeting their aspirations as consumers.

No great knowledge of the world of work is required to discern that producer and consumer values are often in conflict. The manufacture of cars one by one in small workshops might serve the interests of workers as producers, but would hardly serve their interests as consumers in the availability of a cheap, mass-produced model. The advocacy of self-actualization as the reference-point by which work design should be judged is vitiated unless it comes to grips with the role of work in serving purely economic or consumer values. As we saw at the outset, men assess work in terms of what it does *for* them as well as what it does *to* them.

One tempting way out of the dilemma is to assert that the conflict is unreal; that on an enlightened long-term view the structural arrangements of work which best serve man's interest as a producer by enlarging opportunities for self-actualization will also be found to serve best his interests as a consumer by raising productivity. This conviction emerges, sometimes explicitly, sometimes implicitly, from much of the writing of the self-actualization school. In Maslow's words, to organize people for work as if they are 'mentally healthy' adults seeking self-actualization is, in the long run and given certain qualifications, 'the path to success of any kind whatsoever, including financial success' (1965, p. 41). Tavistock Institute consultant-researchers developed the idea of the 'best fit' between technology and social organization, the assumption being 'that in the "right" organization' the job conditions 'required for task performance were always identical with those required to satisfy the social and psychological needs' (Miller and Rice, 1967, p. xii). Examples of the successful application to manual wage-earners of this approach have been documented (Trist, *et al.,* 1963; Rice, 1963). At the higher levels of occupational status the proposition has always been true. Doctors, lawyers, architects, university teachers, research scientists, higher managers and administrators: for all of them the conditions for performing the task effectively are also, for the most part, conditions which provide scope for meeting challenges, carrying responsibility, exercising independence, enlarging knowledge, and enjoying opportunities for achievement and recognition.

It requires the eye of faith, however, to glimpse such possibilities for a large proportion of the world's work. A more balanced judgement would be that scientific management principles such as 'maximal task breakdown' still have much to contribute to industrial efficiency as measured in terms of costs, despite the challenge to their *universal* validity that has been so rightly and successfully mounted in recent years. We cannot resolve our dilemma with the simple formula that 'what is good for people is good for the organization'. Even the Tavistock researchers have been forced to conclude in their more recent work that 'there are settings where elegant solutions of this kind cannot be found or where, if found, they introduce new and intractable constraints' (Miller and Rice, 1967, p. xii).

A category of privilege therefore emerges. Some forms of work enable men to grow towards what their societies define as full human stature; many others do not. It can hardly escape notice that the former are usually accompanied by additional privileges of other sorts in terms of higher income, security, and occupational status. What of the latter forms? It might seem that here man has a choice. He can so design these less felicitous forms of work as to put the emphasis either on extrinsic or intrinsic rewards, instrumental or terminal values, consumer or producer interests. This is one of those propositions, however, in which the abstract mode of expression is apt to veil the social reality. Most individuals have little or no real opportunity to make a rational choice. Some can make a limited choice of sorts between increments of earnings and marginal improvements in intrinsic rewards (Ingham, 1967). But in order to make a rational choice of emphasis as between the full range of intrinsic and extrinsic rewards one must have experienced both sorts in all that they have to offer, and this condition is not fulfilled for major proportions of industrial populations.[4] Instead they tend to be conditioned by a wide variety of socializing agencies to accept a doctrine of work which expects and seeks largely instrumental satisfactions. To these conditioning factors we now turn.

---

[4] Here we touch on the issue of occupational mobility. It can be explored further in Lipset and Bendix, (1959); Harris and Clausen, (1966); and Hunter and Reid, (1968) (which has a large bibliography).

4 DETERMINANTS OF WORK PHILOSOPHIES

One massive socializing agency is the experience of work itself. The kinds of work that are required to be done and the ways in which it is organized embody philosophies of work, whether work-designers and organizers are aware of it or not. Most work embodies a preference for consumer rather than for producer values. It is likely to offer extrinsic rather than intrinsic rewards. Only a small proportion of work, comprising mainly managerial, professional, scientific, craft, intellectual, and artistic labours offers anything substantial in the way of the latter. Whatever the situation in pre-industrial societies—and for all the Pre-Raphaelite nostalgia we know little of the medieval experience of work—the modern criterion of job design is likely to be in terms of man's interests as a consumer rather than his interests as a producer. It is oriented towards minimum costs and maximum output rather than towards self-actualization and fulfilment.

For large numbers of people, therefore, and particularly those in the lower ranks of the occupational hierarchy, the lesson taught by the experience of work is that it must be expected to offer mainly extrinsic satisfactions. Intrinsically, it must be expected to be burdensome, restrictive and often irksome, involving subjection to the control of others and often proving monotonous and stultifying into the bargain. The nature of their adaptive responses will be examined more fully later: here we can note briefly that a common pattern is to lower aspirations or rationalize skin-deep levels of satisfaction into major justifications of one's work. Baldamus notes 'an interpretation of industrial work that has had considerable appeal to managerial executives and professional people: the notion that wage-earners, even at the lower levels of skill, find a great deal of "satisfaction" in their occupation. However, when one looks more closely into the matter, such satisfactions reveal themselves as more or less illusory. They are largely substitute goals or rationalizations which are a function of deprivation, not an independent variable in the motivation to work' (1961, p. 124). In the words of Argyris, 'We could argue that the workers are saying (1) "I must enjoy it in order to live with myself" (thereby reducing the potentiality for dissonance); (2) "I must enjoy it or else I have to go through the extremely difficult task of finding another job" (thereby again reducing the probability of his own unhappiness and discomfort); and (3) "One way to live with the job is to enjoy it"' (Argyris, 1964, p. 70). The existence of these adaptive responses explains the apparent discrepancy between attitude surveys which report a high degree of 'job satisfaction' even among many lower-level workers, and the resignation, pessimism, discouragement and fatalism so often found by sociologists in working-class culture (Argyris, 1964; Goldthorpe, *et al.*, 1969a).

The reference to culture introduces a second major socializing influence. Broad cultural values and ideologies may materially shape attitudes to work and to relationships of subordination and dependency and other variables (Hagen, 1965; Palmer, 1960; Williams, *et al.*, 1966). All values and attitudes capable of being expressed in the work situation, in fact, are potential influences upon orientations to work and upon the social patterns that result. Crozier, for example, suggests ways in which the French value system affected attitudes and social processes in two large public bureaucracies (1964). An aversion to dependency and conflict in face-to-face relationships was carried over into the work situation and resulted in a proliferation of impersonal rules and a tendency towards centralization of decision-making. More generally, it is clear that in a culture where, for example, the ethical code successfully demands of the individual 'subordination to his superiors, respect for his elders, and complete identification with the goals of the house' (Harbison and Myers, 1959; Abegglen, 1958), as in the earlier industrial phases of Japan (now changing), attitudes in the work situation will differ sharply from those of a culture where attitudes are markedly less respectful, as in Australia, Britain and the United States. Cultural variations between societies have also been noted in respect of the relative importance placed on different types of extrinsic reward. Asked to indicate a preference as between a job offering high occupational status and low pay and one offering low status and high pay, a majority of the American respondents to a survey questionnaire, even among the college graduates, opted for the latter, while in Germany and Poland similar studies suggested that white-collar status is given more weight than income (Lipset, 1961).

Equally as important as general cultural values are the values of subcultures. 'Years of experience with varying degrees of frustration, conflict, dependence, apathy and failure influence and become a part of the working-class culture, and are then communicated to the children' (Argyris, 1964, p. 81). From the earliest age, children from manual wage-earning families are likely to be absorbing from parents, relatives and older siblings a multitude of hints and cues as to the expectations that it is appropriate to entertain about work. By the time they themselves enter work their level of aspirations may

already be suitably adjusted downward. This characteristic resignation may extend not only to the job after it is secured, but also the
very choice of job. Thus the pessimism and resignation generated by
job-structures become self-fulfilling prophecies as they are handed
down from generation to generation.

It is clear, then, that a substantial component of the subculture
within which the individual is socialized is itself a product distilled
from generations of experience in a particular type of work situation.
To this extent, the so-called 'action' approach which stresses the
importance of the orientations and aspirations which employees
bring with them into the organization and which shape their frame of
reference and thereby their perceptions and behaviour, need not be
seen as in any way at odds with the approach which stresses the effect
of organization and job design upon the individual. The orientations
he brings with him may be the subcultural consequence of this very
kind of job design.

However, this component of the subculture may be sufficiently
strong in some situations to take on autonomous life of its own which
makes it, in the short and perhaps medium term, independent of the
nature of job design. A management hoping, say, to derive a benefit
by promoting an intrinsic orientation to work among their employees may be disappointed to discover that their proposals to
re-design work in this direction meet with resistance (Pym, 1968).
There may be every reason for their persisting, but the process of
learning a new approach to work may be long and not without tears.
Dockworkers in Britain's port transport industry will come under
pressure to learn a new work culture more appropriate to a re-
organized industry purged of the evils of casualisation and employer
indifference, but the strength of the old docks culture may make this
learning period a long one.

The possibility in situations of this sort is that any impulse to
reform organizational and job design may wither under the apparent
evidence that employee responses are incapable of change. Management may slip back to old practices and attitudes and the consequent
continued 'failure' of employees to change their ways is seen as
further evidence of the futility of attempting reform. This 'self-
fulfilling prophecy' may have even wider expression. Managers who
assume wage-earners to be incapable of aspiring to intrinsic values in
work may for this reason design systems of production which exclude
any likelihood of intrinsic satisfactions being derived. These systems
understandably generate a culture which teaches a purely instru-

mental attitude to work and indifference to management objectives. The 'discovery' that these are the attitudes which prevail among workers will then be hailed as evidence that the productive system was soundly designed and must be preserved.

Although any component of a subculture which has been induced by the characteristic work situation may for a while outlive major changes in that work situation, it may be strongly doubted whether it would survive indefinitely. Employees are likely to learn, however slowly, a new culture and a new orientation to work. It is quite otherwise, however, with those components of the subculture which, though not necessarily generated by the work situation, nevertheless shape orientations towards it. By definition, these will survive changes in the work situation. Important among them in industrial societies is the high—and growing—expectation of a constantly rising material standard of life. This may increasingly divert the individual's interest away from intrinsic rewards to the extrinsic factor of income.[5] Insofar as this occurs, efforts by management to promote employees' concern with intrinsic rewards by re-designing work may meet with little success. Herzberg suggests that American professional men are increasingly preoccupied with extrinsic rewards. 'Professionalism, once a sign of true competence and dedication to excellence in performance, has now become a synonym for gathering the harvest of the hygiene factors of status and money' (1968, p. 184). If the search for extrinsic rewards does come to predominate even in an environment so favourable to intrinsic values as professional work, the effect that can be exerted upon work attitudes by cultural pressures outside the work situation is plain to see. The survival chances of intrinsic values in less favourable work environments would then seem bleak.

The tendency to see work mainly in terms of its instrumental values has been greatly strengthened by certain characteristics of modern, industrial, consumer-oriented society. Industry, business and commerce, with their direct and indirect power over the content of radio and television, motion pictures, newspapers, magazines, and advertising and selling activities, have no interest in promoting the intrinsic values of work. Their interest lies in encouraging the idea that the sole purpose of production is consumption. Thus over a wide range

[5] This point must be kept in perspective by remembering that at low income levels a failure to focus primarily on extrinsic rewards may make it difficult not simply to 'keep up with the Joneses' but also to escape from bad housing, poor diet, ill health, and an unfavourable social and educational environment for one's children.

of goods and services the productive process 'creates the wants that the goods are presumed to satisfy' (Galbraith, 1962, p. 133). Galbraith comments that the urgency of the wants can no longer be used to defend the urgency of the production, since production only fills a void that it has itself created.[6] 'The individual who urges the importance of production to satisfy these wants is precisely in the position of the onlooker who applauds the efforts of the squirrel to keep abreast of the wheel that is propelled by his own efforts. . . . Among the many models of the good society no one has urged the squirrel wheel' (pp. 132, 136).

Modern governments share the preoccupation with output to the exclusion of other rewards in work. Caught between the pressures of ever-rising public expenditure and taxpayer resistance; burdened perhaps with problems relating to the country's external trade; convinced that international political influence and world status are closely linked with economic strength; governments too find them-selves urging economic growth to the exclusion of intrinsic satis-factions. If the latter exist, they are seen as merely incidental by-products; any thought of achieving them at the cost of growth or efficiency becomes unthinkable.

There are yet more fundamental reasons why advanced industrial society comes under strong pressures to be 'growth-oriented'. Popular wisdom is now that the economic apparatus of the modern capitalist society cannot stand still; it must grow or be threatened with instability. The complex interrelationships of production, in-vestment and savings have to be supported by a dynamic of ex-pansion, and any significant and prolonged check to that expansion throws the stability of the whole structure in doubt. Markets, insti-tutions, international trade, currency values: all become geared to the values of growth, competition and efficiency. The society may become, in Rostow's words, 'structurally committed to a high-consumption way of life' (1963, p. 81).

---

[6] Galbraith is speaking here of the United States. There is, of course, 'the other America' (Harrington, 1962), the 'rediscovered' poor who may see the currently-fashionable disparagement of the consumer society as somewhat premature. Large sections of the working class in other countries may feel the same. This leads on to a further point. Galbraith and others writing in a like vein, such as Mishan (1969), are making a social comment of great importance, but it must be carefully disentangled from a certain middle-class sourness towards alleged working class 'affluence' which is apt to emerge in somewhat similar terms. Those who already have their washing-machine, refrigerator, car, and wall-to-wall carpets may find it easy to feel that those still struggling hard to achieve them are displaying an excessive concern with material standards, and that this denotes a society sadly indifferent to higher things.

The social and political problems attendant upon any marked change in these values would certainly be considerable. Thus, supposedly trapped within the pressures of their own dynamics, such societies incessantly promote consumption as the supreme good; if not at home then in export markets abroad. The circularity of the process now becomes evident. Men must be encouraged to consume in order that the institutions of production be preserved in a healthy and stable condition. To what end? To the end of further consumption. To break out of this circularity in order, say, to sacrifice efficiency to intrinsic values in work might require economic and social adjustments on a scale which societies have admittedly come nowhere near mastering.[7]

The very nature of industrial society thus gives its major centres of power a variety of motives for promoting consumer values at the expense of producer values. For many of those who directly or indirectly control or carry responsibility for the use of resources, any widespread demand for intrinsic work satisfactions would limit their freedom or their profits or both; render many problems even more difficult; and introduce a new and troublesome dimension to the parameters of decision-making. Given incentives like these on the part of ruling groups, there is no cause for surprise that, in the words of T. B. Bottomore, 'the working class in all countries has continued to be profoundly influenced by the dominant ideas of capitalist society; . . . by the competitive, acquisitive and possessive conception of human nature and social relations, and in recent times by a view of the overriding purpose of society as being the creation of ever greater material wealth' (1965, p. 73). Reinforcing the actual experience of work, therefore, which for many teaches resignation to the relative lack of intrinsic satisfactions, is a set of values that stresses the importance of extrinsic satisfactions, 'that emphasizes and sanctions the competitive struggle of individuals and groups to improve their lot, to get as much as they can according to the rules of the game. Our society "believes in" people's wanting more than they have and approves their efforts to advance their own interests' (Kornhauser, 1954, pp. 79–80).

[7] This may be all the more reason, of course, for trying to evolve adequate techniques for making such adjustments. If this cannot be done, industrial societies will be trapped for ever within the dynamics of the consumer-oriented society and its absolute value of economic growth. Those who contemplate this prospect calmly are recommended to read Mishan (1969a). He presents a popular version for non-economists (1969b) which, despite its highly dubious rose-tinted nostalgia for 'the world we have lost', remains persuasive.

The local community and the work group, as well as the family, may play an important part in transmitting these and other orienta-tions to the individual. 'The goals a person seeks are those he has "absorbed" from the groups of which he has been and is a member. He comes to act, think, perceive, and feel as his social groups expect him to; he learns to accept the values, and to be the kind of person his society calls for; and specifically, he lives up to what is expected of persons in the status and roles he occupies. What models are set for him as worthy and unworthy goals? . . . The individual learns to want and seek those things he is supposed to want according to the standards of his family, friends, and larger reference groups' (Korn-hauser, 1954, p. 67).

Applying the test of 'cui bono?' may therefore give useful clues when we seek the origins of, or the sources of support for, ideologies and communications which stress consumer values to the exclusion of producer values in work. No hypothesis of a conspiracy by the powerful is needed here; simply a recognition that men with similar interests may well behave similarly even though independently of each other, and that if they are powerful they will find ready servitors eager to volunteer ways of ministering to their requirements. Once successfully promoted and disseminated, these, like other values, may acquire an autonomous role. Power may still be important in promoting their legitimacy and discouraging rival values, but by creating habitual cultural responses which are transmitted to new generations, and by becoming embodied in social mechanisms and institutions, they come to possess their own independent dynamic.

As a result of all this, neither the secularized gospel of work as an inner compulsion nor the humanist view of work as craftmanship has great influence in modern industrial society. 'For most employees, work has a generally unpleasant quality. If there is little Calvinist compulsion to work among propertyless factory workers and file clerks, there is also little Renaissance exuberance in the work of the insurance clerk, freight handler, or department store saleslady . . . For the white-collar masses, as for wage-earners generally, work seems to serve neither God nor whatever they may experience as divine in themselves. In them there is no taut will-to-work, and few positive gratifications from their daily round' (Mills, 1956, p. 219). The factors which therefore come more to the front are the extrinsic satisfactions of income, security and status. Among wage-earners, the principal concern is with the first two rather than with the third. If status is actively pursued, it may be as an instrumental rather than a terminal value, for the relationship between income and status is reciprocal (Wootton, 1955). Such evidence as we have from the Soviet Union reveals many similarities with the West. 'Manual workers . . . find the working environment on balance unpleasant and uncongenial both in its personal and social aspects . . . The pattern of complaints suggests the greater relative importance to the manual worker of pay, and secondarily of working conditions (discipline), as contrasted with the non-manual's concentration on the intrinsic qualities of the job' (Inkeles and Bauer, 1959, pp. 111, 118). We need to remind ourselves, of course, that manual workers who are conscious of having to struggle to survive will feel forced to make income their most pressing preoccupation. Release from compulsions of this kind is, as we noted at the outset, a pre-condition of choice between different values in work. In most industrial countries, however, large proportions of even the least-favoured strata are indeed free from this compulsion, and their preferences are thereby revealing of values.

Yet emphasis on the salience of income, security and benefits must not be allowed to obscure such awareness as there is even among wage-earners of intrinsic satisfactions in work. Blauner, among others, has documented the variations of job structure and design in manual work, and has related them to differences in satisfactory personal experience (1964). It is easy, however, to exaggerate the significance of these variations, for most manual wage-earners and lower-level white-collar workers are hedged about with far more restrictions on independence, on the degree of personal control, and on the scope for full development of abilities than are managers and professionals. The evidence makes clear that intrinsic rewards are valued and their absence regretted (Blauner, 1967). The aspect of control is specially significant since it underlies so many of the intrinsic rewards derivable from work. It includes among its dimensions control over the use of one's time and physical movement—and thus control over the pace of the work process; control over the environment, both technological and social; and control as manifested in freedom from hierarchical domination. It is the relative lack of these forms of control which is apt to impart to manual-work cultures their characteristic features of fatalism and pessimism. These are understandable responses in situations marked by dependency upon the power and decision of others, by corresponding difficulty in predicting one's long-term future, and by a general awareness of close restrictions on the ability to determine one's own destiny.

Evidence of the consciousness of such values in work may seem at odds with our statements about the salience for many manual workers of instrumental aspirations. Yet no conflict is necessarily involved. Men questioned about their responses to work may respond on either of two levels: in terms of how far they have adjusted to work as it is, and in terms of how far they have any picture of work as it might be. In other words, men can at one and the same time (i) expect work to be largely instrumental in nature, (ii) become 'satisfied with' (i.e. resigned to) this situation, and (iii) wish that it could be otherwise—that intrinsic rewards were also open to them. The difficulty of knowing on what level they are responding—along with the fact that they may move between different levels without being aware of it—vitiates many attitude surveys of 'job satisfaction'. Workers may present one picture of themselves when they are speaking from a position of resignation to certain total or partial deprivations (which they have been conditioned to see as largely inevitable), and a very different picture when they allow themselves to dwell on the nature of those deprivations.

5 PRIORITIES IN WORK

The argument thus leads us to consider the crucial importance of practical priorities. Even those employees who are sensitive to the intrinsic rewards derivable from work and who suffer the discontents of deprivation may consider it futile to make the pursuit of such rewards a high priority. In the light of the conditions that they have been taught to expect, such a policy may seem unrealistic. They focus their active hopes upon rewards and satisfactions which seem within their grasp.

It thus seems reasonable to think in terms of high priority and low priority aspirations. The former are those which are actively entertained and pursued. They are experienced as pressing and they appear realistic and within hope of realization. They may well be the aspirations which attract a man to a particular job, which cause him to stay in it, and which constitute the predominant criteria by which he evaluates it. Low priority aspirations are less strongly held or seem unrealistic and beyond reasonable hope of realization, or both. They may nevertheless profoundly affect the individual's behaviour in work. A manual worker who takes, keeps, and values a given job for pre-dominantly instrumental reasons may yet have expressive aspirations which inform his responses to the work situation and management behaviour.[8] A dedicated teacher who finds predominantly intrinsic meaning in his job may feel a sense of injustice with respect to its financial rewards.

The individual's order of priorities may change gradually over the long term or fluctuate sharply over the short term. The reasons are diverse. His values may shift under the influence or sanctions of family, group, community, new leaders, the mass media, or his position in the life cycle. His perception of a value as now coming within reach as a result of a change in power relations or environmental factors may bring it up from low to high priority, just as the perception of a value as passing beyond reasonable hope of attainment may bring it down from high to low priority. His perceptions may undergo sudden short-term changes which markedly, if briefly, invert his priority scale. A dispute may cause the manual worker to react violently against intrinsic deprivations in a way which makes them appear, for a while, his major preoccupation. The vocation-conscious teacher, denied a salary claim, may for a time perceive his job largely in terms of financial injustice. Both may revert when the mood of unusual excitement has passed.

The higher the individual's position in the occupational hierarchy the greater the evidence, on the whole, of concern with intrinsic values in work (Morse and Weiss, 1955; Hyman, 1967). As with manual workers, job-structure itself is of major importance in structuring aspirations—as one moves up the hierarchy one finds that middle-class occupations offer far greater intrinsic rewards in terms of job interest, judgement, discretion, challenge, responsibility and control (Argyris, 1964; Tannenbaum, 1966). Thus a different set of aspirations is created and duly passed on from generation to generation. Those of middle-class origin therefore often learn to aspire to intrinsic as well as extrinsic rewards. To the extent that they come under the influence of values like these they are more likely to take a considered view of their education, their training, their job and the quality of experience that it offers, relating them to a concept of self-development that can realistically be included in their active aspirations for the reason that it seems within reach of achievement. Soviet society is no exception to these generalizations. There, as in America, people 'in the higher status jobs were more likely than the manual groups to choose jobs which permitted "self-expression" and "interesting experience"' (Inkeles and Bauer, 1959, p. 118).

[8] Attention is drawn to the importance of the distinction between satisfaction *with* a job and satisfaction *in* a job in Daniel, (1969); Davison, *et al.,* (1958); and Ross, 1969.

It by no means follows, however, that middle-class persons necessarily attach top *priority* to intrinsic rewards. The same cultural forces
that bear upon manual wage-earning classes bear also upon
managers, administrators, and professionals, who may become
strongly oriented towards the instrumental rewards of status as
reflected in life-styles. Concern with intrinsic values may come to
seem unfashionable, naive, unworldly. An important consideration
here, however, is that in many middle-class occupations progress up
the career ladder may well bring gains in both intrinsic and extrinsic
rewards. For this reason the middle-class aspirant may find difficulty
in recognizing exactly what motives impel him. If he describes them
as a desire for money and status he may be doing no more than
paying verbal tribute to a peer-group fashion. What cannot be
disputed is that for many middle-class persons the quest for more
money and status is often, *ipso facto,* a quest for greater intrinsic
rewards, and an active interest can be maintained in both without
having to sacrifice either. Research among Soviet citizens showed that
'interesting work dominated the desires of the intelligentsia', and
was interpreted by Inkeles and Bauer to 'indicate strikingly the extent
to which they took a decent standard of living for granted and
concentrated on other aspects of the work situation' (1959, p. 118).

The problem of meanings in work is thus a complex one.
Divergent philosophies bear upon men and shape their expectations
and aspirations. Those which stress extrinsic satisfactions have
powerful supporters. Since most work, as at present designed, offers
little in the way of intrinsic satisfactions, those who have an interest
in, or carry responsibility for, maximizing consumer values are likely
to perceive themselves as benefiting if aspirations to intrinsic satisfactions among lower-status employees remain of low priority either
in the sense of not being strongly felt or in the sense of seeming
foolishly visionary. The instrumental orientation stands nevertheless
under permanent threat, as it were, from the notion of individual
personality development, which is a significant strand in the Western
cultural heritage. It would be a bold prophet who asserted that
instrumental orientations would continue indefinitely to predominate within the lower ranges of the occupational hierarchy.

We cannot make sense of much apparently conflicting evidence
unless we introduce a distinction between high and low priority
aspirations. And men differ not only in the nature of their aspirations
but also in the intensity with which they pursue them. Some make but
few and weak demands on work; others make strong demands

over a narrow range; still others demand high satisfaction in respect of all the possible rewards, extrinsic and intrinsic. It therefore becomes necessary to think in terms of the nature and level of the individual's aspirations in work. The diversity of these orientations and levels of aspiration does not result, as might seem likely, in a chaos of conflicting preferences at the organizational level. Individuals belonging to particular social or occupational groups are likely to come under similar social, cultural and subcultural forces and to share a broadly similar outlook. The influence of the peer group or the work group, for example, in socializing the individual into what he is expected to want from work may be specially potent. Moreover, there is reason to believe that a process of self-selection has some effect in bringing men of like orientations together. Within the limits imposed by knowledge, capacity for rational choice, and opportunities for practical expression of that choice, men will select themselves as between different occupations and organizations according to their priorities. Jobs and organizations which offer, for example, mainly instrumental satisfactions may, within the limits indicated above, tend to attract and retain men whose priorities lie in this direction, while those seeking intrinsic rewards may gravitate elsewhere (Goldthorpe, *et al.,* 1968a; Goldthorpe, *et al.,* 1969a; Ingham, 1967). Given this picture of culturally-moulded orientations and varying levels of aspiration, with a process of self-selection operating in widely-differing degrees according to time, place and circumstance, we now need to examine the nature of the interaction which occurs when they are brought to bear upon the social organization of the industrial enterprise. Before we can be in a position to do this, however, we need a conceptual picture of the enterprise itself.

CHAPTER II

The Social Organization of Industrial Work

As one of the many forms of so-called 'complex organization', the industrial enterprise has come under extensive scrutiny both empirically and conceptually. (See the companion volume by John Child in this series). The perspectives from which it can be examined are numerous and are manifested in the wide range of theoretical frameworks and models which different theorists have constructed for their own purposes. Some have selected for special emphasis the formal aspects of organizational structure and functioning, seeing these as a set of rules consciously designed to serve certain ends laid down by the organization's leaders, while others have focused on the 'informal' processes which emerge largely crescively from the spontaneous adaptations of participants either in support of, or in resistance to, these 'official' objectives. Subsequent writers have realized that neither formal nor informal structure could be understood without an examination of both in interaction—and that even this made little sociological sense unless viewed within a total environmental setting of product and supply markets, the state of technical knowledge, and political and socio-cultural contexts. Useful introductory accounts of these theoretical developments can be found in Litterer (1969), Mayntz (1966), and Mouzelis (1967).

But despite growing agreement on certain broad generalities there is still scope for a wide diversity of theoretical presentation as writers devise different frameworks for different selections of empirical data, or develop different conceptual perspectives for their own special purposes. Simon (1965); March and Simon (1958) for example, offers a conceptual framework which stresses the rational decision-making aspect of the organization, but also defines the factors which limit rationality. Burns and Stalker (1961) are among a number who have developed a distinction between the Weberian model of bureaucratic organization, with its precisely-defined roles, reliance on rules, hierarchical differentiation, and stress on discipline and vertical inter-actions (which they term the 'mechanistic' type), and a far more flexible and open variety (the 'organic'), which they see as better adapted to conditions of rapid environmental change, and which is characterized by more diffuse role definitions, more reliance on 'professional' orientations, greater use of lateral interactions and less stress on discipline and hierarchy. The capacity of an enterprise to survive and prosper depends heavily, they argue, on whether its functioning follows the organizational patterns appropriate to its task and environment. One major reason why it may not is that the 'working organization' may be distorted by (i) the political system, which relates to internal struggles over the distribution and regula-tion of power, and (ii) the status structure, which produces rivalries and conflict between members over rights and privileges. Woodward (1965, 1970) has related task and type of productive system to a conceptualization of the enterprise in such terms as the number of levels of management, spans of control, amount of written com-munication, ratios of staff to hourly-paid workers and of direct to indirect labour, and other dimensional factors. Pugh *et al.* (1963) have developed a conceptual scheme on similar lines in terms of specialization, standardization, formalization, centralization, con-figuration, and flexibility, seeking thereby to provide operational measures for comparative study. Etzioni (1961) has focused on the different patterns of compliance found in different types of organiza-tion. Katz and Kahn (1966) have set up a Parsonian-type open system model comprising five basic subsystems serving the needs of produc-tion, supportive operations, maintenance, adaptation and manage-ment. It has been argued that a number of these theoretical per-spectives show signs of a convergence towards a 'systems' approach to which many strands of sociological and social-psychological theorizing are contributing (Buckley, 1967).

These examples are chosen from a wide and varied field merely to illustrate the style of organizational theorizing and to suggest that there is no 'one best way' of conceptualizing the social structure of the enterprise. In the succeeding pages, certain components will be selected simply because, in drawing attention to what is important for the present essay, they serve the analytical needs of much that will follow.

In seeking to isolate what for our analytical purposes are essential components, one difficulty presents itself at once. The social organi-zation can be found in very varied forms ranging from the sophisti-

B

cated to the primitive. The danger exists that if the more elaborate forms are taken as the model then certain components may be taken as basic which in fact are not basic at all. The defining characteristics must be pruned to the minimum. This does not mean, however, that the more complex and sophisticated developments will be ignored, for the analysis will seek to present a dynamic picture of how internal and environmental forces generate such developments and thereby bring about constant modifications in the structure. The initial sketch of the social organization now to be presented is an abstraction—a picture of a notional state of affairs before individual and group interactions and responses to environmental factors have wrought their effects upon the fabric. In this way, it is hoped, there can be presented not only a picture of industrial work and the social forms to which it gives rise, but also a view of the dynamics that make those forms what they are.

1 THE SOCIAL ORGANIZATION OF THE ENTERPRISE

As men pursue their experience within the organization, we may assume a process of explicit or implicit assessment to be taking place as they measure that experience against such aspirations as they may entertain. Clearly their experience has a number of different aspects. It will be assessed by the individual, according to his aspirations, along various dimensions of extrinsic rewards such as money, environmental conditions, status, and social satisfactions; along dimensions of intrinsic rewards such as job interest, challenge, creativity, autonomy and other paths to self-actualization; and along dimensions of participation in decision-making which may have extrinsic or intrinsic value or both. Before this assessment process is explored, however, we need to define the corresponding constituent elements of the social structure of the work organization, for it is the individual's location in this social structure (referred to hereafter as 'the social organization'), which determines his experience.

The essence of organization is regular, standardized and recurrent behaviour. The social organization therefore consists of patterned uniformities of behaviour which persist for varying lengths of time. The regularities and uniformities are structured into the behaviour by norms—a norm being defined here (as in the *International Encyclopaedia of the Social Sciences*) as 'a rule, a standard, or pattern for action'. It will be assumed for analytical purposes that all organizational behaviour is structured, regulated or guided by some norm or combination of norms. If certain patterned uniformities of behaviour give way to different uniformities, a change in structure has taken place as a result of a change in certain of the norms.

As in the case of the norms which govern behaviour in the wider society, organizational norms are of several different kinds. One major category, of course, consists of explicitly enunciated rules formally promulgated by those in superordinate positions. These rules are likely to cover most aspects of the work sequence —recruitment, training, work roles, relationships of super- and subordination, financial and other rewards, promotion, discipline, dismissal, production methods, the use and maintenance of the material technology, accounting and other control techniques, and of course many other aspects not requiring specific mention here. Some of these rules will be wholly or partly determined by law emanating from an external political agency and, varying with the society, covering such issues, perhaps, as safety, welfare, production standards, or terms and conditions of employment. Another category of norms consists of explicitly enunciated rules formulated and articulated by subordinate groups—for example by groups of crafts-men or professionals who may bring certain self-regulating practices to bear upon their own role-behaviour. A further category comprises informal understandings generated within superordinate and sub-ordinate groups. While not as explicit as articulated rules, they may nevertheless effectively govern behaviour—indeed may do so more effectively than explicit rules. This category includes customs, con-ventions, and social *mores*. Finally, organizational norms include formal rules and informal understandings that are concerted and jointly sponsored by superordinate and subordinate groups. The question of the extent to which the various constituent groups of the organization are governed in their behaviour by these different types of norms is of course a matter for empirical inquiry.

2 SUBSTANTIVE AND PROCEDURAL NORMS

The distinction drawn earlier between substantive and procedural orientations can be used to express a conceptual difference between substantive and procedural norms. Procedural norms are those rules and understandings which structure and regulate the decision-making methods by which norms are formulated. Substantive norms, emanating from these decision-making procedures, cover, as we have noted, every aspect of organizational activities. Of course, the formu-lation of norms is not the only activity of decision-making pro-cedures. They are also concerned with the application of norms.

What this really means is that decisions constantly have to be taken, explicitly or implicitly, about which norm or norms are to be used in dealing with a particular situation, problem, or instance. Against the background of this distinction between procedural and substantive norms, we turn now to examine certain necessary components of the social organization.

Minimally, the social organization comprises systems of roles, of sanctions, and of communications. Without these there is no organization. The concept of role may include up to four separate elements which need to be distinguished. Each role includes a technological behaviour system of norms which define the task activities. Secondly, it includes a set of norms designed to focus attention upon the goals defined for the organization by its leaders; specify the kinds of behaviour necessary for achieving those goals; lay down modes of personal conduct; set out the duties and responsibilities of the individual towards the organization; and embody values deemed by its leaders to be required of all the organization's members. Thirdly, some roles include elements which endow them with control over the methods and conduct of work. Inspectors, checkers, work-study engineers, supervisors, production planners, quality controllers, budgeting and accounting functions; all are roles which could be included in a special category of 'control mechanisms' which standardize performance, ensure quality, plan the work, appraise the performance, and set the tone for the firm's activity. These are specific aspects of a general requirement of the social organization which needs examination in its own right—relationships of super-ordination and subordination. The top management of the organization will allocate the 'right' to issue directives and orders, determine policies, pronounce judgements on relevant issues, define standards, settle controversies and generally act as leader or guide to other participants. Rights and duties relating to such activities are therefore hhe fourth element of the role system. The norms defining these rights and duties are, of course, procedural, the decisions which emerge being about substantive norms or their application.

The second major element of the social organization is the normative system of sanctions through which superordinates seek to regulate and control the behaviour of subordinates. Every sanction has its positive and negative aspects. Financial rewards, promotion prospects, praise and approval, transfers to more desired work, and any other form of gratification are positive but also have a negative aspect in that they embody a conditional clause threatening their withdrawal or witholding if the required behaviour is not forth-coming. Conversely, negative sanctions such as reprimands, fines, suspension, dismissal, demotion, and any other form of deprivation all have a positive aspect embodied in a conditional guarantee that they will be lifted or not be imposed if the desired behaviour is followed. The superior can therefore control behaviour either by bestowing some gratification and threatening to withdraw it or by inflicting some deprivation and offering to remit it.[1]

What is the basis of the ability to apply sanctions? Here we shall follow Emerson (1962) and Blau (1964) in seeing this ability as deriving from a relationship of dependence in which one person is dependent upon another for the securing or the continued availa-bility of something that he values. The entity to which value is attached may be scarce resources, approval or symbolic rewards, or life itself. Etzioni categorizes the bases as physical, remunerative, and normative; the first deriving from physical force, the second from command over scarce resources, and the third from the 'allocation and manipulation of symbolic rewards and deprivations' through such channels as 'the allocation of esteem and prestige symbols, administration of ritual, and influence over the distribution of "acceptance" and "positive response" ' (1961, p. 5). Thus to deter-mine the ability of A to apply sanctions to B one must ask questions like: What does A have at his disposal that B wants? How badly does B want it? Does B have any alternative sources of supply?

Insofar as managements have control over the supply of whatever men value, they are able to control and regulate behaviour by making a supply available under the threat of withdrawal if the required behaviour is not pursued. They can grant or deny men access to an income—and therefore livelihood. They can adjust the level of that livelihood and manipulate possibilities of promotional advancement. They can bestow or withdraw status. They can transfer men to more satisfying or less satisfying work, and display signs of approval or disapproval as encouragement or threats. In some societies they can recommend the bestowal of state honours. In all societies there are defined circumstances in which they can call upon the civil power and even perhaps the armed services to apply physical force against those who transgress certain norms.

This array of sanctions at management's disposal can be categorized according to analytical requirements or convenience. For

---

[1] In the absence of the conditional clause, neither the bestowal of gratifications nor the infliction of deprivations would achieve the desired regulation of behaviour.

example, we can conceptualize the differential distribution of financial rewards as 'pay structure'. Similarly, we can abstract the differential allocation of status and conceptualize it as a status system.

The third and last major basic component of the social organization is a communications system. Its analytical importance hardly needs labouring. The very concept of social organization presupposes the communication and exchange of information and meanings. But this cannot, of course, be left to chance. The information to be transmitted and the mode of transmission must be structured by a planned communication system.

Our notional picture of the basic components of the social organization therefore includes technological behaviour systems, sets of more general behavioural norms, control mechanisms, a system of sanctions, a status system, and a pattern of communications, all buttressed by relationships of superordination and subordination. We can also abstract from the general behavioural norms the values expected of all participants, and from the communication system the orientation and indoctrination of new members, and introduce a concept of management ideology and its function of serving management goals by socializing members into desired orientations and patterns of behaviour. Management ideology has other functions besides this, as will emerge later, but this is an important one. Ideology has proved a slippery concept since Marx used it in at least three different senses, but one important analysis distinguishes the rules and concepts that 'are part of the very stuff of social relations' from the 'rules and concepts *serving to strengthen or undermine* those relations' (Plamenatz, 1963, p. 345). The latter we may call ideological.[2] Management ideology seeks to legitimize, in the eyes of organization members, not only the goals defined by the organization's leaders but also the social organization which is designed to serve them. By these means it hopes to strengthen its chances of securing willing compliance from its members, which means here not simply obedience, but also a disposition on the part of the subordinate to use whatever discretion he has in decision-making to further the ends of organizational leaders. The essence of willing, as against forced, compliance is well expressed in a passage by Bendix. 'In modern industry the

[2] 'A theory or opinion which purports to describe some aspect of reality, or a moral or legal rule, or a concept used to express such a rule or to encourage obedience to it, is *ideological* when its function is to maintain or challenge some part of the social order, or (as Marx might have put it) of the system of social relations; and a theory or opinion is ideological also when it serves to allay fears and create hopes' (Plamenatz, 1963, p. 344).

cooperation needed involves the spirit in which subordinates exercise their judgement. Beyond what commands can effect and supervision can control, beyond what incentives can induce and penalties prevent, there exists an exercise of discretion important even in relatively menial jobs, which managers of economic enterprises seek to enlist for the achievement of managerial ends' (1956, p. 251).

We now have a view of the organization as a structure of roles and social relations which include relations of superordination and subordination, and an ideology which seeks to legitimize this social order in the eyes of its participants. Earlier the social organization was referred to in terms of patterned uniformities of behaviour structured by norms. Insofar as any organization consists of people acting in ordered, structured ways, it may be described as a complex of norms which create the order and the structure. So far we have looked at sets of procedural and substantive norms, many of them explicit but some implicit, which top management seeks to induce participants to accept by a combination of persuasion and sanctions. As already seen, if the uniformities of behaviour structured by these norms give way to different ones, the structure has changed. This means that the distinction frequently drawn in organizational literature between 'formal' structure, as officially prescribed by organizational leaders, and 'informal' strutcture, as created spontaneously by subordinates, may be confusing if it creates an impression of two systems. There is only one organization—people cannot behave in two different ways at once. The uniformities of behaviour which they actually follow constitute the social organization. This is why the view just presented of a structure rationally designed by top management to serve their goals is merely a notional basis on which to build. Subordinates frequently adapt their role or some other component of the social organization in the service of goals which top management would repudiate. The patterned uniformities of their behaviour may be structured to some extent by norms which are not management norms, upheld by sanctions which are not management sanctions. In such situations it is their adaptations which constitute the relevant aspects of the social organization, not some mistaken impression, wish or aspiration which may exist in the minds of top management or within the pages of an organization manual. Nevertheless, the norms articulated or aspired to by management will remain a crucial variable in the situation if management seeks to enforce them. The behaviour of subordinates then becomes an issue of contention. Management tries to structure it in terms of their own norms;

informal work groups or formal organizations such as trade unions try to structure it in terms of theirs, both sides using sanctions and ideological appeals. At the moment we are concerned with management. What resources lie to hand for their use in this endeavour?

3 AUTHORITY AND POWER

Reference has been made to the relationships of superordination and subordination which management's procedural norms seek to maintain between the members of the organization. The reason why hierarchy is so crucial for the organization's leaders is that it facilitates the making of decisions over which they can hope to exercise some control. Acceptance of the norms covering these relationships is therefore the key to the acceptance of all other norms. The degree to which subordinates legitimize the procedural norms governing decision-making, and the degree to which they legitimize the substantive norms emanating from those procedures, are simply opposite sides of the same coin. The problem of 'authority' is therefore understandably a central issue. Few problems in social and political science are more confused and confusing. Perhaps the most persistent conceptual error is to see it, as Etzioni does (1961), as a special variety of power (Blau, 1964; Buckley, 1967; Giddens, 1968; for useful discussions). Here it will be viewed as a relationship in which the superordinate is perceived by the subordinate as having the right to make decisions which must be accepted as binding. The idea of discussion or argument is not excluded, since what is involved is what Simon terms 'the right of the last word' (1965).

However authority is defined, few writers fail to see it as being bound up in some way with legitimacy. Authority is said to lie in the *right* to expect and command obedience. It will not do, however, to infer that authority exists simply because management norms have conferred this right upon certain specific roles. What if the subordinate does not acknowledge the right? It is he who confers legitimacy upon the superordinate's claim for obedience—or withholds it. For example, the norms of a craft work group—upheld mainly by shared values but in the last resort by group sanctions against the individual—may repudiate the right of any supervisor who is not of their own craft to command their obedience. In other words, the norms of the group clash with the norms of management. In this situation of normative conflict, the group is refusing to acknowledge the rightness of management norms about this particular relationship of subordination and can therefore be said to be withholding legitimacy from them. And if authority has to do with legitimacy then management is not, on this particular issue, wielding authority. In other words, authority is not an attribute which can be built into the social system rather as one builds motive power into the technological system. It is a relationship which requires appropriate behaviours from both superordinate and subordinate. It is one in which the subordinate extends 'consent' to the order-giving role of the superior, i.e. legitimizes the norms governing this relationship.[3]

Simon offers a useful notion when he writes that in an authority relationship the subordinate 'holds in abeyance his own critical faculties for choosing between alternatives and uses the formal criterion of the receipt of a command or signal as his basis for choice' (1965, p. 126). As we have seen, this does not exclude the idea of discussion or argument. Its usefulness lies in expressing the nature—once the 'last word' has been spoken by the superior—of that voluntary submission, that voluntary placing of oneself under the direction or command of the superior, which is the essence of an authority relationship. It is this quality which marks it off from a relationship in which the subordinate is forced to submit to norms which he does not legitimize. In a relationship of that kind certain patterns of behaviour are being imposed upon him 'against his will', i.e. without his having extended consent.

This is not to say that sanctions have no place in an authority relationship. I may fully legitimize certain norms which seek to regulate and control my behaviour and yet, in a moment of weakness or temptation, try to evade or transgress them. The citizen who regards the fiscal system as perfectly just may nevertheless smuggle a watch through the Customs or falsify his tax declaration; the worker who accepts the need for 'no-smoking' regulations in the factory may nevertheless succumb to his craving if he gets the chance. If the offence is discovered, sanctions will be forthcoming in the form of punishment. But if I legitimize the norms in question, I am also likely to regard the punishment, too, as legitimate provided I perceive it as 'fitting', i.e. not disproportionate to the offence. There is, indeed, an

---

[3] This does not exclude the possibility that his consent may have been secured by the use of pretence or deception which leaves him ignorant of certain facts, implications, or probable consequences. The pejorative use of the term 'manipulation' covers these cases, though manipulation is sometimes seen as a separate method of controlling behaviour. Needless to say, the authority secured by such tactics lasts only as long as the subordinate remains ignorant, and his discovery of them is likely to modify sharply his frame of reference towards management's legitimacy for some time into the future.

B*

important sense in which I 'consent' to my own punishment. I shall, of course, be aware that my behaviour is being regulated and controlled, but I legitimize the regulation and its methods. In such circumstances I am unlikely to experience the sanctions as being coercive in nature; that is, as forcing me to behave against my consent. The punishment in question is unlikely, therefore, to inspire me with a sense of grievance and injustice.

From such considerations as these we can conclude that even within a relationship of subordination that is fully legitimized by the subordinate, and that we are therefore defining as authority, the superior may consider that, given human frailty, he cannot rely for organizational predictability upon good will and must uphold the norms by means of sanctions. Authority relations are therefore perfectly compatible with sanctions in both their positive and negative aspects of rewards and punishments.

If even those relationships of subordination that are fully legiti-mized by the subordinate need to be underpinned by sanctions, organizational leaders are likely to feel the need to lean far more heavily on sanctions in situations where these relationships are not legitimized. Here management is seeking to regulate and control men's behaviour along lines and by means to which the latter have not extended consent. The attribute of 'rightness' which the sub-ordinate extends to the superior in an authority relationship is absent. He is therefore being forced to submit to certain norms, as it were, 'against his will'.

His response to this situation is likely to be very different from that in an authority relationship. Since sanctions are being used to impose a pattern of behaviour which he perceives, for any one of a number of reasons to be examined later, as illegitimate, he is likely to feel that he is being pressured or in the extreme case coerced into conformity. It is in such circumstances that we are most likely to feel that power is being exercised against us. Popular usage of these terms varies, of course, but it is probably true for many that power carries con-notations of pressure or coercion applied against one's consent. To differentiate situations where sanctions are used to enforce con-formity to norms which the subordinate perceives as illegitimate from situations where they are used to uphold legitimized norms, the former will be referred to here as power relations as against the authority relations which described the latter.[4] The ascription of

---

[4] Such is the diversity of popular usage of these terms that any choice of definition for conceptual and analytical purposes cannot avoid seeming to some extent arbitrary.

legitimacy or otherwise extends, of course, to the exercise of the sanctions themselves. Where the sanctions are perceived as legitimate, they can be regarded as part of an authority relationship. The case is different in respect of a power relationship. When I am conscious of being subjected to power, the sanctions used to compel me to conform to rules which I do not legitimize will likewise be perceived by me as illegitimate. This applies to their positive as well as their negative aspect. A Communist employee who sees the private-property rights of his employer as illegitimate will feel just as strongly that his dependence is being 'coercively' exploited when he receives his pay packet (with its conditional threat of withdrawal), as when he is threatened, say, with three days suspension (with its conditional promise of remission). By their very nature, however, punishments are likely to evoke the deeper resentment. This response will be qualitatively different from the response to punishment in an authority relationship. In the latter the subordinate is likely to feel that he has simply received his just desert. In the former he is likely to generate a sense of grievance and injustice.

In summary, then, there are fundamental differences between authority and power as these terms are being used in the present essay. In the former, subordinates legitimize the order-giving role of the superior and although sanctions are deemed necessary to deter or punish transgression, these too are legitimized. In the latter situation sanctions are used to impose upon others norms of both substantive and procedural kinds which they do not legitimize, and since this behaviour is forced upon them without their 'consent' they are more likely to experience this pressure or coercion as power.

We now need to inquire into the practical significance of this distinction. Why should it matter whether management uses power or authority to uphold its norms regulating superordinate and subordinate relations? The answer lies in the fact that, since rights are correlative with obligations, a person who accepts the rightness of a superior's demand for obedience feels, in the last resort, obliged to

---

Power, for example, has been variously identified with prestige, influence, eminence, competence, knowledge, dominance, rights, force, or authority (Bierstedt, 1950; Dahl, 1957; Goldhamer and Shils, 1939). Some might wish to define the use of sanctions even within a fully-legitimized relationship as 'power'. The need for a clear, sharp distinction, however, between the nature and consequences of legitimized and non-legitimized situations, along with the need to minimize complexities and complications in exposition, has prompted the definitions presented here. They are close to, though not identical with, those used by Buckley (1967).

obey. The quality of this pattern of compliance is likely to be very different from that prevailing where compliance can only be secured by the exercise or threat of sanctions which the subject perceives as illegitimate. It is the difference between willing cooperation and a forced obedience under duress—obedience which is withdrawn whenever the coercive sanctions are not immediately in evidence. Here lies the vicious circle from which some industrial managers find escape so difficult. Finding its authority failing, management falls back on the coercive sanctions of power, only to find that this further undermines its own legitimacy, which in turn prompts the intensified use of power.

The significance of a relationship of subordination which is not legitimized by the subordinate but is upheld simply by management's use of power lies not merely, however, in the quality of compliance. Such a relationship legitimizes, in the eyes of the subordinate, whatever action he may be disposed to take to oppose management power with counter-power if he can mobilize it.

It does not follow from all this that a management operating by the norms of economic rationality will necessarily perceive it as disadvantageous to their interests to rely on power rather than authority, assuming they are free to choose. There are three possible reasons why they may choose power. Firstly, they may not aspire to the higher quality of performance that can follow from authority relations as against power relations. Secondly, they may so aspire but lack the knowledge or conviction that superior results would ensue. Thirdly, they may be positively convinced by a weighing of costs and benefits that, so far as they are concerned, the cultivation of authority relations would not justify the costs in terms of time, care, and compromise. What kinds of structural circumstances might validate this conclusion by the norms of economic rationality? A system of production in which the employee could be so tightly controlled and 'programmed' in his work behaviour by technology and other forms of regulation that quantity and quality of output was only insignificantly affected by whether he offered willing co-operation or forced compliance might provide such validation. There would of course be many other factors to evaluate. Forced compliance might vent its frustrations in high absence, sickness, accident and turnover rates, along with covert resistance to change. But power might be able to control even these provided there was enough of it. In Britain, between the two world wars, massive unemployment on a scale unprecedented before or since gave managements great power and made many employees desperately anxious to do nothing which might threaten their livelihood. The state may exact penalties for absenteeism, as in the Soviet Union (McAuley, 1969). Even if employees possess sufficient power to be able to manifest their discontent in these forms it cannot be assumed without enquiry that the costs necessarily exceed those of cultivating authority relations. Much of the 'human relations' literature has made this assumption too readily. The point is one to which researchers into management's personnel and labour relations strategy, past and present, might usefully pay more attention.

It follows from the foregoing that the greater the extent to which the desired performance depends on the willing cooperation and initiative of the employee, the more prejudicial to performance becomes the exercise of compulsion against him and the greater the importance of normative agreement—perhaps in some roles full normative commitment. That there is widespread recognition of this in industry can be deduced from the fact that managers, research scientists, and other professionals of various kinds are rarely subjected to detailed compulsions in their task activities. In such cases the costs of foregoing normative agreement tend to be readily perceived as exceeding the costs of cultivating it. As lower participants become increasingly able and disposed to mobilize power they too can make desired performance depend on their willing cooperation by threatening to limit or withdraw participation altogether, thus forcing management to try to cultivate authority rather than rely on power. As already suggested, however, management's strategy here will depend on a complex weighing of costs, utilities, and aspirations.

4 THE BASES OF LEGITIMACY

It is with these qualifications in mind that we turn to inquire into the possible bases of managerial authority. In other words, by what means do managers seek to induce subordinates to perceive their rule as legitimate, and thus extend willing compliance and cooperation?

We are here concerned with the ideas and values by which management hopes to validate its procedural norms. In this quest for legitimacy, ideologies are pressed into service in the hope of promoting agreement on these values. They are aimed not only at subordinates but also at the wider society in the belief that, if they succeed in modifying expectations of subordinate behaviour at work, social pressures of various kinds will help to induce acceptance by the subordinates themselves.

The types of appeal are many and diverse, varying over time and between countries. They vary, too, according to whether they receive physical or moral support from the state. The state may, for example, support employers in seeking to induce universal agreement that private property in the means of production confers certain 'rights' upon the owner. These include the principle that, in entering into a contract of employment, the employee legitimizes the employer in directing and controlling his activities 'especially in relation to time, place, content and method of work' (Ross, 1969, p. 13) and legitimizes, too, the employer's use of sanctions if necessary to maintain this obedience. One aspect of the process of promoting the legitimacy of this principle may be the propagation of the idea that the contract of employment is based on free consent between parties of equal legal status. To the extent that employees can be induced to accept propositions of this sort they will legitimize the employer's order-giving role and thereby perceive it as authoritative.

But there are, of course, many other kinds of appeal which employers and managers make for support of their rule. They may invoke the Social Darwinist principle that success in the competitive struggle proclaims their fitness and thereby their entitlement to govern, or that their special contribution to national wealth justifies them in their leadership (Bendix, 1956). More recently, in the United States, the focus has been upon the 'modern' 'socially conscious' private enterprise system which, by its success and creative dynamic, its professional orientation of social responsibility as against the old 'exploitative, harsh capitalism', and its enlightened concern with 'human values' (Cheit, 1964), justifies management in their appeal for social support. In the Soviet Union, the source of the manager's formal legitimacy derives from the backing of the Communist Party hierarchy, and the ideological pressure is directed towards ensuring that the hierarchy is accepted as the sole final authority for the proper interpretation of Marxism–Leninism (Granick, 1961).

Alternatively the appeal in the Third World may be to the legitimacy enjoyed by the nationalist regime which liberated the masses from imperialism. In Japan the manager's legitimacy has rested heavily on the persistence of feudal and family values which shaped industry as they shaped other institutions (Abegglen, 1958). Even in Western societies the force of tradition and custom can endow managers with legitimacy in the eyes of their subordinates. This may be important, for example, in explaining the unchallenged writ that may run within long-standing family firms—and equally the sudden collapse of authority that may follow a sudden change in their circumstances.

Charismatic leadership may be important. The position of the charismatic leader rests on an identification between leader and led of such a kind that he is able to crystallize, articulate, and shape the practical expression of normative aspirations among his followers. Once again, cultural components are obvious: Hitler had massive charisma for Germans, none for Englishmen. In a society where expertise *per se* commands great respect, managers may be able to justify their rule by demonstrating efficiency and superiority of judgement, even where subordinates feel no great enthusiasm for the objectives being pursued. If managers believe that subordinates attach value to such procedural aspirations as 'worker participation', 'democratic involvement', joint decision-making and the like, they may seek to strengthen their legitimacy by modifying the procedural norms accordingly, hoping thereby for the procedural-normative agreement which will mean substantive agreement. A wide range of possibilities exist for procedural change and can be arranged in sequence of significance. Subordinates may receive the right to have information; to protest against decisions; to make suggestions; to be consulted; or to participate directly or through representatives in a joint process of decision-making or collective negotiation. As with all the other possible sources of legitimacy, subordinates may or may not share the relevant values. If they do not, management will gain nothing by such a change. If they do, they may, as we have already noted, value procedural participation for terminal or instrumental reasons or both. A terminal preference reflects ideological or cultural values which may or may not be adequately met by the procedural changes. If the preference is an instrumental one, subordinates will value the new procedural norms—and reward management with the sought-for legitimacy—only insofar as they prove effective for the pursuit of substantive aspirations. Instrumental success may, however, result in the new procedural norms becoming valued for their own sake by promoting such principles as self-respect, dignity and independence.

Insofar as subordinates are —or can be brought to be—strongly committed to the value of a continuously rising material standard of life, managers may hope to strengthen their legitimacy by trying to meet subordinate aspirations in respect of material rewards, welfare, and fringe benefits. Since this is one of the appetites that grow by what they feed upon, it is apt to prove an unstable base for authority.

Yesterday's luxuries are today's necessities; the horizons of satisfaction ever recede, and management may find themselves expected to meet aspirations that rise faster than their productive ability —especially when the demands of other constraints are taken into account. Their authority may be correspondingly unstable. This is a specially uncertain base for the reason that material rewards are palpable, precisely measurable, and therefore all too easily comparable. Shifting relationships between rewards can quickly generate a sense of grievance. We also get a sense here of the part that may be played by class or caste divisions which structure and limit aspirations of different groups. As these divisions weaken, aspirational limits weaken with them. Normative references long maintained by custom dissolve, thus giving freer play to the growth of more expansive aspirations.

Finally, insofar as managers perceive the values sought by subordinates to be those of 'integration into the factory social system', or 'personality development', or 'psychological growth', or self-actualization, they may try to serve them not only by such procedural changes as are mentioned above but also by 'permissive' or 'supportive' supervision, 'employee-counselling' and other types of 'human-relations' programmes (Likert, 1961; Baritz, 1965), or by changes in job structure (Katz and Kahn, 1966). They may combine these with an ideology designed to persuade subordinates and society at large that the industrial organization is, in essence, a cooperative harmony of common goals which only fools or knaves choose to disrupt, and which thereby renders theirs a legitimate government (Fox, 1966).

5 PATTERNS OF AUTHORITY RELATIONS

All these diverse bases of managerial authority rest on normative agreement upheld by shared values. It follows that should management behave in ways which are based on, or directed towards, values other than those by which subordinates are legitimizing management's role, or in ways which fail to embody those values adequately, the authority relationship comes under potential threat. For example, if subordinates are legitimizing that role on the basis of management's professed concern first and foremost with employee interests, authority relations will be threatened if management are perceived as giving employee interests low priority. If legitimacy is offered on the basis of management's presumed respect for professional standards, it may not survive an instruction from management that standards be cut in order to gain a short-term competitive advantage. The case is equally clear if we suppose management to issue orders which conflict with a subordinate's moral principles. Thus the shared values promoting legitimacy create a 'zone of acceptance'[5] within which management's writ of authority holds for the subordinate, but outside which their behaviour may be perceived to be, as it were, 'ultra vires'.[6]

But managerial authority may be undermined not only by a failure of management to embody adequately the shared values in their behaviour, but also by a movement away from those values by subordinates. Employees who once acquiesced in the assertion that property rights and the freely consenting equality of the parties to the employment contract legitimized the employer's rule may come to see the situation differently. Experience may dispose them to accept the leadership of those who argue that since the assumption of equality is a mere legal fiction which masks gross economic inequality, the employer's rule and his use of sanctions must be considered illegitimate. The employment relationship will then come to be seen not as based on consent but as essentially coercive in nature. This exercise of power by the employer will be regarded as justifying the mobilization of counter-power by employees collectively in an attempt to introduce parity in their dealings with him. The more nearly they succeed the less they are likely to experience the relationship as one of coercion.

There are, of course, many other possible shifts in the values of subordinates. Approval of the sorts of behaviour encouraged by the philosophy of Social Darwinism may give way to respect for a policy of 'live and let live'. Deference to the rich, the powerful and the successful may decline relatively to sympathy for the poor, the weak, and the unsuccessful. Liberation from the imperialist yoke may come to be taken for granted and disenchantment spread to industrial as well as political governance. New prophets may arise and exploit their charisma to impart a new turn to aspirations. Feudal values in such countries as Japan may weaken as the ethos of 'progress' and 'modernity' lead employees and their unions to adopt the prefer-

[5] The phrase is Simon's (1965), though he approaches it somewhat differently.

[6] Cultural differences in this respect can be striking. In most Western countries the shared values offer only limited scope for managerial intervention in the private lives of their employees. In Japan, industrial employees legitimize a situation in which 'the company and its activities and programs penetrate the life of the worker far beyond the work situation itself', including arranging marriages for the women (Abegglen, 1958, pp. 69, 75).

ences and emulate the behaviours of those in countries like the United States which are perceived as supreme embodiments of that ethos. In the reverse direction, a shift away from the extrinsic and towards the intrinsic rewards in work would deeply undermine managerial authority if they pursued their present priorities. The design of work and modes of industrial operation would need to be profoundly different in a producer-oriented from those of a consumer-oriented society.

But given the existence of shared values, the commitment to these values by either side can be strong or weak. This means that there can be strong or weak support for the tacit or explicit agreement on the procedural norms regulating the relationship of subordination. Thus there can be strong or weak authority. Accordingly it may be useful to consider degrees of commitment *to* management rule as being on a common scale with degrees of commitment *against* it. This would give us a continuum ranging from total acceptance of authority at one end to total rejection at the other. Examples of total acceptance are rare in industry, but illustrations may be found in other spheres. Since total acceptance means unquestioning submission to substantive norms or instructions, examples must be found in the utter commitment to the religious or charismatic leader, in the behaviour of suicide troops in war, or in the doctrinal subservience of members of extremist authoritarian political sects. At the other end of the scale, total rejection of authority is an expression of complete normative breakdown. Revolutionaries or extreme militants may completely reject the procedural norms on ideological grounds. Since both procedural and substantive legitimacy are commensurate, and their repudiation of the former is total, it follows that they cannot be appeased by substantive concessions. Indeed, in order to justify their continued militancy, extremists are likely to respond to concessions only by raising their demands, even if only to avoid cognitive dissonance.[7] Their ideology requires them to keep up the fight and they must have something to fight about.

In these polar-type cases the substantive outcome of the particular hierarchical relationship in which he is involved is irrelevant to the subordinate. In these contexts he has no substantive aspirations. But few organizations reveal such extremities. More frequent are

[7] Social psychologists observe that the individual tends to strive towards consistency or consonance between the various beliefs and opinions he holds, and between these beliefs and opinions and his behaviour. Inconsistency or dissonance produces psychological discomfort and motivates the person to try to achieve consonance.

situations where commitment to values which either support or reject the established procedural norms, while not total, is nevertheless very strong. Members of some religious sects accept rigorous and detailed regulation of their private life of a sort which they would reject from any other source. Workers in Communist countries may likewise lend themselves to management purposes by exceeding official production norms and readily accepting rationalization in the manner of 'heroes of labour', 'shock workers' and Stakhanovites (Dobb, 1942). The devoted employee of long standing in the paternalist family firm in the capitalist West may uncomplainingly endure much. Other examples are the members of a *kibbutz* workshop; the leading spirits in a small production co-operative; and fervent nationalist employees in a newly-developing country. Examples of situations displaying strong commitment to values which reject the established procedural norms are naturally more apparent in societies which permit open challenge than in those which do not. In the West one may find the militant shop-floor worker who rejects all or many of the values which support procedural-normative agreement in industrial organizations. He may refuse to acknowledge the rights attached to private property in the means of production; deny that private enterprise serves anybody but property-owners; cherish a contempt for managerial competence, and despise the emphasis on material progress. Clearly if he extends any legitimacy to management at all it will be minimal.

Insofar as authority relations do prevail in the industrial organizations of the West, they are probably most widely characterized, so far as subordinates are concerned, by a low-key acquiescence. Of all the values which can legitimize managerial rule, those which appear to be coming to predominate in these societies are those which relate to substantive aspirations for a continuously rising material standard of life, and to procedural aspirations for participative decision-making machinery through which substantive gains can be made and protected. If this is the case then it suggests a predominantly instrumental and utilitarian type of involvement of the subordinate in the industrial organization (Etzioni, 1961, arrives at the same destination but by a very different conceptual route).

As we have seen, this is apt to prove a somewhat unstable base for authority relations. We must not overlook, however, the degree to which it may be buttressed by the habituated behaviours created by early socialization. From childhood we are all trained in obedience, though social classes differ sharply in how far their members are trained in giving orders as well as obeying them. As children we are urged to obey parents, teachers, policemen, and public officials simply *because* they are parents, teachers, policemen and public officials. Our mentor may or may not add—'and if you don't you'll be punished'. Even if he does, we are usually left in no doubt that the principal reason why we should obey is that we *ought* to obey; that it is right for the functionary concerned to expect our obedience. We also learn that if punished for transgression we are receiving no less than our just desert. These are lessons in the behaviours appropriate to subordination. The importance of the family, the group, the school, the community, the society at large, in shaping our perceptions of legitimacy is therefore crucial. In the case of any particular individual, of course, socializing influences brought to bear may or may not conform to the predominant pattern.

So far as the majority are concerned, however, by the time they take up employment they are trained to accept that they must work for a living, that this normally involves employment in a privately or publicly owned organization, and that they there come under a generalized expectation that they will accept the orders of persons appointed to govern them. This generalized expectation is likely to be supported, in the case of private industry, with certain propositions about the 'rights' of 'ownership', and in the case of the public sector, the 'right' of public officials. These expectations and their supporting propositions are likely, for many people, to be only vaguely conceived, and to have the status of traditional rather than rationally evaluated behaviours. Their effect is nevertheless crucial, for they ensure that the employer or manager receives an employee who is already socialized and trained in obedience.

Increasingly, however, over the period of industrialization these socializing processes have in many societies been supplemented by others offering a less accommodating perspective. Trade unions, while supporting management legitimacy in general and helping to socialize members in the behaviours appropriate to their subordinate roles, have also trained them to reject management prerogative over certain limited types of decision and to support the union in demanding joint decision-making in those spheres. Other values not necessarily generated only by trade unions may also bring new challenges by employee groups to the traditional bases of managerial authority, as when workers increasingly judge the economic system by whether it can supply them with a continuously rising standard of life.

In summary, most work organizations in most societies are likely to be found in the middle ranges of the continuum of power and authority. Only a tiny minority of employees are likely totally to deny all legitimacy to the procedural norms which structure the decision-making roles of those who rule them, and a still tinier minority are likely to offer total submission. The specific basis and strength of authority relations in any given organization is of course a matter for empirical enquiry, and national patterns vary widely. The values which provide the basis differ considerably and can be found associated in different combinations. The significance of a free market in values is, however, plain to see. Management will have an enormous advantage in maintaining its authority in societies where it enjoys the support of a state apparatus which controls the dissemination and teaching of ideas and values. In other societies managerial authority is permanently under threat from new values or from new interpretations of existing values.

In the West, much of the history of personnel techniques such as profit-sharing, co-partnership, paternalism, industrial 'betterment', industrial welfare, the 'human relations' movement, 'permissive' management and the like, is a record of the search for new, or for the strengthening of old, legitimations. But what happens when the search fails? We need to remind ourselves of the resource available to managers when their authority falters, breaks down, or cannot come effectively into existence because the shared vulues necessary to uphold normative agreement are only weakly held or have never existed. This resource is, of course, power. In the event that the value-commitment by subordinates is not adequate to uphold the procedural norms of decision-making, management can turn to power.

6 SANCTIONS AND POWER

We have seen that the procedural norms of decision-making which regulate relations between superordinate and subordinate may be upheld by shared values. Characteristically, however, organizational leaders discover that they cannot rely on consensus alone to ensure the very high degree of social order and predictability of behaviour that they deem necessary. Any concept of the industrial organization which presents it as a system within which subordinates consistently offer full legitimacy to their rulers on the basis of strong commitment to shared values is of no use as an analytical tool. Commitment to these values on the part of subordinates is unlikely to be sufficiently universal, total, and unswerving to suit management goals—which we shall be examining later. The question of compliance with the normative system thus becomes problematical.

The dynamics of the situation are not far to seek. The degree of observance of norms by the individual is the outcome of an interaction between the strength of his commitment to the values underlying the procedural norms and his substantive or procedural aspirations. The aspiration concerned may be of profound significance or merely trivial. The situation may be simply that of an employee in, say, a chemicals plant longing to break a no-smoking rule. Or he may be deeply aggrieved about a pay issue and lack confidence that the disputes procedure can give him a fair and speedy hearing. Or he may feel that management's assertion of prerogative in respect of a certain category of decision-making—relating, say, to 'lay-offs' or plant closures—is an affront to his rights and dignity as a person.

To the extent that his aspirations are not being fulfilled, a strain is put upon his commitment to the decision-making procedures that are producing the incongruence between aspirations and reality. The weaker his commitment to the values underlying those procedures, the more likely it is that norm-observance will break down under a strain of given intensity. The subordinate then flouts a rule, disobeys instructions, refuses to accept an order, ignores a union-management procedure agreement for settling grievances, or in some other way transgresses the prevailing procedural norms.

The strength of this response, however, varies, and the variations are important. Three broad types may be distinguished. The first is a common one in all organizations. As we have seen, men may accept the organizational norms and the values underlying them and yet be tempted to evade those they find specially irksome or specially easy to evade. The worker in a chemicals plant may, for example, accept the rightness of the rule prohibiting smoking and yet transgress it if he can. Despite the normative agreement, therefore, management may perceive a need for sanctions which punish the transgressor and thus deter a cumulative flouting and eventual breakdown of norms.

As already noted, however, these punitive sanctions designed to uphold the procedural norms of decision-making are not necessarily perceived by the transgressor as illegitimate. If he legitimizes the norms he may well legitimize sanctions designed to uphold them, provided he perceives the punishment itself as fitting. In such a situation, the application of sanctions will not be perceived as the exercise of coercive power.

In the second type of situation, the tension between the individual's normative aspirations and his commitment to the values underlying the prevailing norms is severe enough to break that commitment. There is now a condition of normative conflict. This normative breakdown is of far deeper significance than the first situation where the individual, despite his transgression, still extended basic consent to the norms concerned.

One solution obviously open to management is to adjust the norms to suit the subordinate's aspirations. In this way they can maintain legitimacy and therefore authority. But in doing this they may create an unacceptable incongruence with their own aspirations. They may see no way of adjusting the normative system in such directions as to serve the aspirations of both themselves and their subordinates. They may be tempted in this situation to use sanctions to impose the relevant norms. Since the subordinate is withholding legitimacy from the norms at issue, he will also withhold legitimacy from sanctions designed to enforce them. This will seem to him an exercise of power, justifying evasion or the mobilization of counter-power. Management may not be aware of these and other negative consequences or, if they are, convince themselves that they are either unimportant or easily subject to control. This may not, of course, be true. Even short-term consequences may be significant, and long-term consequences still more so. If incongruence for subordinates is severe, persists over a long period, but is kept latent by the exercise of power, all commitment to once-shared values may eventually disappear. It may even pass into a commitment totally and ideologically opposed to the value system held by management.

This is the third kind of situation. The organization may include employees with a value commitment which is ideologically opposed to the values which underlie the organization's procedural norms. No action by management can promote their own legitimacy for employees in this category. Management cannot hope to strengthen the value commitment of these employees to the procedural norms, since no such commitment exists to be strengthened. Neither can they reduce incongruence by meeting the subordinates' substantive aspirations since, as we have already seen, total rejection of procedural norms and the values that support them cannot be assuaged by substantive concessions. There may be very few persons measuring up to this extreme definition, but their role as leaders may be of great practical importance in some situations. Only by the use of power can management hope to control their behaviour—assuming that management aspires to control, which is not always the case.

Neither the second nor the third types of situation would arise if organizational leaders, or others acting on their behalf or in their interests, could control either the strength of the subordinates' commitment to shared values or the nature and intensity of their aspirations. Even in totalitarian societies, however, thought control has not yet reached this stage, though managements in such societies enjoy a considerable advantage as compared with their counterparts in pluralistic societies, where management or state influence in these respects has to compete with that of other groups within a relatively free market in ideas and values.

The distinction between the first situation, on the one hand, and the second and third on the other, is conceptually crucial and, though perhaps not always easy to detect empirically, of considerable significance for management—and perhaps government—policy. In a discussion of social deviance, Merton makes a similar distinction between the 'aberrant', who acknowledges the legitimacy of the norms he violates, and the 'nonconformer', who challenges the legitimacy of the social norms he rejects (1966). The practical importance of the distinction has already emerged. The application of punitive sanctions against the aberrant does not necessarily undermine the legitimacy of management rule. Applied against nonconformers, they will arouse strong resentment and resistance in the second type of situation and implacable bitterness in the third.

Thus the question of whether a particular instance of rule-breaking is correctly diagnosed has practical implications. Incorrect diagnoses are, however, constantly being made. No systematic investigation has been pursued, but certain probabilities of the most likely errors can be suggested. Perhaps the commonest is to diagnose situations of the second type as being of either the first or the third. Managements and governments confronted by industrial disputes in which employees are breaking rules—in Britain a current preoccupation is with the flouting by 'unconstitutional' strikers of procedural norms governing the handling of grievances—frequently diagnose them in terms of the first or third types of situation. Either the strikers are presumed to have committed themselves to total observance of the relevant norms, however incongruent these may at times seem for their own aspirations, or it is assumed that they are bent upon weakening or even destroying the organization. For both these diagnoses the prescription which often suggests itself to managements and governments is the application of punitive sanctions. Men who violate norms to which they are presumed to have committed themselves must be compelled to do what they know to be right—to behave, as it were, in accordance with their better selves. Men who are bent on weakening or destroying organizational order must be prevented by power from doing so.

In fact the situation may be of neither kind. Without even remotely aspiring to destroy the system, men may put it at risk by acting from a deep sense of injustice towards certain of the norms which govern them. What, then, explains the assumption made under one of the diagnoses above, that they must be regarded as having committed themselves to these norms? Such an assumption may derive from the observer's belief that when men take up employment they automatically place themselves under management prerogative, which they are then morally bound to obey. More probably in the Western world, the norms in question—and this applies specially to procedural norms for settling disputes—are the subject of an agreement between management and unions. The assumption will therefore be that the union members are bound by the agreement made through their representatives. Unfortunately for this assumption, it is becoming increasingly clear that, in a situation where men's procedural aspirations for a voice in determining the immediate circumstances of their working life are rising, far greater care is needed to secure genuine normative agreement than is often manifested by management and union representatives. It is all too apparent that the mere signing of an agreement by representatives commits the employees to nothing. Many 'unconstitutional' strikes develop out of situations marked by such managerial and union incompetence, weakness, normative confusion, and bad communications that it is difficult to argue that the strikers are fairly committed to anything. Unless there is a real winning of consent based on full rank and file understanding of issues, implications, and alternatives, the norms which result from union-management agreement may carry no greater authority than those imposed unilaterally by management alone. If, in such a situation, men are coerced into norm-observance in the mistaken belief that they are simply being compelled to do what they must know in their heart to be right, their sense of injustice becomes further compounded. In Durkheim's words: 'But if the conquered, for a time, must suffer subordination under compulsion, they do not consent to it, and consequently this cannot constitute a stable equilibrium' (1964, pp. 2–3).

Similar consequences flow from wrongly diagnosing a situation of this type as an instance of the third, where it is presumed that the transgressors are ideologically motivated towards destruction of organizational order. One of the difficulties of diagnosing correctly is that persons so motivated may emerge as leaders of groups which, while nowhere near the same ideological extremity of irreconcilability with management values, find themselves, perhaps as a result of past management and/or union incompetence and weakness, in a condition of utter normative confusion and frustration where all reference points and standards are in a state of flux or dissolution. In such conditions the only behavioural guide which seems compatible with self-interest is self-assertion through power. This can easily be expressed in the terms of the present analysis. Location in a normative system defines rights as well as duties. But since it is not so much one's absolute position in these respects which has the predominant importance, but rather one's position relative to others, the value to the individual of the normative system owes much to its ability to assure him of a relative position that he perceives as fair and just, and to protect him in that position. If his position is subsequently changed for the worse without his consent by others gaining a relative advantage, the reference points and standards which previously spelled justice have now disappeared. The normative system no longer offers him protection. If he can muster no power to restore the situation he may lapse into demoralization. If, on the other hand, power is accessible, either for him as an individual or in concert with others, there will be a strong temptation to use it. Feeling free now from any self-imposed constraints arising out of commitment to a normative agreement, he resorts to self-assertion through power. The greater the degree of normative confusion that prevails, the more difficult he will find it to judge what degree of self-assertion is 'fitting' and appropriate. It is in such a situation that he may follow a leader who, because of his unqualified ideological rejection of managerial rule, can offer a clear and unambiguous call to action. Management, in turn, may then resort to counter-power to force the situation back to normative agreement, possibly through compromise.

Ideological leadership of this kind may also emerge, of course, in more straightforward situations where management has long frustrated strong normative aspirations among employees. What commitment there is among employees to the values supporting management rule may become eroded. The way is then clear for leaders to emerge with an ideological commitment against such values. Aspirations for higher pay, more security, or greater job control may become infused with resentful doubts about the whole basis of management rule. Should management subsequently seek to restore its authority by making concessions, it may be puzzled to find that the policy of buying peace does not succeed. What has happened, of course, is that value consensus has been replaced by value conflict to such an extent that normative concessions no longer provide a quick direct route towards the restoration of authority.

This type of situation is recognizable in practice where employees perceive every act of management as suspect. Whatever is seen by management as being in *their* interests is interpreted by employees, necessarily and by definition, to be against *their* interests. Managers who inherit such a situation and aspire to restoring full authority relations face a long, testing process of building up some measure of agreement on basic values.

We are not finished yet, however, with examples of incorrect diagnosis. Sometimes the case in which men in a 'type two' situation are being led or represented by men in a 'type three' situation is diagnosed as being wholly type two in nature. In other words, the extreme demands and sentiments expressed by the few are assumed by management to be the genuinely-felt injustices experienced by the many. Searching their consciences, they deduce that if these demands are conceded, peace will follow. They therefore set about buying off hostility. But this only results in the leaders raising their demands, for the reasons explained earlier. Concession follows concession and employee expectations are raised accordingly. Eventually management decide that organizational survival is threatened, and stand fast. In the belief, created by management's past behaviour, that if pressed hard enough management will once more give way, leaders blunder into pitched battle. After great loss on both sides and destruction of employee expectations, a new normative order is agreed or imposef.

One important issue raised by these diagnostic difficulties is that industrial societies in which there is considered to be a problem of organizational order, but in which the dominant opinion seeks to minimize the use of coercion, may well find it necessary to ask a difficult question. In what circumstances can it properly be assumed that employees have committed themselves to normative agreement, thus rendering them justly liable to punitive sanctions should they engage in rule-breaking? Such a question requires careful definition of the social processes which are to be taken as having established normative agreement. Absence of these would render punitive sanctions inappropriate in any situation where the object was to promote and support authority as distinct from power. The contribution of the social psychologist in terms of perceptions, frames of reference, attitude change and communications would of course be crucial here. It might, for example, be established that no normative agreement can be said to exist in conditions where either party has failed to understand the issues; is not aware of the possible alternatives of action; does not appreciate the consequences of his choice, or for some other reason cannot be regarded as morally bound. When we apply these considerations to large numbers of employees whose participation in decision-making can only be an indirect one through representatives, the practical difficulties speak for themselves. Yet the fact remains that unless some approximation to these conditions is achieved, the possibility exists that agreements may be signed in their name which employees do not perceive as legitimate, and which can only be upheld by power. Industrial societies which seek to minimize coercion may need far more attention directed to the nature of normative agreement, the conditions which must obtain if something like equality between the parties is to be achieved, and the criteria by which it is to be judged that normative agreement has in fact been arrived at.

7 POWER RELATIONS AND LEGITIMACY

The upshot of the preceding discussion, therefore, is that there is a variety of situations in which organizational leaders are likely to resort to sanctions which may be perceived by subordinates as power. Managers discover that even in the most favourable circumstances they cannot rely on normative agreement alone to support the hierarchical relations which they perceive as necessary. Power fills the gap, though depending on their own aspirations and perceptions they may, of course, in view of the negative responses which tend to be generated by the use of power, seek to minimize it by promoting and strengthening authority relations.

We have discussed forms of managerial power and traced their origin to control over resources. But power-dependence theory draws attention to the fact that dependence may not only lie in one direction. Employees are dependent on management for income, but management is also dependent on employees to get work done. In respect of the employees' dependence on management for access to a livelihood, the power which management derives thereby varies inversely with the range of alternative opportunities open to job-seekers. When job-seekers outnumber jobs, they are more dependent on the employer than he on them, which leaves him with the balance of power. The reverse situation, however, produces a marked shift in this balance. When jobs outnumber job-seekers, his dependence may be the greater, and power shifts accordingly. One need look no further than this for the great significance of governmental full-employment policies, now widespread, which reduce the 'reserve army' of un-employed far below the levels once tolerated.

However, the power derived by individuals, groups and classes from control over resources is not only manifested directly in re-lationships at the organizational level. Quite apart from the general political aspect, which does not concern us here, this power can also be brought to bear indirectly to mould ideas, attitudes and values in the wider society in ways which closely affect organizational relations. If legitimacy rests on values held in common between superordinate and subordinate, then any group which can dominate the promotion and acceptance of values holds the key to legitimacy. The part played in totalitarian societies by state or party control of the agencies of socialization and communication is plain to see. Even within pluralistic societies, however, power tells. Control over resources confers great advantages for any sustained and thorough dissemination of ideas. In private-enterprise societies powerful groups have used this control to promote, for example, a universal belief in the sanctity of property rights and the legitimacy of the sanctions derived from them. They may be able to call many agencies of socialization into their service—education, religion, the mass media, writers, journalists, and many others prepared to peddle their wits, brains and training in return for being kept in a manner to which they hope to become accustomed. We are also concerned here 'with ideologies of manage-ment which seek to justify the subordination of large masses of men to the discipline of factory work and to the authority of employers' (Bendix, 1963, p. ix). At the organizational level, too, employers and managers are likely to propagate ideologies designed to establish the legitimacy of their position and what they do with it. In pursuing these efforts their very power may induce the subjected to internalize the appropriate ideas and values. Thus, in relation to work and property, power may be used to promote the very system of values through which legitimacy is claimed. Power can at once provide the engine behind the socialization processes and condition the subjected to accept the messages which they transmit. Far from power being regulated, as Parson argues (Giddens, 1968), by common value-orientations, power has been used to socialize the powerless into accepting values which justified the existing distribution. These values may then develop an autonomous life of their own, shaping interactions and institutions quite independently of the power which originally promoted and disseminated them.

But the analysis cannot stop there. It is convenient at this juncture to anticipate points that will be made more fully later. Scarcity of labour can, as we have seen, produce a shift in power relations in favour of employees. Given the right to pursue their aspirations freely through independent associations, the more favourably placed groups may be able to mobilize their power with the aim of imposing or negotiating changes in the prevailing organizational norms. This mobilization is achieved through organization. By submitting to norm-governed behaviour of their own structuring, they achieve collective control of an economic resource—their own labour. This control over a resource they then try to apply to the normative-regulation process, either by forcing management to accept their norms or by obliging them at least to come to compromise agreements in a process of joint regulation. Consciousness of this power that lies to hand may itself stimulate aspirations. Value components in their own culture or some other culture to which they make reference—values to which they have previously been denied access—may now seem within reach. Concepts like freedom, equality, respect, and fairness may become invested with new practical meanings as these emergent crystallizations of power take hold of elements in the cultural heritage and make them serve new ends and new interest groups. New ideologies seek to legitimize these endeavours and undermine those of management, and the possession of power makes possible their dissemination. They, too, shape interactions and institutions, changing the content of social disputation and conflict; modifying classes and class relations. Major social change, including significant adjustments in power and class fortunes, may result from new values or re-interpretations of old ones which owe nothing to any engineering by dominant social groups and may in fact be resisted by them.

The foregoing discussion is directly relevant to the debate between so-called 'integration' theory, highly influential in the United States under the intellectual leadership of Talcott Parsons, and 'coercion' or conflict theory of the sort more prevalent in the work of European sociologists, especially those in the Marxist tradition. Dahrendorf presents the issues incisively (1959), and Giddens (1968) gives other references. The debate is intricate. Here it must suffice to say that whereas integration theory conceives of social structure in terms of a functionally integrated system held in equilibrium by certain patterned processes based on common norms and values, conflict theory views social structure as being held together by coercive power but yet producing within itself the forces which maintain it in an endless process of change.

In fact, the structure and dynamics of the industrial enterprise are altogether more complex and subtle than can be accounted for by either the integration or the coercion model. Insofar as there is an absence of normative agreement between superordinate and subordinate, management norms may be enforced by power. But there may be a measure of normative agreement which, to the extent that it prevails, enables subordinates to legitimize management's superordinate role and the use of sanctions. Some part of this normative agreement may well have been engineered through the superior material and psychological resources enjoyed by the power-holders. But unless the power-holders take steps to ensure their own monopoly, events that are unplanned or at least unplanned by them may cause a shift in power relations—such as a labour scarcity produced by a sustained boom in free market economies, or by full employment policies pursued by governments. There may follow a quickening of normative aspirations that owes nothing to any engineering by dominant social groups. Normative conflict may follow and force managerial adjustments in both substantive and procedural norms.

Empirically, therefore, enterprise norms are more likely to be supported by a mixture of power and authority than by either operating alone. If we think in terms of a continuum with pure power and pure authority at opposite extremes, most enterprises are likely to be found in the middle ranges. The situations in which subordination is enforced by a more or less continuous exercise of power tend to stand out as pathologically conflict-ridden; those in which authority's writ runs relatively unblemished are viewed as rare showpieces.

8 THE SOURCES OF NORMATIVE CONFLICT

We have traced the exercise of power in organizations to the fact that the adherence of participants to procedural and substantive norms is problematical, and that insofar as organization means planned, predictable behaviour its leaders are likely to see themselves as obliged, at least as a last resort, to use power to enforce such behaviour. This leaves open for the moment such questions as how much planning and predictability is sought, what level of performance is aspired to, and what other methods are available and used before the last resort is reached. The question which now calls for closer examination is: what makes the adherence of subordinates to organizational norms problematical?

It will be recognized that in exploring the exercise of power against transgressors we are, by definition, excluding the disciplining of Merton's aberrant who basically accepts the prevailing norms but who, from weakness, strong temptation or whatever, transgresses those he finds specially irksome or easy to evade. There is no normative conflict here and he may well not perceive the punitive sanctions as power, for there is an important sense in which he is giving 'consent' to their imposition. The case of the nonconformer, however, is very different. How are we to conceptualize the causes of the normative conflict which produces him?

One way into this problem is to see the organization as a coalition of stakeholders (Rhenman, 1968, for a statement and further reading). Stakeholders are defined as individuals or groups who depend on the organization for the realization of their goals and on whom, in turn, the organization is dependent for its continuance. Their participation therefore rests upon their receiving certain minimum inducements and upon their making a certain minimum contribution (Simon, Smithburg, and Thompson, 1950, for a full statement of this view). They include not only a wide and diverse range of employee groups but also shareholders, consumers, creditors, suppliers, the local community, central government, and others which require no specific mention here.[8] As will be seen later, stakeholders can also be seen as constraints on management, though we must be careful to remember that management itself is a major stakeholder,[9] the nature of whose stake has yet to be examined.

Such a perspective invokes the picture of a convergence of 'interests' towards a pattern of collaboration which, given two conditions,

[8] Even this passing reference to a complex issue brings out the conceptual problems of defining 'organizational boundaries'.

[9] More precisely, as will be seen later, the management system consists, not of one homogeneous group of individuals with similar goals, but of a plurality of stakeholder groups with goals that are by no means the same.

enables them all to get at least an acceptable minimum of what they want. The first condition is that they are coordinated with sufficient skill by top management, both in relation to each other and in relation to the organization's numerous environments, to ensure that the organization can continue to offer the minimum inducements for continued participation by each of the interests. The second condition is that the aspirations of the stakeholders remain compatible on at least some minimum level at which all are prepared to continue participation. It is not enough, therefore, simply to postulate 'interests' or stakeholders. We must always direct our attention to their aspirations—or to express the same point in different terms—to the way they perceive and define the situation for themselves.

No great knowledge of industry is required to identify a number of incompatibilities which may emerge. Suppliers may demand a 'long term' for delivery; customers will normally press for a short one. Employees may demand a wage level which threatens shareholders' hopes for a high dividend or consumers' hopes for stable prices. Managers may seek a free hand to introduce labour-saving equipment or rationalization policies while employees demand security and assert property rights in the job. Governments may try to impose stable prices at a time when managements are under strong pressures to raise them, or may press industries to raise the proportion of output going to export when management would prefer to cultivate more convenient and possibly safer markets at home.

When the employer or manager declares, to a group of recalcitrant workers: 'We are all in this together', he may well be reciting a truism in the sense that all the stakeholders may feel dependent for what they want upon the continued existence of the organization. But he may shrink from the implications of consciously recognizing that their wants may not be easily compatible. He may seek to subsume them all under a general assumption that what really matters are economic values alone, and that if only the stakeholders pull together they can facilitate his leadership role and enable him to increase the share of everyone—profit-receiver, consumer, and employee alike (Nichols, 1969). There are at least two major weaknesses, however, in this view. Firstly, it has long been clear that when men demand 'more', they often mean not only absolutely more but relatively more than some other group or groups. Convictions about justice are at stake as well as goods and services. This casts light on an important difference within the world of values. There is one realm of values of which it can be said that 'to share is not to take away'. For example,

c

social values may include the notion that there are certain modes of behaviour that we may adopt towards a man which embody 'the respect due to him as a human being'. Now A may be enjoying the benefit of these behaviours while B is excluded. But if, subsequently, they are extended to B also, A will not have to give up his enjoyment of them. In order for B to receive this respect it is not necessary for A to go without it. Insofar as we are concerned with the respect due to men as men, B can receive it without A having to give up his. In other words, it can be said of this value that we can 'share' without 'taking away'. This is obviously not the case, however, with respect to the value placed on material goods and services. A and B may agree to collaborate to maximize economic wealth, and B may agree to accept A's direction and thus make collaboration more effective. To this extent, they hold the same values and B is able to legitimize the norms governing the relationship, which is therefore one of authority. But when it comes to sharing the wealth produced, A's gain may be B's loss. In other words, so far as a continuously-rising material standard of life is concerned, this is a value which we cannot share without 'taking away'. Thus even shared values can generate conflict.

The second major weakness of the view which exhorts the stake-holders to focus on their common interest of maximizing economic wealth is that the organization by no means offers only economic values. It can also offer its members the chance to exercise power, pit themselves against challenges, do work which they find satisfying, enjoy congenial social relations, find psychological security, or simply live a quiet life. The pursuit of economic values may threaten any of these for particular persons or groups at particular times. These facts alone are sufficient to explain divergencies between the members of the manager's constraint-set. What is at issue is not only how wealth is distributed, but how it is produced in the first place.

This brings us back to the point that much depends on the compatibility of the aspirations of the various stakeholders. It is sometimes argued that organization imposes objectively-rational requirements of behaviour upon each of the stakeholders—that claims should not be pressed to the point where the organization's survival is threatened. But this is much too simple and static a view. A powerful stakeholder may enlarge his claim in the belief—which may or may not prove valid—that other stakeholders will submit or that management can be driven so to conduct organizational affairs as to accommodate this enlarged claim without depriving the other stakeholders. If other organizations are accessible, threats can be made that the stake will be withdrawn and contributed elsewhere. Under these pressures managements are constantly making major or minor readjustments in their coordination and deployment of resources so as to meet the shifting incidence of stakeholder claims. The dynamic and continuous nature of this process means that it is characterized, on management's part, not so much by weightily argued grand strategy, but rather by tactical day-to-day improvisations, shifts and contrivances. The business ideology, currently fostered in some quarters in the United States, of the dedicated professional management disinterestedly weighing stakeholder claims and ensuring that each receives 'justice' pays little respect to a far less tidy reality (Nichols, 1969). The reality is characterized by a management which is itself a stakeholder striving, in the light of its own aspirations, to coordinate the contributions of a coalition of other stakeholders whose claims to some extent run parallel but to some extent diverge. This helps to explain the appeal of 'growth' as a primary objective for company managements (Galbraith, 1969). A policy of expansion may make possible higher financial rewards all round and also create many opportunities of promotion to jobs of higher pay, status and interest, thereby enabling management to accommodate quite a wide range of stakeholder aspirations including, of course, their own.

A view of management as striving to accommodate the interests of a range of diverse stakeholders draws attention to the fact that discretionary decision-making is involved. This raises the question of accountability. In the nineteenth century the interests of the stakeholders were deemed to be protected by the impersonal forces of the market, which closely constrained managers to take decisions which in the long run were in everyone's best interests. Whatever the truth then, there would be considerable agreement now that the market no longer, for good or ill, constrains managerial behaviour to this degree. For a variety of reasons, managements of large corporations find themselves 'administering' and 'managing' prices, wages, and demand (Galbraith, 1969; Shonfield, 1965) and enjoying some discretion in the process. There need be no cause for surprise that uneasiness should be expressed about this managerial power and to whom and to what extent it is accountable (Cheit, 1964). More precisely, three questions can be asked of management in any industrial society. What mechanisms exist through which the various stakeholders can hope to influence the ways in which management exercises its discretion? Do these mechanisms favour some stake-holders as against others? By what values or ideologies are these mechanisms—or their absence—on the one hand justified, and on the other, challenged?

These questions cannot be pursued here, but it is from some such analysis that we can draw the answer to the question which opened this section—how are we to explain normative conflict in the terms of our present theoretical framework? Briefly the answer is that, the nature of the coalition being what it is, and the nature of employee aspirations being what they often are, management sometimes feels constrained to govern contrary to the interests of employees as they themselves see them. We have already noted and criticized the idea that management's role in this process is that of disinterested mediator concerned only with some criterion of the social good. As a major stakeholder, management brings its own aspirations to bear. The management stake obviously needs to be examined.

9 MANAGEMENT ASPIRATIONS AND GOALS

As in the case of lower participants, management's substantive aspirations may be for such extrinsics as money and status, or such intrinsics as challenge, achievement, personal growth and self-actualization. Procedural aspirations may be for more power or authority, either for its own sake or instrumentally to achieve ends which may be either self-regarding or altruistically directed towards the supposed interests of other persons, other groups, or society as a whole. Again, cultural variations between societies are apparent (Haire, *et al.,* 1963; Harbison and Myers, 1959).

In bringing their aspirations to bear on their work situation, managements are faced with a set of constraints. Here we take up again the notion of stakeholders. The nature of the constraint set varies within and between societies, but the range from which these constraints are drawn includes the product market (where management has to concern itself with the demands and shifting tastes of consumers and the threat, if any, from competitive organizations and products); factor markets (where the interests of suppliers, including suppliers of finance in the form of shareholders and creditors, make themselves felt); the state of the arts (in the form of productive methods and techniques, which may bring their own compulsions to bear); the political environment (in the form of policy or planning pressures from government, parties, or political agencies of any description); the socio-cultural environment (including public opinion and the law); and finally, the substantive and procedural aspirations of the other members of the organization.

It is a matter for empirical enquiry as to which of these and possibly other constraints are operative. If the organization is to survive, all the constraints in the set must receive a certain minimal attention. If they do not, consumers go elsewhere; suppliers withdraw service; techniques become too obsolete to be viable; political agencies invoke the power of the state; the law enacts its penalties; or the members of the organization refuse to continue participation.

In asserting that all the constraints in a given manager's constraint set must receive a certain minimal attention if the organization is to survive, it is important to remember that survival is not inevitable. Management may not aspire to survive, or, though aspiring, may lack the requisite knowledge, skill, resources, or luck. Economic or sociological theories which attempt to identify market sanctions against managerial inefficiency in terms of lost trade, declining profits or bankruptcy are constantly confronted with evidence that managerial inertia can persist even in the face of ruin. Such a situation can arise, perhaps, from a change in methods or markets to which management fails to adapt. Industrial history can show many family firms, for example, which have proved unable to meet the organizational challenges posed by growing size or technological or market change, and which have foundered or been absorbed as a result. In any case, the 'needs of survival', on which some conceptual models rest so heavily for explanations of managerial behaviour, tell us little, for the range of variation in the vigour and mastery with which work organizations are conducted over and above mere survival level is very great.

The question of which constraints in their set bear most heavily upon management depends upon such factors as their society's institutional arrangements—which greatly affect the power with which a particular constraint can, as it were, present its claim—and the values and expectations which society brings upon management's execution of the role. In a fully-planned society, for example, where free markets have been abolished and where productive decisions are centralized in planning agencies, the power of the consumer interest may be so limited as to exercise only a negligible constraint on management. If employees are forbidden to mobilize their own power through independent, collective associations, or are restricted in their mobility from job to job, they too may constitute only a weak constraint on managerial decision-making.

Similarly the technology may be static; the law ineffective; public opinion indulgent; political agencies sympathetic; and suppliers lacking in bargaining power. Conversely, management may find itself operating in a fiercely competitive free enterprise market with rapidly-changing products and technology; hedged about with rigidly-applied legal regulations; subject to political pressures supported by a censorious public opinion; and facing factor markets where the suppliers of raw materials, finance and labour all enjoy superior bargaining power. Clearly the range of possible combinations of constraints is wide and calls for empirical exploration in each case.

Faced with its particular constraint set, management shapes its goals accordingly. In the process it will select a certain constraint or constraints as salient in the sense that management perceives it as specially important for its goals and as calling for special attention. The significance of this is certainly not that non-salient constraints will necessarily be ignored. In the first place, the quest for survival involves, as we have seen, some degree of concern with all the constraints that present themselves. And in the second place, management may manifest a concern with a non-salient constraint which goes well beyond that required for mere survival if it perceives it as having instrumental value for the service of a salient constraint. The more powerfully a non-salient constraint asserts itself the more likely it is to receive this kind of attention. To make this point, incidentally, is to draw attention to the fact that the salience or non-salience for management of a given constraint is not necessarily determined by its power or lack of it.

It is not necessarily the case, of course, that the service of non-salient constraints will be perceived by management as having any instrumental value for the service of its salient constraints. The demands of the former may well be perceived as being in direct conflict with the demands of the latter.

The fact that one or more constraints in its set will be perceived by management as salient has a further significant aspect. An important managerial activity is the so-called 'search' process through which is generated the flow of initiatives, ideas, research, and programmes for development. Management's choice of saliency among its various constraints will have a considerable effect on the nature of this search process, insofar as the choice will itself determine what sorts of action occur to the searchers as being worthy of consideration.

It remains now to illustrate these abstractions by practical examples. Galbraith has argued that in Western capitalist societies the prevailing mode is for management to seek, as a first priority, a secure minimum of company earnings sufficient to make accustomed payments to shareholders and to provide a supply of savings for reinvestment (1969). But this he sees as a means to what for them is a more important end—the service of their own aspirations through autonomy and growth. In our terms this would rank as a non-salient constraint perceived by management as having instrumental value for the pursuit of their aspirations towards greater power and status. Once their own safety and autonomy are ensured by a minimum level of company earnings, the predominant choice of management, argues Galbraith, is to seek the greatest possible rate of corporate growth as measured in sales. This therefore represents their salient constraint. Again, in the terms of the present analysis, other constraints such as employee aspirations and political pressures might be perceived by management as being in direct conflict with the salient constraint.

Galbraith's view of what he believes to be the prevailing orientations of corporate managements is wholly or partially shared by some theorists (Baumol, 1959; Marris, 1964), but is contested by others who, for example, assert that for analytical purposes one need only assume the prime goal to be long-run profit maximization, or is challenged prescriptively by those who argue that corporations ought to be conducted primarily in the interests of the stockholders (Hayek, 1960). Rubner has emerged as another doyen of shareholder rights who, in the course of a stimulating discussion (accompanied by a valuable bibliography), asserts that 'A mixture of paternalism and contempt for the functionless shareholder is typical of the mental outlook of the modern director' (1966, p. 78).

The debate about business objectives, both in its descriptive and its prescriptive aspects, relates closely to the continuing controversy about the nature and extent of the divergence between ownership and control (see Child, 1969a, in this series for discussion and references, and Nichols, 1969). The connection lies, of course, in the degree of management independence which gives them some freedom to choose which constraints to treat as salient.

Whatever the facts about the dominant modes of management goal-behaviour, the total range of modes that can be found is wide (Webber, 1969). Profit-seeking behaviour and growth-seeking behaviour may between them cover a major portion of the field, but it is possible for salience to be given, for example, to employee aspirations by seeking forms of social organization which embody certain ethical principles to which a leading management figure or some wider group of participants is committed. Public honours may be sought by giving salient concern to political pressures or to objectives defined by government as being 'in the public interest'.

When we turn from private enterprise to the public sector of capitalist societies and to publicly-dominated economies, differences are at once apparent which affect management's constraint set. Suppliers of finance, for example, may occupy a very limited place. Care is needed, however, in making inferences about probable management behaviour. The private shareholder may disappear, but if governmental constraints—possibly now more assertive—place emphasis on the criteria of financial performance, management behaviour may change little.

Other possible differences in constraint sets may result from differences in the position and power of consumers, political agencies, employees, and the law. Management's attitudes towards the various members of its constraint sets may be affected accordingly. Managements in fully-planned economies may feel a need to pursue their goals by at least appearing to serve their political masters. 'The Soviet manager is oriented to production. Volume of output is the acid test of his work. Marketing is no problem; finance is a trivial concern. But the purchasing department is the rock on which the factory organization stands, for supply shortages lead to production shortages. A good procurement man is above price' (Granick, 1961, p. 280). Employee aspirations may be an important instrumental constraint from the point of view of production norms, but consumers may come a long way behind.

Given the crucial importance to such groups as consumers, employees, shareholders and governments of managerial aspirations, goals, and the choice of salient constraints, it is not surprising that, where possible, these groups seek to exert influence or power, direct or indirect, to mould those aspirations and choices. This can be done by strengthening some constraints and weakening others, or by acting upon management's values through socialization or ideological persuasion. Consumers may organize themselves or try to insist on competitive markets or price controls; shareholders may form militant movements or support take-over bids; employees may form unions, demand changes in procedural norms and promote counter-ideologies; and the state may discourage or encourage monopoly, impose legislation of many different kinds to structure management choices, and promote certain values and ignore others. The range of this state activity is, of course, enormous, but of special relevance to the work experience of employees are the diverse ways in which the state can affect the organization's procedural norms on which their substantive circumstances depend. These procedures of decision-making can be shaped by encouraging or discouraging trade unionism, collective bargaining, and all the concomitant expressions of collective action which these involve; by requiring—or not requiring—managements to set up consultative or decision-making councils representative of subordinates as well as themselves; or by imposing devices of accountability which ensure some power or influence to lower participants. Certain experimental forms in this field have attracted considerable attention and debate in recent years, notably the so-called 'workers' management' of Yugoslavia (Blumberg, 1968, for discussion and bibliography), and 'co-determination' in the coal and steel industries of West Germany (Blumenthal, 1956; Shuchman, 1957, Spiro, 1958). Of all the forms of participation in decision-making in the West, however, collective bargaining or joint regulation is by far the most important and securely rooted (for a comprehensive review of the situation in a wide variety of countries, see *Participation of Workers in Decisions within Undertakings,* International Labour Office, Geneva, 1967). The relative merits of different forms of participation have been newly canvassed in recent years as a result of fresh stimulus to the long-standing debate on 'industrial democracy' (Clegg, 1951 and Clegg, 1960, for earlier statements; Blumberg, 1968, for a challenge to this perspective).

Much of what has been said so far in this section about management aspirations and goals refers more specifically to top management. It would be wrong, however, to suppose that all levels of management can be subsumed within the same perspective. In referring to management as a stakeholder, it would be more appropriate to see different levels or groups within the management system as having different stakes; as facing different constraint sets; and as therefore having different goals. For example, the head of an industrial company's maintenance and construction department may see one of his goals as being that of resisting all proposals to put internal company work out to contract with specialist maintenance and construction companies, fearing the consequences to his own future position and status (Chandler, 1964). This may conflict with

c*

the goals of other management groups who might have their own reasons for seeking to reduce costs or inconvenience by calling upon outside services. Some of the implications of regarding the management system as a plurality of interest groups will emerge later.[10]

10 MANAGEMENT CULTURE AND NORMATIVE CONFLICT

Management's choice of constraint saliency is of course a direct expression of values. In discussing the probable nature of management goals we need therefore to examine the values that tend to predominate in management culture. This is a culture which has spread outwards from Western Europe to become increasingly worldwide. It has three major components which are closely related. The first is the value-system of economic rationality analysed by Weber (1964), prominent in which are such principles as the measured weighing of utilities and costs; the use of money as the universal measure of value; and the importance of maximizing-behaviour and of capital accounting. The second major component is the value-system of economic growth: the philosophy which measures national success by performance in the international league-table of Gross National Product. This philosophy is now virtually worldwide and completely transcends fundamental differences in political and social systems. The third component is the closely associated notion of technological progress; the philosophy that finds terminal as well as instrumental value in extending human control over material resources. These three components constitute the dominant culture of industrial societies—the culture in which managers are trained before and during incumbency of their role. Here we link up with the themes of the first chapter, where we noted the heavy emphasis of modern social values on production-for-consumption, on material costs and utilities, and on efficiency and productivity. These are orientations that are highly valued; by the same token they are highly rewarded.

Top managers are therefore likely to choose their salient constraints from among those which relate to financial accounting, production technology, and the promotion of markets for the goods and services produced. It is through the medium of these constraints that they are likely to perceive their aspirations as being most fruitfully pursued. Insofar as they are able to shape the substantive

---

[10] The work goals of professionals (such as scientists and technologists) in the organization also have their special interest (Glaser, 1963; Kornhauser and Hagstrom, 1962; Prandy, 1965; Ritti, 1968; Strauss, 1964).

and procedural norms of the organization, it will be these salient constraints that are likely to have the preferential influence on the shaping. Other constraints will be met, but only insofar as this is necessary for survival or serves instrumentally a salient constraint. Included among these others are, of course, the aspirations of the employees. As we have noted, employees may be able to mobilize enough power to force management to pay very close attention to their aspirations. So far as they are concerned, however, there is a great difference between a situation in which management pursues employee interests as a primary concern, and a situation in which it pursues them only insofar as they are compatible with some other primary concern. The implications for the managerial frame of reference within which search is conducted for possible policies are profound. In the second situation, a whole range of possibilities which might serve employees' aspirations will not only fail to receive serious consideration, but will simply not occur to the minds of policy-makers and planners for the reason that their frame of reference cannot be expected to generate such initiatives.

The argument leads us, therefore, towards certain crucial propositions. Depending on managers' substantive and procedural aspirations, there is a probability that they will perceive their concern with employee interests to be no more than instrumental to, if not conflicting with, their primary interests and will seek to define organizational norms accordingly. This does not of itself imply conflict. To the extent that employees are totally committed to the same values as management, they may accept that management must be the judge of priorities. In terms of procedural aspirations, they may define for themselves a role of submission to managerial rule and therefore to the substantive norms that management decrees. Such value-consensus may not, however, exist. Employees may well dispute the value placed by managers upon minimizing labour costs, upon pleasing consumers or shareholders in preference to themselves, upon seeking new technology to replace old skills, upon developing new products or new markets whatever the threat to the expectations of lower participants. It is for these reasons that the adherence of employees to management's norms must be considered problematical. It is in these terms that we need to discuss the possibility of normative conflict.

CHAPTER III

Adaptations to the Social Organization

At this point we may suitably pull together the principal strands of the exposition that have emerged so far. We began with the question of what the individual seeks from his work, presenting the issue in terms of extrinsic and intrinsic values. In relation to the organization these values manifest themselves as the individual's normative aspirations, substantive and procedural. These aspirations may or may not be met by the norms prevailing in the organization. Or to express the same notion in a different way, the normative system insofar as it affects him may be congruent or incongruent with his aspirations. The organizational norms will of course owe a great deal to management, who design them according to the values embodied in *its* aspirations. To the varying extents in which the individual's normative aspirations are met by the norms prevailing in the organization, there exist varying degrees of normative agreement. Normative agreement provides the basis of an authority relationship. Authority therefore rests ultimately on shared values—on an identity between the values underlying the subordinate's aspirations in work and those underlying management's norms.

To the extent that the individual's normative aspirations are not met, there is a state of normative conflict and a corresponding lack of authority. If management's norms are to prevail in these circumstances, they can only be upheld by power. Given the resulting lack of legitimacy, employees are likely to consider themselves justified in seeking to evade or change them if they have the opportunity.

Judged by certain of the components of the Western cultural heritage, such as equality and the prime importance of the individual personality, some measure of normative conflict might seem, on the face of it, to be highly probable in societies influenced by that heritage. For in pursuing a set of values within which those of economic rationality commonly predominate over those of equality and concern for the individual personality, managements usually deem it expedient to construct normative systems marked by extreme inequalities and by a tendency to see persons as means rather than ends.

These inequalities extend to every aspect of the social organization. Generally speaking, opportunities for pursuing substantive and procedural aspirations tend to diminish as we move from the top to the bottom of the structure. Whether we are concerned with extrinsics such as financial rewards, fringe benefits, status and security, or intrinsics such as job interest and opportunities for challenge, achievement, responsibility, decision-making and other contributants to self-fulfilment, the scope tends to narrow as we descend the hierarchy from top management to unskilled labourer (Tannenbaum, 1966).

It is practicable to devise ways of measuring and comparing these job attributes, so it must not be supposed that we are appealing to merely impressionistic evaluations of work. One study by Turner and Lawrence, for example, presents 'task attribute rating scales' which systematically order different jobs in terms of such dimensions as variety, autonomy, interaction, knowledge, skill and responsibility (1965). Such attempts to evolve operational measures for reducing the imprecision of more general comparisons is akin to the work of Woodward (1965, 1970) and Pugh *et al.* (1963) in searching for empirically measurable variables for use in organizational analysis. It might well be that a combination of these lines of inquiry would be necessary in trying to measure certain other job attributes—such as, for example, what the job offered in terms of direct or indirect participation in decision-making.

It requires little detailed research, however, to establish the general point being made here—that jobs located towards the top of the hierarchy provide scope for wider and deeper aspirations than do jobs located towards the bottom. Relatively viewed, multiple advantages at the top of the structure may be compared with multiple disadvantages at the bottom. Setting aside for a moment the question of the level of aspirations, positions at the top seem likely to offer the possibility of a high degree of normative agreement; positions at the bottom a high degree of normative conflict.

1 COMMITMENT AND ALIENATION

Of considerable significance here, both conceptually and empirically, is the question of normative commitment to the role or the organization. Normative commitment implies what Etzioni calls 'moral involvement'—a 'positive orientation of high intensity' (1961, p. 10). Top management sees this in terms of 'loyal identification with the aims of the company'. Translating into the present framework, it could be analysed as follows.

If normative agreement between the individual's aspirations and the prevailing organizational norms extends to intrinsically-valued norms which, in the terms of Western culture, are said to encourage and promote psychological and personality growth, this agreement could be said to touch greater depths within the individual than agreement which is limited, say, to financial rewards, with their implication of a more utilitarian and segmental, though not necessarily weaker, attachment. Insofar as normative agreement does extend to these deeper levels of the individual's response he is likely to experience it as more nearly total than segmental, with the result that, as we say, his 'personality' becomes 'involved'. Given such a depth of normative agreement, the individual will feel 'identified' or 'committed'. It follows that commitment of this nature is more likely to be found in the upper than the lower ranks. The former tend to be 'more involved and personally identified with their work, and their attitudes toward the organization itself are more favourable. These relationships are so general that students of organization may react with surprise when exceptions to them are found (Tannenbaum, 1966, pp. 39–43). The condition of commitment is one which many managements would like to see universal throughout their organization. They usually fail, however, to understand the necessary preconditions for it—namely a work situation which provides scope for the individual to exercise and develop what he feels to be his deeper self, as against a work situation which hedges him closely about with restrictions, controls, and precisely defined programmes for action. The social relations of industry offer few perspectives more ironical than that of a deeply-committed management recoiling with puzzled contempt from the manifest indifference of their hourly-paid workers to everything other than the principal aspiration that holds them within a system which management itself has designed—the size of the pay packet.

Even among manual workers, however, differences between the task attributes of varying types of work can be significant enough to result in different degrees of commitment. Turner and Lawrence, comparing worker responses to forty-seven very different jobs spread over eleven American industries, found that among rural small town workers, whose aspirations included 'a relatively large amount of variety, autonomy, interaction, skill, and responsibility', the more 'knowledge, skill, and sense of responsibility, intrinsic to the work, the more likely was worker response to be characterized by very low absenteeism, suggesting a favourable kind of involvement in the task' (1965, pp. 36, 93).[1] The much greater differences in task attributes as between manual and, say, high-level administrative, technical, scientific, and intellectual work, could be expected to produce correspondingly sharp differences in commitment.

Discussion of commitment also invites attention to what is often regarded as its opposite—alienation. At once we face a problem. If commitment describes a state of normative agreement which extends to the intrinsic values in work, are we to define alienation as a state in which the individual aspires to such fulfilment but is denied? Such a definition is often implied (Feuer, 1962). But let us consider two examples. An ambitious young executive, eager not only for money and status but also for challenge, autonomy, responsibility and power, chafes at having to wait. An hourly-paid worker on the shop floor, convinced that he would be unrealistic to hope for challenge, autonomy, meaning, responsibility and power in his work, suppresses any aspirations he may have in these directions and cultivates indifference to virtually every aspect of the work situation other than its financial rewards, which he finds generally satisfactory. Figuratively speaking he repudiates a major part of his nature which might otherwise cherish normative aspirations towards intrinsic values in work. Which of the two is alienated? The executive can hardly be said to be alienated from a mode of activity which he is only too anxious to enlarge and extend, or from an organization with which he is only too anxious to identify. It does not seem plausible, therefore, to define alienation in terms of frustration, which implies continuing orientation towards a given goal. Of the two, therefore, it is the hourly-paid worker who must be considered alienated.

This is, of course, Marx's approach. For the early Marx, 'total man is the one who would not be mutilated by the division of labour. The man of modern industrial society . . . has acquired a specific form as a result of a particular trade. He remains imprisoned for the greater part of his existence by this specialized activity, and hence he leaves unused a number of aptitudes and capacities which might be developed' (Aron, 1968, p. 146). Under private ownership of the means

---

[1] This is but one aspect of a wider inquiry, which is discussed and compared with other relevant research in Shepard (1970).

of production, the worker not only loses control over the product of work but also over the process. Work, the essential activity which defines man's humanity and through which he realizes himself, loses its essential characteristics and becomes merely a means of obtaining a livelihood (Bottomore and Rubel, 1963). The link is plain to see between the philosophy of work implicit here and the doctrine of William Morris, the craft ethic analysed by Wright Mills, and current notions of self-actualization. Labour, for Marx, was alienated because it had become a commodity sold to others and not a form of self-expression. Deprived of opportunity for self-expression in the very activity through which he could hope to realize himself, man therefore lost his sense of self and identity. But whereas for Marx alienation was a temporary affliction from which men would be released with the passing of capitalist society, for Tocqueville, Weber and modern critics it is a product of industrialization and mass society *per se* (Nisbet, 1967). Alienation is seen as a consequence of the organization of work itself and the abolition of private property carries no implications for change in this respect. A communally-owned industrial system may be just as consumer-oriented as a privately-owned one, and just as concerned with what work does *for* people to the exclusion of what it does *to* them. In other words—to restore continuity with the preceding analysis—if work is the activity through which man realizes himself, then a situation in which he repudiates or ignores the self-realizing aspects of work is a situation in which he repudiates his own essential nature. Thence derives the language of 'self-estrangement'. The young executive is not, therefore, alienated, because far from repudiating his own nature, he is only too eager to give it full scope.

Here, then, we are defining the alienated worker as one who is cut off from certain kinds of work experience to which he himself does not aspire. Thus he can be alienated yet perfectly satisfied. The concept therefore clearly embodies the assertion of normative aspirations on behalf of others. We are saying that certain kinds of experience would be good for people though they themselves do not realize it. More precisely, the concept embodies (i) the empirically testable belief that certain types of social condition result in certain psychological states, and (ii) the non-empirical value that some psychological states, and the behavioural patterns that flow from them, are intrinsically superior to others. 'Marx pointed to meaninglessness of work and a sense of powerlessness to affect the conditions of one's life, dissociation from the products of one's labour, the sense of playing a role in an impersonal system which one does not understand or control ...' (Lukes, 1967, p. 151). Whether men were conscious of this or not, a change in social conditions could provide them with a life experience which they would value more highly once they had come to know it. The modern self-actualization school argues, in essence, along the same lines. They share, with Marx, a moral ideal of man which they variously describe as healthy, normal, natural, mature, or self-actualizing. This ideal can be realized or denied by the normative system which structures the work situation.

In describing alienation as a consequence of work organization we are faced with the need to give it concrete meaning. This is not easy. Blauner, however, has taken up Seeman's attempt (1959) to give alienation a multi-dimensional definition and applies the notions of powerlessness, meaninglessness, isolation, and self-estrangement to the varying forms and structures of modern industry (Blauner, 1964).[2] Alienation is viewed as a quality of personal experience; a general syndrome comprising a number of different objective conditions and subjective feeling-states which emerge from certain relationships between workers and the socio-technical systems within which they are located. Blauner's analysis is valuable in correcting any view of industrial work as a homogeneous entity and showing the diversity of personal work experience. But what is the relationship between alienation and that vaguest of much-used concepts, job satisfaction?

We know that workers can be alienated in the sense that their location in the social organization precludes any normative commitment to the job or the enterprise and yet, for certain periods at least, have a firm attachment because their aspirations towards instrumental satisfactions are being well served (Goldthorpe, 1966; Goldthorpe *et al.,* 1968a). Blauner suggests that alienated workers are 'dissatisfied' only when they have 'developed *needs* for control, initiative, and meaning in work' (p. 29—his italics). 'Needs' are, of course, what are being referred to here as priority aspirations. Yet many inquiries appear to tap a widespread incidence of such needs according, for example, to Argyris (1964) and Touraine (1965). The notion of priorities in aspirations may help here by enabling us to suggest that many workers, despite being conditioned to a largely instrumental view of work, partly by agencies of socialization and partly by the experience-given conviction that intrinsic satisfactions

---

[2] In a subsequent paper (1967), Seeman stresses self-estrangement as the key dimension.

are not for them, nevertheless have certain aspirations in this direction which remain passive for most of the time, but can be tapped by attitude surveys. Their situation has behavioural consequences in that their largely instrumental and calculative attachment cannot be expected to demonstrate normative commitment towards, and identification with, the organization. Moreover, these lower priority aspirations may not only aggravate disruption at moments of special excitement, but also sharpen the vehemence with which the active aspirations—the ones within reach—are themselves pursued.

Empirically the whole field of inquiry into job satisfaction and occupational preferences is a difficult one. Attitude surveys which put simple 'sponge' questions get answers from the vast majority of people in all occupations saying that they are satisfied with their jobs. But the methodological weaknesses of this approach are many. What precisely is the source of their satisfaction—the pay, the working conditions, the social relationships, the work itself, the simple fact of being able to conform to a universal social expectation? It is doubtful if more than a small proportion of respondents know themselves, and there are many other difficulties (Blauner, 1967; Hyman, 1967). However, while the ambiguities of assessing absolute levels of job satisfaction are considerable, it is possible to speak with greater assurance about relative levels of satisfaction experienced by members of different occupational groups. All surveys show satisfaction declining steadily as one descends the occupational status scale (Herzberg *et al.*, 1957). Evidence from the Soviet Union has a general similarity with that from the West. 'Professionals and business administrators overwhelmingly report job satisfaction; the per cent satisfied generally decreases as we descend the occupational hierarchy . . .' (Inkeles and Bauer, 1959, pp. 103–4). Even absolute levels of satisfaction can be probed to some extent by asking appropriate questions. Perhaps a more sensitive indicator of latent dissatisfactions and frustrations is to ask people at all occupational levels whether they would choose another line of work if they had the chance to start their working life anew (Blauner, 1967). Managers and professionals show majorities opting for the kind of work they are doing already, whereas among manual workers a majority of even the skilled would have preferred to do something else.

2 RELATIVE DEPRIVATION

Evidence therefore supports the expectation that the inequalities embodied in the normative system are likely to result in normative commitment at the top of the hierarchy and in an increasing probability of normative conflict as we move down through its successive levels to the bottom. Yet, viewed in this light, industrial societies are remarkable not for the degree to which they are rent by disorder but by the degree to which they appear to meet the aspirations of many of the parties involved. Order tends to be the prevailing condition. Although the inequalities certainly constitute a formula for maximum discontent at the base of the hierarchy, tapering off to a minimum towards the top, the extremes are often less far apart than might be expected. Managers may be more discontented than one would be inclined to predict, and lower participants less. Since the social and political consequences of this tendency are profound, it has naturally attracted some attention. A number of recent writers have sought to explain why in Britain, for example, 'considerable and abiding inequality does not apparently give rise to deeply divisive conflicts in which the existing social structure, political institutions included, is frequently and fundamentally called into question' (Goldthorpe, 1969b, p. 192).

There already exists in our analysis the source of explanation for this in the norms and values which differentially shape men's aspirations at different organizational levels. It is worth stressing, however, at this stage of the argument a concept that helps us to understand the relationship between inequality and grievance. This is the concept of relative deprivation. It draws attention to a process which contributes towards acquiescence and order in situations which otherwise appear rich in potentiality for conflict.

Runciman notes that 'dissatisfaction with the system of privileges and rewards in a society is never felt in an even proportion to the degree of inequality to which its various members are subject. Many people at the bottom of society are less resentful of the system, and many nearer the top are more so, than their actual position appears to warrant' (1966, p. 3). His explanation is that 'the aims of the less fortunate are channelled towards positions which are likely to be feasible for them rather than positions which will only be attained by those whose starting-point was much higher'. By contrast, 'those who had ... been successful seemed to have had their aspirations heightened by success. Success, therefore, can itself provide the external stimulus by which comparisons are heightened, whereas those who are forced to adjust themselves to lesser achievement will reduce their aspirations in accordance with their experience' (pp. 26, 29). It follows from this that men's aspirations are likely to grow the faster once their position has begun to improve; a fact which explains how industrialization and rising standards have promoted the worldwide 'revolution of rising expectations'.

The notion of relative deprivation presupposes the notion of reference group. The part played by reference groups in determining aspirations about rewards and status in work is too obvious to need labouring (Lipset and Trow, 1957). So-called 'coercive comparisons' in terms and conditions of employment have become, under conditions of labour scarcity, a source of inflationary pressure in the national economy (Turner, 1957; Taylor and Pierson, 1957). Large occupational groups seek an improvement in their position for no other reason than that another group with which they habitually compare themselves is already enjoying such an improvement. In the absence of a productivity increase, concessions to this claim must prove inflationary.

The mitigating consequences of the relative deprivation effect are considerable. If lower participants were habitually to compare their position with the financial rewards, status, autonomy and intrinsic job interest of higher management, it is difficult to see how industrial society in its present form could maintain its legitimacy. It might be supposed, therefore, that powerful groups would take an active interest in encouraging people to adopt the most modest reference groups which they could be persuaded to accept, since this would contribute to order and stability of the *status quo*. This would conflict violently, however, with an even more pressing objective of those who control the industrial systems of advanced Western countries, which is to promote ever-rising levels of consumption. People must be taught to want more. The more ambitious the comparative reference group, the greater the urge to consume. Thus for those with an interest in maximizing consumption, the more ambitious people's reference groups become, the better.

As yet, however, the reference groups typically chosen lean towards modesty rather than ambitiousness. In terms of extrinsic rewards, lower participants compare themselves with other lower participants, or those whose standards seem within achievable range, rather than with those at the top of the hierarchy. And in terms of intrinsic rewards, lower participants are often conditioned, as we have seen, by experience, by agencies promoting consumption values, and by class or work-group expectations into making few claims in this direction. Such aspirations as exist in this range may remain passive except at moments of crisis or special excitement.

This does not, as we have noted, mean that behavioural responses are not affected. The industrial system pays a price for its elaborate division of labour and its highly unequal distribution of autonomy, control, and responsibility. That price is the relative absence of normative commitment among a high proportion of its lower participants. If a man's relationship to his work is structured so as to exclude all but a minimal degree of discretion, judgement, challenge, responsibility, autonomy, and skill, there remain only the extrinsic satisfactions and, as we have seen, theorists of the self-actualization school such as Argyris, Maslow and Herzberg argue along with Marx that these cannot provide the basis for psychological growth and commitment.

The concepts of relative deprivation and comparative reference group therefore remind us, should we need reminding, that industrial systems of the existing type are only made possible by the widespread, habituated acceptance of values which support great inequalities of rewards and extreme hierarchical differentiation of status and decision-making roles. However, as already noted, if we rest content with this emphasis alone we ignore a major dynamic of change. New values—or more probably new interpretations of existing values—may quicken aspirations and promote discontent among employees with the prevailing norms, thus generating normative conflict. This may focus on any one or a combination of the substantive norms which directly or indirectly affect financial rewards or security or status or any other aspect of working conditions, or on the procedural norms which structure the ways in which decisions relating to these or any other organizational norms are taken. In order to trace the variety of responses to normative conflict and the consequences, we need to clarify the conceptual relationships between aspirations, organizational norms, and work goals.

3 WORK GOALS AND CONGRUENCY

The individual's aspirations in work may be said to constitute his general strategy. He aspires, say, to more money, or more security, or more job interest, or more autonomy. The specific tactical aims and objectives which he sets himself in order to realize these aspirations are his work goals. For example, in one kind of shop-floor situation an individual paid by the piece who aspires to more money may define a goal of maximizing his output. In another situation an individual paid by the piece with a similar aspiration might define a goal of minimizing his output—with the aim of compelling management to raise piece rates. Thus for any given aspiration, goals may differ according to the situation. They may also change at very short notice as the situation demands. They are the individual's currently-preferred methods of pursuing his aspirations within the normative system as it affects him.

If the normative system is fully congruent with his aspirations, his work goals will be fully congruent with the normative system. In other words, if the organizational norms are seen by him to offer full scope for realizing his aspirations, the consequence will be that he can accept the norms that seek to define his behaviour. His goals are coincidental with the task behaviours and objectives laid down by those norms. If, on the other hand, the normative system is incongruent with his aspirations, his goals are likely to take forms which diverge from these task behaviours and objectives and to be incongruent, therefore, with the normative system.

It might seem, on the face of it, safe to assume that the objectives of the organization's leaders would always be furthered by their subordinates having goals which were congruent with the normative system, and handicapped by their having goals which were incongruent. This cannot, in fact, be assumed. Situations may arise in which leadership objectives would be best served by action which diverged from formally-prescribed operating practice, and ill-served by action which followed that practice meticulously. Crises, unforeseen contingencies, and opportunities for informal innovative practices which raise efficiency are examples of such situations. With these provisos in mind we turn now to examine the diversity of possible goal-responses which individuals may offer to a situation which they perceive as one of normative conflict.

4 NORMATIVE CONFLICT AND ADAPTIVE RESPONSES

There are two basic types of response to normative conflict. In the first, awareness of incongruencies which are perceived by the individual as beyond his power to change causes him to withdraw from the situation. In the second, the individual takes positive action designed to prevent and reduce incongruency—and by the same token to defend and increase congruency.

Withdrawal may be complete, as measured by labour turnover, or partial, as measured by absenteeism and the sickness rate. Some would include here the accident rate. All are affected by many factors (Kilbridge, 1961), but the views have been advanced that 'accidents are in part used, however unconsciously, as a means of withdrawal from the work situation', and that absence phenomena generally 'reflect the quality of the relationship of the person to the employing institution' (Hill and Trist, 1962, pp. 23, 27). Withdrawal is not, however, necessarily physical in nature. The individual may withdraw from active involvement in his work into apathy and indifferent performance. In the second basic type of response, positive action on the normative system takes many different forms, but in general it follows from a disposition on the part of the individual (i) to ignore, manipulate or change the relevant norms in ways which are congruent for his own aspirations, and (ii) to defend himself against incongruent consequences produced by the manipulations and changes effected or proposed by others. Two further distinctions are important. The action may be effected either by the individual alone or in concert with others; and it may either be imposed unilaterally or introduced through an agreement of some description with opposing individuals or groups.

Both these basic types of response are manifested in behaviour. But we must not overlook the possibility that normative conflict may remain latent in the sense that it receives no behavioural expression of any kind. Theoretically, at least, we have to allow for the possibility that management power may be so absolute and all-pervasive that no outlets are available to the individual for manifesting his discontents—not even by withdrawal behaviours. Such a situation is very rare, but totalitarian regimes may offer examples of an approximation to it. In the Soviet Union, absenteeism may bring severe penalties, and when an employee seeks to exercise his legal right to give notice he sometimes finds that administrative devices and social pressures from party or 'enterprise committee' succeed in changing his mind (McAuley, 1969). There can be few situations, however, in which the employee has no way of venting his discontents upon the organization responsible for causing them. Insofar as he does have ways we are concerned, of course, with manifest behaviours.

The two basic types of manifest response differ sharply. Withdrawal is a generalized gesture of rejection specially apt to be made, perhaps, by those who perceive no methods by which they can act upon the specific norms which cause their discontent. Although withdrawal behaviours and other types of response are not mutually exclusive, there is some evidence that withdrawal is favoured by those without effective means of remedying their grievances (Sayles, 1958; Scott, *et al.*, 1963; Turner, *et al.*, 1967). The other manifest forms of action have the common characteristic of being directed towards specific norms perceived as disadvantageous. Action may take the form of evading, manipulating or changing the existing norms, thereby setting up, as the standard of reference for one's behaviour, norms of one's own choosing. The individual may be able to adopt his own norms without being noticed—or more precisely, without being noticed by anyone who wishes to challenge his action. Very few normative substitutions go unnoticed by someone. If this change renders the normative system less congruent for the observer's own aspirations, he may either feel compelled, if he occupies an inferior power position, to submit to the change, or decide to challenge it. It is the latter situation, in which an individual or group seeks to modify the normative system in ways which are then challenged by other individuals or groups, that we usually think of as conflict in the behavioural sense.

5 THE MERTONIAN PATTERN OF RESPONSES

A more detailed classification of adaptive responses—including responses to situations perceived as congruent as well as those perceived as incongruent—extends to a list so similar to that postulated by Merton (1957) for a very different context, that it seems pointless to invent completely different terms. His categories will therefore be used, with the caution that some divergencies of usage are inevitable. Responses by the individual range over the whole Mertonian gamut of conformity (for which a better term in this context might be simply 'acceptance'), innovation (convergent and divergent), ritualism (used in a different sense from Merton's), retreatism, and rebellion.

The first type of response is that of full acceptance of one's location in the normative system. One pursues one's goals by accepting and working through the existing norms. Convergent innovation refers to covert or overt individual initiation of change in organizational norms which benefits top management goals as well as the individual's. Divergent innovation, ritualism, retreatism, and rebellion, on the other hand, are all situations in which incongruencies produce a divergence between the individual's goals and the behaviours prescribed by the organizational norms—divergence of a kind which does not benefit top management goals. Divergent innovation refers to covert individual initiation of change which furthers the individual's goals but not those of top management. Ritualism implies a situation in which, given incongruency, the individual interprets his best interests to lie in invoking certain norms as a form of pressure upon management. In every organization there are certain norms—such as those, for example, relating to safety, quality, and formal procedures of many diverse kinds—which, if given exaggerated observance can prejudice operations. This produces the paradox whereby 'working to rule' can in extreme cases bring the organization to a standstill. There are many situations short of this, however, where ritualism, in the sense of insistence or over-insistence on the observance of certain norms, can be a potent instrument in the struggle for power and control (Crozier, 1964). Retreatism implies withdrawal. 'Defeatism, quietism and resignation are manifested in escape mechanisms which ultimately lead him to "escape" from the requirements of the society ... It is ... a privatized rather than a collective mode of adaptation' (Merton, 1957, pp. 153, 155). Rebellion constitutes an overt challenge to top management goals.[3] On an individual basis it is difficult to sustain except from locations near the top, where, however, it is unlikely to be pressed for quite different reasons, as will be seen later.

Adaptive responses on a collective as against an individual basis may be either innovative, ritualistic, or rebellious. Individuals may concert to apply covert innovative practices, to enforce certain organizational norms purely for their own tactical purposes, or in some other way to make an open challenge to management. Since the collective aspect derives from the need to mobilize more power than is possessed by the individual alone it is not relevant to the 'acceptance' and the retreatist forms of adaptation. As we shall see, these collective responses bring out the importance of the work group for the individual's aspirations. For example, 'groups allow full retreatism only inasmuch as they are weak and discouraged. Successful groups prohibit retreatism completely' (Crozier, 1964, p. 199).

It remains now to apply these categories to the goals of the different levels of management and to those of lower participants.

6 MANAGERIAL ADAPTATIONS

Top management is in a privileged position inasmuch as its role is so diffusely defined that, given its command over resources, it has wide scope for shaping the normative system to accommodate its own aspirations. Insofar as it can do this, its goals will of course be congruent with that system. Even the Soviet manager, surrounded

---

[3] Rebellion may range from revolt directed against only *some* of the norms to revolutionary action aimed at overthrowing the whole normative system. This distinction can be related to the discussion of 'the bases of legitimacy'.

with a fine mesh of state-imposed norms, is in practice usually able to shape them to suit his needs and interests (Granick, 1961). As already noted, however, the requirements for survival will impose a set of constraints. Unless the goals managers set themselves are adequate to meet these minimum conditions they leave themselves open to organizational extinction or being replaced by other leaders.

The position of middle managers is a complex one. They are likely to feel their location in the social organization to be more congruent for their aspirations than do those at the bottom of the hierarchy. Yet their goals are certainly not identical with those of top management. Their dependence upon higher management for approval, support and promotion is itself a differentiating factor, for dependence introduces its own frame of reference which by definition cannot be shared by those upon whom the dependence rests. Another factor distinguishing middle management from its superiors is its more immediate exposure to the day-to-day pressures on the shop floor. These two factors alone may result in goals which relate less to top management goals than to a satisfactory personal accommodation of conflicting pressures coming from above and below (Dalton, 1950b). This is likely to be equally true for lower managers—the so-called 'first-line' supervisors or foremen. Widespread recognition of this has resulted in the cliché notion of 'the man in the middle' (Roethlisberger, 1945). It has been said also of the Soviet foreman, as of his Western counterpart, that he 'has achieved success only as he has taken up a position independent both of management and of the workers he supervises. If he tries to execute all of management's instructions, enforce all rules, and sternly combat work restrictions, he can only succeed in cutting his own throat. On the other hand, he cannot fully identify with the workers under him; for if he does not maintain some pressure upon them, management will soon fire him. . . . In short, the foreman must try to be the shop-floor mediator between management and the workers' (Granick, 1961, p. 242).

These characteristics of their work situation may combine with others to render foremen much more disposed than their superiors to pursue their interests through collective action where this is possible. It is likely that, given organizational and technological complexity, middle and top management will increasingly be expected to hold formal qualifications in higher education or training, and that the foreman promoted from the shop floor will find his future prospects to be limited . With his status also undermined by a proliferation of managerial specialists, by the growth of hierarchy, and by new channels of communication between higher management and his work-group subordinates which often by-pass him altogether, the foreman seems diminishingly ready to identify himself with management. Ground between the nether millstone of an increasingly self-assertive and powerful work group, and the upper millstone of a management which expects of him a degree of control for which it no longer provides the structural pre-requisites, his status, role obligations, and rewards may come to seem so uncertain as to call for collective action with his colleagues if he is to achieve some control over his work situation.

The adaptations of the middle manager, on the other hand, are likely to take the form of individual, unilateral action of the innovative kind. He may feel able to propose changes that are congruent with his aspirations and resist changes that are incongruent by legitimizing his advocacy or obstructionism in terms of top management goals. If he cannot clothe his behaviour in this respectable garb of service to 'the organization's best interests', he may act covertly, conniving with other managers engaged in similar manipulations of the norms. His role as manager is likely to endow him with some command over resources and thus enable him the more effectively to pursue his goals on an individual basis. Individual action is likely to seem preferable, and his goals are unlikely to include overt collective action for private ends unless it can be legitimized by reference to top management goals. The reasons are two-fold, both deriving from the fact that the manager is on a career ladder. First, progress up the ladder depends on the grace and favour of his superiors, which means that his orientation to their goals must appear clear and unequivocal. Second, there is room at the top for only a few, which means that he makes his way up the ladder by his individual efforts in competition with his fellows. Even if he does experience some incongruency in common with his colleagues it is rarely in his interests to act in open concert with them. 'Rebellion' is therefore unlikely. This does not preclude the emergence of covert cliques and alliances. A managerial clique may seek 'to increase the status and reward of one or all members; to get more support in job activities; to find social satisfactions; to hide facts or conditions that would be frowned on by superiors; to escape unpleasant situations or annoyances; to get more privileges, ... and to share the limelight with superiors' (Dalton, 1959, p. 53). A managerial clique is different, however, in certain crucial respects from an overt collectivity such as a shop-floor work group. While its members take cues from each other and concert tactics and strategy, they are likely to implement these shared understandings in their separate individual capacities and not as a collectivity. Among managers, 'internal power struggles . . ., are largely denied and must be cloaked. . . .' (Dalton, 1959, p. 227). Thus there is no place for any principle of representation and formal leadership such as exists among collectivities of lower participants.

Managers may not confine their alliances to other managers. Within the complex coalition of stakeholders that is the enterprise, different issues bring about shifting alliances as stakeholders group and re-group for the purpose of exercising power or influence. The participants may include stakeholders who in conventional terms are regarded as 'outside' the organization. For example, with respect to the issue explored by Chandler (1964), that of the American company contracting-out some of its maintenance or construction work, the forces in favour of this policy may consist of several company management groups, an 'outside' contractor, a craft union which organizes his employees, and possibly spokesmen from the local community, along with others. Those arrayed against in temporary solidarity may be other company management groups (e.g. those in maintenance and construction), informal groups of their workers, and an industrial union which represents them. Such examples underline the fact that for many purposes it is not useful to see 'management' and 'labour' as two monolithic blocs facing each other in simple confrontation. It is more fruitful to regard each issue in management-labour relations as having its own particular interest-group structure and pattern of bargaining relationships.

Further examples of alliances between management groups and other stakeholders for specific purposes would not be difficult to find. A management faction may join with a powerful shareholder interest to impose a policy upon other management factions—a takeover or merger, a new product or marketing strategy, a palace revolution or a re-allocation of responsibility and power. Alliances may even bring in representatives of government or other public agencies where these have an influence in business organization, pricing, markets, production policy, labour relations strategy or some other relevant issue. The conventional notion of what constitutes organization boundaries may impede perception of these groupings, which are more fruitfully explored, perhaps, in terms of the full diversity of stakeholder interests, many of which are ordinarily seen as 'outside'.

Alliance activities of this kind are not, of course, the only types of response practised by managers. Retreatism is far from rare, expressing itself in the form of a strategy which aims at survival and the quiet life until retirement age. Ritualism among lower and middle managers in bureaucratic contexts has been well documented by Crozier (1964).

Only in more recent years have sociologists fully recognized these diverse managerial practices and manipulations designed to serve their own goals. Elton Mayo wrote as if the management system was inspired solely by the logic of efficiency and that only manual workers were prone to informal manipulations of the social organization (Baritz, 1965). The manipulations and group supports practised by managers are now fully documented. They are brought to bear upon all the constituent elements of the social organization—roles, authority, control systems, sanctions, status and communications.

The management role structure offers examples. This can be 'variously distorted by personal ties and sentiments' (Dalton, 1959, p. 256). These operate to support those who are failing in a role, and may take the form of protective demotions or promotions to less publicly-visible roles, or the movement of failed line officers to staff roles for which they have no particular qualification, or the retention of people on the payroll for offices which they virtually no longer fill. Roles such as that of 'personal assistant' may be created more to inflate a particular manager's status than for any serious purpose which is expected to be served. The role content of the various offices changes as aggressive managers invade and usurp spheres of responsibility once commanded by others. Departmental roles acquire vested interests in relation to other departments, and may become private pressure groups in that they have their own particularistic and parochial interests to defend and promote. Managers may develop loyalty to the autonomy and the specialized function and ideology of their department. Conflict between departments may develop, causing decisions to become increasingly oriented, perhaps, to the strategy and tactics of inter-departmental jealousies and power manoeuvres (Harrison White, 1961). Chandler, for example (1964), traces in empirical and theoretical detail the relationships which may develop between company maintenance services and other departments, showing how power relations and concepts of 'rights' to certain types of work become exploited in complex struggles which bring in allies and opponents from 'outside' as well as 'inside' the organization.

Cliques may manipulate the power structure to serve sectional interests. Line officers, for example, may form alliances to defeat the efforts of staff specialist groups to change production methods or introduce new methods of control. These and other staff innovations may be opposed for fear that they will 'bring personnel changes, break up informal arrangements, reduce their authority or enlarge that of rivals (including staff people), and bring reorganization with possible change of superiors' (Dalton, 1959, p. 100). This may lead staff specialists to withhold improvements if they believe that defeat would be inevitable or that to force an open confrontation would prejudice their personal future.

Control systems may suffer considerable distortion and evasion (Dubin, 1968; Jasinski, 1968). For example, operating managers may sacrifice maintenance and replacement needs in order to minimize short-run production costs, if these are used as a criterion of performance (Dalton, 1959). Pressures on foremen for greater output may drive them into covert deals with work groups and with each other which loosen overall management control. Managerial distortions of cost and production records are known to achieve considerable ingenuity. Infringements of safety and health regulations may be connived at if they benefit output. Production rules may be ignored for the same reason. For the worker, the inspector and the foreman, the development of a satisfactory social environment, the minimization of conflict, and the development of tolerable social relations may become a major end, leading to the mutual toleration of rule-breaking (Bensman and Gerver, 1963; Crozier, 1964). Senior managers may connive for the sake of a quiet life. In one situation, a desire by production and staff managers for certainty in the variables important to them, cost and accountability, led them to oppose uncertain experimentation, stringent standards of quality, and novelty in products (Harrison White, 1961).

The system of rewards and punishments has great instrumental value for personal goals, since it is a source of control over others. Soviet managers, under pressure from planning agencies to maximize output, may permit a loosening of piece rates in order to win the good will and high effort of their workers, thereby ignoring official instructions (Granick, 1961). There are many other ways in which the organization's material resources and services lend themselves to unofficial use as supplementary rewards to influence the behaviour of others in desired directions. The exploitation of expense accounts is notorious, and it has been known for managers who are scrupulous in this respect to come under pressure from the unscrupulous to change their habits (Dalton, 1959). Private use of organizational resources is sometimes seen as a legitimate supplementation of salary. In addition, of course, cliques may operate a private ranking scale of approval and prestige through which they reward those conforming to group norms. By the same token, such a scale can be used as an instrument of punishment. More tangible sanctions can be imposed by witholding cooperation, failing to pass on vital information, or dropping derogatory hints to third parties. Recommendations for promotion and appraisal reports are not invariably impartial. Status is often an explosive issue. The manipulation of symbols can become a preoccupation—the size of offices and the nature of their furnishings, the number and colour of telephones, the room and even the table at which meals are taken in the staff canteen.

Communication systems become involved in most of the manipulations already enumerated. The desire to defend or advance the rights, privileges and powers of a position may reduce the effectiveness of communication, in that subordinates may treat instructions and decisions from superiors merely as data to be used along with others in arriving at their own decision. Information passing up the hierarchy may be withheld or falsified in order to conceal shortcomings, thus disabling higher management from making fully rational decisions (Crozier, 1964; Evan, 1961). Information and decisions passing down may also be distorted for reasons of self-interest.

All these are examples of how the normative system can be moulded by managers in the pursuit of their goals. It is important to recall that the results need not be disadvantageous for top management interests, which may be furthered rather than prejudiced by certain kinds of informal supplementation by subordinates. It may, for example, be beneficial for top management goals if particular departments or managers extend their power over resources, achieve higher status, or elbow colleagues aside. Hence the necessity for a distinction between innovative practices that are convergent with, and those that are divergent from, top management goals.

The aspirations which inspire these managerial manipulations are drawn from the whole spectrum—material rewards, security, social satisfactions, esteem and status, autonomy, and self-actualization, including the exercise of power or authority. The forms taken by the resultant goals are clearly shaped by the fact that career interests and ideology are normally of overriding importance in obliging managers to abstain from overt, collective action. They must therefore pursue their needs through private manipulations, cliques, covert alliances, and overt action which can be rationalized in terms of service and loyalty to top management goals.

The position of professionals such as technologists and scientists in the upper ranks of the hierarchy may in some cases be somewhat different. 'They move freely, and would like to move much more freely, between posts in governmental, university, and industrial establishments. The career is not enclosed by the pressure either of "loyalty to the firm" or of "best prospects" within the individual firm' (Burns and Stalker, 1961, p. 33). Moreover, for this very reason rewards may depend upon their preserving the full, clearly-defined status of professional. They cannot, however, count upon the organization doing this for them. In one sense professionals, like apprenticed craftsmen, fit somewhat uneasily into modern, complex organizations. 'For the individual firm the technologist is an alien element; he does not fit into the factory system in the same way as other functional specialists, since these are no more than bits of the general management-entrepreneurial function. The actual information held by the technologist, as well as his training and skill, has value outside the firm' (Burns and Stalker, 1961, p. 33). Every organization is in some respects unique, and usually contains some powerful members who would like to tailor the professionals to their own specific requirements, trimming and modifying duties and responsibilities accordingly. This blurring of role definitions might eventually mean, however, the submergence of the professional identity and status on which social conventions about rewards depend. To defend themselves against this breakdown of their separateness, with its threat to their special status and privileges, professionals may look partly to their own associations. These associations, led by salaried officers whose own goals become bound up with the survival of professional identity, emerge as vested interests in their own right as they build up horizontal links between professionals in different organizations. An important consequence of professional consciousness is the 'tendency for fellow professionals to give at least as much weight to professional loyalties as to the firm's interests when judging one another's performances' (Banks, 1964, p. 51).

The expansion of the so-called 'science-based' industries with their increasing technological complexity and employment of professionals may increase these and other problems of the working relationships between expert specialists and general 'line' management (Barnes, 1960).[4] The nature of the potential difficulties can usefully be studied within the conceptual framework of 'cosmopolitans' and 'locals' (Gouldner, 1957). However, there are signs that discussion of these difficulties may have exaggerated them and over-generalized their extent. Lawrence and Lorsch (1967) and Glaser (1963) among others have shown that great care is needed when attempting to generalize about professionals in organizations, for their orientations clearly vary with the nature of organizational sub-environments and the consequences for their own work. (For other references in this field, see Box and Cotgrove, 1966; Kornhauser and Hagstrom, 1962).

7 THE ADAPTATIONS OF LOWER PARTICIPANTS

The adaptations of lower participants may be either individual or collective. If individual, they can take the forms of acceptance, innovation, ritualism or retreatism; if collective, the forms of innovation, ritualism, or rebellion.

We have already noted that the manager is on a career ladder and dependent for advancement on the favour of his superiors, and we have seen how this is likely to discourage overt collective action with his colleagues unless it can be legitimized by reference to top management goals. The position of most lower participants differs at almost every point. They are not on a career ladder. Promotion is not an important possibility, for example, for most wage-earners. Since the prizes are negligible there is no point in running a race. Yet a race between workers would be beneficial for management if it weeded

---

[4] Some observers (e.g. Blauner, 1964; Vollmer and Mills, 1962) also note a tendency for the technology of these industries to invest some of the manual occupations with higher status and intrinsic interest, and thereby to make possible a higher degree of commitment or involvement on the part of the workers concerned. Conceivably it could happen, therefore, that the incidence of behavioural problems in these situations shifts somewhat, with those at the lower levels becoming less marked and those at the higher levels more so. One may speculate further that, given take-overs, mergers, and the vagaries of government contracts, professionals and other specialists whose security is threatened may be more readily disposed than general line managers facing the same threat to seek collective defence through professional associations or white-collar unions, though they may well face dilemmas as to which of these two forms to choose (Prandy, 1965; Strauss, 1963; Strauss, 1964).

D

out the less fit and raised the level of effort. In these circumstances, the race would be of a somewhat peculiar kind with negligible prizes for the winners but heavy penalties for the losers. Thus far from accepting competition among themselves, wage-earners have a *prima facie* interest in suppressing it, and this can only be achieved through collective action. Moreover, this collective action can be pursued openly with no disadvantage to themselves since there is no personal advancement to be prejudiced by management disfavour. Besides providing defence against incongruency resulting from competition, the collectivity can also act positively to increase congruency. Thus we are led towards the theory of 'employee collectivities'. Individuals may feel they have a common interest in combining to take action to enlarge the congruency of their location or to remove or resist incongruency. The common interest usually extends to individuals in other organizations and other industries; indeed, on some issues, to all collectively-organized groups who share the position of dependent wage or salary earning and subjection to managerial rule.

This is not to suggest that lower participants who seek to act upon organizational norms can achieve nothing except through a collectivity. Individual manipulations of norms are open to everyone to some degree. A rule against smoking may be evaded by frequent visits to the lavatory. Safety or health regulations may be ignored in the interests of higher output and earnings. Production methods may be privately modified to suit personal convenience or preference. Materials may be embezzled for private use. Yet the area of discretion and the control over resources are usually so effectively circumscribed for the lower participant that he often sees collective action as the only effective medium through which to realize his purposes.

8 ACTION BY EMPLOYEE COLLECTIVITIES

The relevant collectivity may be either the immediate work group, the wider work group, a trade union's local organization, or the union's national organization—or some combination of these. Similarly, any particular pattern of behaviour may be legitimized by one or more of these collectivities but be regarded as illegitimate by the others. Thus, in the analysis which follows, any systematic attempt to relate these diverse possibilities to the forms of action undertaken would be impossibly cumbersome. The word 'collectivity' must be taken to mean any of these levels, depending upon circumstances. Unquestionably the richest single source of information and insight for most of the issues raised in this section is Slichter, Healy and Livernash (1960), which can be taken as a general reference on a wide range of collectivity behaviour—and management response.

Firstly, the collectivity may act upon roles. It may seek to impose upon management its own definition of work roles; as for example when its norms lay down who may do which tasks; whether given tasks may be sub-divided, and how tasks are to be allocated. It may seek to determine the role relationship with the material technology, as with machine-manning norms, and with the question of who is entitled to operate certain tools. Collectivity norms may bear upon role-definition in yet another sense, in that they impose upon each individual member of the collectivity an ethical obligation to act with his fellows in applying and defending unilaterally-devised work norms. There are also many issues relating to the recruitment and training of people in roles about which the collectivity may try to impose its own norms. Apprenticeship regulations and the 'closed shop' are the most obvious examples. Attempts such as these to modify the normative system may serve a variety of goals for group members. They affect the immediate fortunes of individuals in respect, perhaps, of material rewards, security, status and autonomy. They also affect the integrity and cohesiveness of the collectivity.

Role-behaviour as prescribed by management may be moulded by the collectivity in still other directions. Some role definitions result in excessive monotony, boredom and fatigue. The occupants may accordingly seek relief through talking, joking, horseplay, gambling, prolonging tea-breaks and similar diversions. Group norms may also have a bearing on the deployment of roles in space and time. They may seek to influence the allocation of individuals to and between jobs, gangs, departments or shifts. They may preclude the use of shift work or of staggered work patterns—perhaps partly to protect social relationships outside work with family and friends. Changes proposed by management in the role structure and the deployment of roles may be resisted if they threaten rewards, valued social relationships, security, status or autonomy. Technical or organizational change may be opposed, for example, if it seems likely to eliminate jobs or reduce piecework earnings or overtime which has become a regular contributor to the pay packet (Somers, *et al.,* 1963). It may threaten to destroy long-established work teams or disrupt hitherto satisfactory relationships with supervision. The whole future of a job or a group may be put in doubt. The status of both within the workplace may be undermined if downgrading or demotion seems likely. Autonomy and independence may be in danger—many studies have indicated the strong resentment generated when subordinates are deprived of the ability to organize and control their own work (Touraine, 1965). Part of this resistance derives from the fact that the ability to organize and control one's work is itself a source of power against management; power which can be used for all kinds of purposes. Some part may be bound up with self-esteem and status. But another part may be concerned with personal satisfaction in work. Such motivations may be combined in group efforts to protect or restore the control of work organization which is threatened by management rationalization (Touraine, 1965).

Many collectivity norms of the types just referred to, along with others yet to be mentioned, may have the effect of hampering management in their pursuit of lower costs or higher output, though this depends, of course, on the nature of management aspirations. For this reason they are dubbed 'restrictive practices' (Fox, 1968; Weinstein, 1965), though colloquialisms abound, such as 'ca' canny', 'make-work rules', 'feather-bedding' and other variants. The sensitiveness shown by management, unions, and the public in Western industrial societies about restrictive practices provides further insight into the predominant cultural meaning of work in these societies. It must be justified primarily by market or utilitarian criteria. Work which cannot demonstrate its worth in these terms is suspect and is felt to require convincing arguments in its support. In an effort to supply them, workers operating restrictive practices designed to protect their livelihood have offered many diverse rationalizations—safety for themselves or the public, the importance of 'maintaining quality' irrespective of market considerations, the 'true' long-term interests of the industry, trade, or occupation. Apparently the argument which they have felt likely to be least socially acceptable, and which they have least often used, is that it is better for the individual to be paid for work which is not 'needed' than to undergo enforced and unwanted idleness imposed by 'market forces' and suffer unmerited hardship in the process. This is not, of course, to suggest that these societies have ever totally repudiated responsibility for individuals excluded from 'needed' work. Even before the protective legislation of the welfare state there was poor relief. But support of this kind has usually been applied through specific channels and institutions differentiated from the organizations of work themselves, and those forced to seek it have had to accept a sharp cut in income and status—further evidence of the value placed on 'productive work'.

Other societies work to different precepts. In Japan, for example, many companies accept that 'established' workers must be retained and paid even when work of the normal kind is not available. Substitute activities may be provided which could not be justified by strict economic criteria. This is a further indication of the altogether more diffuse role played by work organizations in Japanese society.

It is not only the perceived interests of individuals which lead to collective responses experienced by management as 'restrictive' or 'obstructive'. The structure and disposition of the collectivities themselves may be such as to impede change. Technical or organizational innovations may strengthen the position and future prospects of one union group at the expense of another. Depending on the degree to which the members of the threatened group have internalized the values of the collectivity, they may resist the innovation even though it promises individual benefits.

Control mechanisms may be of a kind which places them beyond manipulation or modification by work groups—such as when they are built into the productive process and operate automatically. But others are more vulnerable—work groups may, for example, apply their own sanctions upon inspectors if quality standards are deemed too rigorous, or may frustrate supervision by deciding collectively about their own pace of work. Production records and job tickets may be manipulated. Work measurement, a potent instrument of managerial control, may be obstructed.

Relationships of subordination may likewise come under challenge by collectivities. Craftsmen may refuse to accept instructions from any supervisor who is not a member of their craft and its appropriate union. Limits may be imposed on management's rights to apply punitive sanctions such as fines, suspension or dismissal. Collectivities may press upon management the establishment of a jointly-operated 'grievance procedure' or appeals system. This enables an individual member or group of members of the collectivity to seek redress of a grievance by going beyond the immediate superior to a higher rank and, if no acceptable settlement is reached, to proceed by stages up the hierarchy of command. This is an important change in the decision-making procedure, and therefore in procedural norms.

The field of punishments and rewards offers many examples of self-protective group behaviour. Attempts to limit management's disciplinary right to apply punishments have already been noted. Attempts may also be made to regulate the promotion process in order to minimize favouritism or other forms of arbitrary action by management, and to promote such work-group norms as selection by seniority as against managerial norms of selection by merit. In the realm of pay, the ramifications are considerable. Men's aspirations as regards pay relate not only to absolute levels, but even more to the question of how their reward compares with that received by others. There is little need to emphasize the threat to managerial legitimacy that ensues when a work group or occupational category feels unfairly rewarded. The structure of rewards therefore has profound significance for the whole question of order within the organizational community (Meij, 1963; Taylor and Pierson, 1957).

Pay cannot be separated from the other half of the 'effort bargain'—the work to be done for it (Behrend, 1957). Workers need to secure and maintain what they feel to be an equitable relationship between the two. If it is felt that a fair wage is not being received, group norms may be directed towards limiting work performance to a level which is felt to secure this relationship. They may also actively seek to prevent any change in this relationship in management's favour. Under payment-by-results schemes, for example, work groups may limit their output for fear that too high a level of earnings will convince management that piecework rates or 'allowed times' are over-generous, and that they will find themselves doing the same amount of work for less pay (Lupton, 1963). Piecework systems can easily lead to inequalities in pay that are difficult to justify. They can hinder mobility of labour or changes in working methods when a worker who is earning a high rate on one job becomes unwilling to move to another where the rate is known to be 'tight' or where, through unfamiliarity with the task, his speed of work will drop. Another incongruency for work groups under incentive schemes may be wide fluctuations in earnings, so they can sometimes be found manipulating the system to avoid them—to management's disadvantage. Work group norms of fairness operate in still other ways. If one group strikes a favourable bargain on piece rates when new methods are introduced, other groups may demand adjustments to their own rates to restore differentials. As earnings of piece-workers rise, there may be pressure from time-workers in the same establishment (e.g. maintenance workers) for their rates to be raised also (National Board for Prices and Incomes, 1968, for analysis of problems arising from incentive schemes and a review of the literature).

There is also the familiar problem of systematic overtime (Whybrew, 1968). In situations where workers have been encouraged to rely on a high level of overtime earnings, an improvement in work arrangements which is advantageous for management may be highly disadvantageous for work groups if it seems likely to reduce earnings by reducing overtime. The whole practice and expectation of long, regular overtime result in many inefficient work procedures. Jobs begun during the normal working day are spun out to be completed on overtime. Artificial distinctions may be created between occupations so as to provide work for colleagues in other trades. Sickness absence may be increased so that men have to be brought in at premium rates to fill the gaps. Work groups seek to get overtime shared equally among members regardless of job needs and individual skills. Managers who come under great pressure from workers to maintain heavy overtime may tend to become casual about the use of labour, to lose the habit of counting the cost of extending the working week, and to stop asking whether it is really necessary. All these are examples in the field of pay where work groups seek to modify organizational norms in directions more congruent for their aspirations.

The status of the job or the work-group in the hierarchy of the workplace may be important for individual members or the collectivity or both. Groups may therefore manoeuvre to enhance their relative position or to oppose any adverse change in it. This may not be, however, the only status effect. The individual seeking status who cannot achieve it in the formally-prescribed hierarchy may seek it through leadership within the anti-management culture of a disaffected work group. Obstructionist tactics may be adopted partly to acquire prestige in this informal hierarchy which turns the formal status system upside down.

The communication system may also be affected by work group goals. The need of lower participants to seek out the real power centres where the effective decisions are made which govern their working lives; the need to bring their influence to bear at the point where it matters; the need to appeal over the heads of lower management—these impulses frequently lead work groups to press for arrangements through which they can short-circuit the operational lines of communication. Patterns of interaction may bear little resemblance to the organization manual, with foremen and supervisors becoming dependent on work-group leaders for the latest information, gossip or rumour about top management intentions. Another possible effect of collectivities upon communications may be crucial. Leaders may screen information passing from management to their members, and from their members to management, if they deem it in the interests of collectivity unity, policy, or resolution. Their practice in this respect may, of course, be infused with considerations of personal power or prestige which are difficult to disentangle from considerations of 'collectivity need' as the leaders define them. The effects of this screening vary from subtle modifications of meaning to outright distortion of fact. The ideology fostered and disseminated by the collectivity is also likely to have an effect on communications in that it provides the frame of reference through which they are perceived. Ideology is itself therefore, as we shall see, a resource in the struggle for power.

Power brings us to the most fundamental consideration of all. We have been considering the goal-responses which emerge when people find themselves in a position of normative conflict, defined as a situation in which priority aspirations are not being met by the organization's prevailing norms. In this context it is presumed that individuals and groups will do their best to change the norms which structure, define, and regulate their work situation. If they do not find the prevailing norms congruent with their aspirations they will try to substitute norms of their own choosing. But by changing the normative system they may well make it less congruent for the aspirations of other individuals or groups. These may offer resistance. Where no agreement can be reached about the change, the possession of power makes possible the imposition of change by one individual or group upon another.

Three illustrations of the dynamics of the process will serve to pose, and answer, certain questions about its operation. How can such behaviours as high absenteeism, bad time-keeping, excessive time off for sickness, and poor work performance be described as a substitution by the individual of norms of his own choosing in place of those prescribed by management? The answer is that when the individual perceives the normative system as failing to meet his aspirations, one generalized way out is for him to substitute, in place of management norms prescribing 'a fair day's work' conscientiously done, informal group norms which embody the proposition that the employer's indifference to employees' interests justifies their indifference to his (Fraser, 1968; Fraser, 1969). Thus derive behaviours characterized by the slogan 'Couldn't care less'. But we have argued that in the absence of agreement normative change can be imposed by power. Management hardly agrees to withdrawal behaviours. Can the individual be said here then to be behaving with reference to norms of his own choosing which he introduces through his own power? The answer is that he can. Some degree of power is needed by the individual even to manifest withdrawal behaviours. A tight labour market can provide it by enabling the individual to leave in the confidence that another job will be available, and by deterring management from punishing the lesser withdrawal behaviours lest employees be driven away. At a minimal level of power, such responses as these to normative conflict may come, say, from un-skilled workers in low-status occupations who have a modicum of market strength but no effective collective organization. At a maximal level of power they may come, say, from those who lack collective organization but enjoy a very strong market position, such as skilled secretaries in a large city.

The second example is a group which has the ability to mobilize collective power and which prefers to identify specific organizational norms which they find incongruent for their aspirations and substitute equally specific norms of their own. This tactic contrasts with the generalized rejection characteristic of those who practise withdrawal behaviours. The group may, for example, reject a management norm which prescribes maximum effort on a payment-by-results scheme and substitute a group norm limiting the output of each member. They may be able unilaterally to impose this norm on the appro-priate level of management if the manager believes that, should he resist, the group will use its power to obstruct him in pursuing his own goals—which may well diverge from those of top management. He too, therefore, substitutes a norm of his own choosing—the work group's—for the officially-prescribed norm. He submits to this situation, but can hardly be said to extend agreement and therefore remains uncommitted to it. It is not a case of normative agreement which has legitimacy for him. Moreover, he is likely to feel the need to conceal the situation from top management, so the communica-tion system, too, is now affected.

The third example is of the situation, historically the most common, where management exercises superior power in imposing its own normative system upon lower participants who may or may not have aspirations to change it but who in any case cannot muster the ability to challenge their rulers. Managerial action of this kind may, for example, follow the discovery that norms which are incon-gruent with their own aspirations, such as restrictive practices, are prevalent within the organization. They may then use power to compel employees to change their behaviour. Forced to submit, the

D*

employees will not have extended agreement to this situation and it will have no legitimacy for them. They can be presumed to evade or change it whenever the opportunity occurs—or to resort, perhaps, to withdrawal behaviours if no opportunity occurs.

Power is therefore the crucial variable. Individuals may hold enough power to achieve change single-handed, but most lower participants have to mobilize it through collective organization. The whole purpose of the collectivity is therefore to shift the balance of power, and many of its strategies can only be understood in the light of that purpose. But what kinds of factors determine whether or not employee collectivities actually develop?

9 STRUCTURAL FACTORS AND THE GROWTH OF COLLECTIVITIES

Organizations, occupations, and the societies in which they are located vary considerably according to whether they make it easy or difficult for cohesive interest groups to form and mobilize power against management. The literature on this aspect is now considerable. A general statement about the position of modern industrial wage-labour is worth reproducing. 'The outstanding features of the work situation of modern wage-labour are, on the one hand, the physical separation and social estrangement of management and workers, and, on the other, the physical concentration and social identification of the workers themselves. Not only is the worker separated from management through the physical layout of the factory, but also socially through the impersonal and standardised relationships that result from the institution of technical and economic rationality. The work situation of the modern large-scale factory is one where instrumental action is at a premium' (Lockwood, 1958, p. 205).

This is not all. 'The calculability, rationality and discipline of machine production call forth relations between management and the workers that are specific and impersonal . . . The whole atmosphere of the productive unit is conducive to impersonal antagonism. Such relationships are further reproduced outside the factory through the operation of the labour market where labour is treated as a commodity. A social situation is created in which the workers' experience of the impersonality of the factory bureaucracy is widened and generalized into a sense of class division. The same organization of factory production throws workmen together, physically and socially, and provides the prime basis for their collective action'.

Within this generalized picture there is room for wide variations of specific circumstances which may promote or hamper combination. The numerous studies made of these different structural situations include those by Cunnison (1966), Goldthorpe, *et al.,* (1968a), Kuhn (1961), Lupton (1963), Sayles (1958), Scott *et al.,*(1963), Scott *et al.,* (1956), Woodward (1965). They cover not only situations which exemplify Lockwood's generalized description and thereby create the ideal soil for combination, but also situations such as the one described by Cunnison and Lupton in which the normative system, while creating severe incongruencies for workers' aspirations, structures the setting in such ways as to make collective action extremely difficult to organize.

Analysis in detail of the technological and social conditions which favour or discourage collective organization is too large a subject to be pursued here, but some indication can be given of the kind of factors at work. Marx noted, for example, that workers in small workshops who laboured side by side with their employers associated with them informally, developed personal ties with them, were markedly less class-conscious and less involved in workers' organizations than workers in large establishments. Many others have followed him. 'The personal ties of small-shop men with their employers tend to weaken their identification with organizations predicated on a conflict of interests between workers and employers. To the small-shop man the problems of the boss are more persuasive, and the chances for individual recognition and rewards through personal relations with the shop owner are felt to be greater than in larger shops . . .' (Lipset, Trow, and Coleman, 1956, p. 152). In the larger establishments, management is remote and the union is near, visible, and important; in the smaller, the union is remote and the owner and foreman loom large.

Studies of the kind already referred to illustrate the very different types of social order created by different patterns of division of labour and work flow. They range from situations which bring men together into closely-knit, cohesive, solidary groups, to situations which leave them isolated and competitive. A major stress which appears to characterize some of this literature is that 'the technology of the plant—the way jobs are distributed and flow into one another and the nature of the division of labour—moulds the types of work groups that evolve within the plant . . . The technological structure . . . exerts a major influence on the source of motivation and morale, the work group' (Sayles, 1958, p. 4). This kind of analysis brings out the importance for collective action of such variables as whether the job organization brings men together or splits them up; the relative position of the group on the promotion ladders within the plant; its relative size and importance; whether jobs within the group are similar or dissimilar; whether their work is indispensable in the short-term; and how far management can measure work load and pace. The importance of the last point has been illustrated by Crozier, who shows how 'areas of uncertainty' can be exploited to serve the power interests of individuals or groups who occupy strategic positions in relation to those areas. In a situation otherwise dominated by specific and precise norms, the possession by an individual or group of an area of role behaviour which cannot be governed by specific and precise norms bestows a measure of discretion. This discretion can be exploited as a source of power. Thus, observes Crozier, 'new power relationships develop round the loopholes in the regulatory system. Groups fight for control of the ultimate strategic sources of uncertainties ... Subordinates try to increase their amount of discretion and utilize it to oblige higher-ups to pay more for their cooperation' (1964, pp. 111, 160).

Other studies examine the structural and social settings of non-manual workers (Bain, 1967; Bain, 1970; Blackburn, 1967; Lockwood, 1958; Prandy, 1965). Again, a quotation from Lockwood describing the position of many clerical workers prior to bureaucratization illustrates the sort of analysis which can help to illuminate potentiality for collective action. 'The management of clerical work is not carried out with the same kind of impersonal discipline that is a common feature of factory organization ... The division of labour not only splinters the work-force among departments and through occupational differentiation, but also brings clerical staffs into relatively close and enduring relations of cooperation with managers and supervisors'. The working relationship 'introduces a personal and continuous element into office organizations and obviates the harsh, impersonal and purely instrumental character of the command which industrial sociologists are beginning to single out as an important source of latent hostility on the part of the factory worker' (Lockwood, 1958, pp. 78-9).

While it is not necessarily the intention, analysis on these lines may create the impression of a simple and direct relationship between the nature of job design, work organization and work flow on the one hand, and the existence and character of collective action on the other. This would be to ignore a whole range of other variables, some of which are internal to the organization, others external. The former include, for example, the structure of rewards, anomalies within which are a potent stimulus to collective action among competing groups (Turner, Clack and Roberts, 1967). The latter include the labour market and the policies of trade unions, employers' associations, and governments. Equally important are the aspirations of both management and lower participants and the goals to which they give rise. As we have seen, lower participants do not constitute a *tabula rasa* on which the social organization imprints certain predictable perceptions. The differing nature of aspirations means differing intensities of the will to organize and to seize the opportunities available. Groups with a strong will towards collective action may be able to surmount considerable obstacles put in their way by the social organization. Craftsmen who have fully internalized a traditional ideology, for example, can maintain solidarity even when thinly scattered throughout a plant in a way which would defeat less motivated workers. Conversely, groups with only a weak will to organize may fail in circumstances which seem objectively more propitious. The aspirations determining strength of will are themselves shaped, as already seen, not only by consciousness of the availability of power but also by such external factors as societal, community, or subcultural values and roles, and by such internal ones as management policies and ideologies, the example set by other groups, and so on.

A vivid example of the way in which social solidarity created by circumstances outside the work situation may be carried over into it and greatly strengthen union effectiveness and aspirations towards job control appears in a report issued by the Commission on Industrial Relations about a group of companies in the British engineering industry. A high proportion of the employees were Indian and Pakistani immigrants, especially Punjabis. 'Among Punjabi immigrants there is an unusually high degree of social cohesion which has its basis in kinship or in life in the same locality. The latter is itself a reflection of the social organization of the villages which many left as members of families of small peasant proprietors or land workers. This social cohesion is carried into the workplace by the Punjabis. . .' (Flanders, 1970, pp. 19–20). They then used their strength to control recruitment and promotion, thereby further reinforcing their own cohesion by fostering powerful mutual obligations.

Perceptions are therefore shaped by a frame of reference which is only partly determined by the social organization itself. We must always take account of 'the way in which workers' own definitions of the work situation (their work-roles included) may significantly determine their attitudes and behaviour in this situation, to some extent independently of its "objective" features;' definitions which may derive not only from their role as workers but also from 'their various other social roles as members of families, communities, social classes and so on' (Goldthorpe, *et al.,* 1968a, p. 45).

The formation, growth and character of employee collectivities are affected also by management attitudes. The factor of 'employer recognition' has always been important in the history of trade union growth, but in Britain today, for example, it has special importance in respect of unionism among white-collar workers. White-collar unionism is at a high level in the public sector and at a low level in the private. Lockwood (1958) explains this in terms of bureaucratization—the private sector is marked by a large number of small firms and relative lack of uniformity in working conditions, whereas the public sector is characterized by large establishments and work groups, rigid classification of jobs, uniform scales of pay, explicit criteria of merit, the proliferation of impersonal rules, and increasing 'social distance' between management and lower employees. Bain, however (1970), argues that perhaps an even more important determinant of variations in the degree of white-collar unionism is differences in the extent to which employers resist demands for recognition and pursue policies designed to discourage or prohibit their staff employees from joining unions. The reasons for these policies he duly explores, though there is insufficient space here to follow him (see Kassalow, *et al.,* 1965, and Sturmthal, 1966, for international comparisons of professional and white-collar unionism).

Employer attitudes towards unionism among their wage-earning employees have often been strongly influenced by the structural features of their enterprise and their industry. The nature of product and supply markets; the degree and the nature of competition; the cost structure of the business; government pressures with respect to price and wage movements; these have often been important in modifying or reinforcing purely personal, class, or status sentiments. Employers may also be influenced by the collective policies of employers' associations (Munns, 1967; McCarthy, 1967). For at this point we need to note that, just as lower participants may feel that they have certain interests in common, so may employers and top managements. The nature of the common interest may relate to legislation, commercial and trading procedures, or market regulation. 'Market' here may be the product market or supply markets, including that for labour. The interest in the labour market may be that of presenting a united front of power to trade union demands, or of eliminating wage undercutting by supporting the union in its enforcement of minimum wage rates throughout the industry. Clearly these collective policies constitute another 'external fact' which top management must take into account in determining strategies towards combination among employees.

In totalitarian countries the nature of management response is likely to be determined by the fact that they enjoy full support from the state's coercive powers in denying employees the right of independent collective action. Societies vary profoundly in the degree and nature of encouragement or discouragement offered by the state apparatus and the law towards independent combination among employees (Brown, E. C., 1965, Deutscher, 1950; McAuley, 1969; Sturmthal, 1957). Here there is space only to point to the most extreme of the contrasts. In most countries of the West, the use of coercive sanctions by organized labour against employers—including the government as employer—is allowed, and trade unionism and collective bargaining are not only permitted but encouraged and supported by legislation. The opposite extreme is characterized by the Soviet Union, where trade unions serve as but 'a mild and strictly limited check on the short-run administrative interests of the industrial managers, which might run counter to the state's long-run interest in maintaining that modicum of satisfaction among the workers required for their long-run efficiency' (Rostow, 1954, p. 70). Given the successful propagation by state power of an ideology which asserts 'that there cannot be a conflict of interest between management and worker, or between the worker and the state' (McAuley, 1969, p. 253), employee aspirations appear to have adapted to the situation. McAuley's study reveals that some sections of the workers are prepared to voice objections to management policy and demand rights embodied in state norms and plans, but declares that the labour force as a whole 'lacks any tradition of pressing for improvements ... There is no tradition of single-minded "unionism" nor any marked pressure from the workers' (p. 251). She and other researchers (notably Brown, 1958, 1960 and 1963) warn, however, against underestimating the influence of Soviet employees over their managers, and Brown (1960) argues that the power of unions at plant

level is increasing and, on certain issues, is leading to an encroachment on managerial prerogatives which might startle even Western
managements. Nevertheless, such activities are contained within
strictly defined limits.

By comparison with the Soviet Union, where there is little sign that
this denial of union independence generates any serious resentment,
other states which suppress independent unions have not been so
fortunate. In Spain a militant tradition which survived the civil war
has repeatedly clashed violently with state forces in attempts to secure
independent unions, resulting in a sequence of civil disorders over
recent decades about which most of the West has appeared to remain
in ignorance.

CHAPTER IV

Employee Collectivities

Now that the analysis has reached the stage at which collectivities[1] have been formed, an entirely new element is introduced. So far we have been concerned with the attitudes and responses of individuals. The formation of collectivities has been presented, in fact, in terms of the aspirations of individuals. But a collectivity is a concentration of power. Once that concentration of power exists, an additional determinant has appeared on the scene. For if an individual comes within the ambit of a collectivity's power, the collectivity may, quite independently of his attitude towards collectivities and his original aspirations and goals, be able to bring him into membership and mould his attitudes and responses thereafter.

Insofar as he can be brought to share the collectivity's values he will be able to legitimize its procedural norms and thus accept the leadership and direction of its officers. His behaviour within the work organization is now therefore subject to an additional source of authority besides that of management. The same considerations apply to sanctions. The leaders of the collectivity, like those of any other organization, find that they cannot rely on goodwill alone for the necessary predictability of behaviour. They therefore make use of threats to withdraw gratifications or of promises to remit deprivations in order to control the actions of their members. Trade unions can expel, suspend, fine, or debar from office; work groups can disapprove, 'send to Coventry', impose financial penalties, or force management to use their powers of dismissal. These sanctions, too, may be legitimized by the members.

Even if the individual does not legitimize the values, norms and sanctions of the collectivity, power can be used not only to bring him into membership but also to keep him there. The implications of this are fundamental. As soon as this new level of social structure, the

[1] Although the social organization itself is a collectivity, the term is here confined, for convenience, to combinations and associations of employees.

employee collectivity, has been created, explanations of the behaviour of individuals who come within its ambit of power—which is
in no way fixed or static, but may expand or contract—must include
consideration of this power relationship. Obviously the power of
collectivities varies. Some are too weak to be able to exercise effective
control, but at the other extreme the collectivity's power over the
individual may be very great.

This means that the growth of collectivities cannot be related to
simple propositions about the volume of discontent or conflict;
neither can their strategies be related to a mere summation of
individual aspirations. Evaluations by the individual of the congruency or incongruency of his location, and of joining or not
joining a collectivity, must be seen in the context of his power
vis-a-vis the collectivity. His position may leave him little effective
choice. We turn now to examine the nature of the collectivity in more
detail.

1 THE NATURE OF THE COLLECTIVITY

When a collectivity is formed, a group of individuals create a social
organization with officers and functionaries in a role structure. The
object is to construct an agency which can mobilize power. Every
employee has some power, but for lower participants it is normally
insignificant compared with that of top managers. Since the social
organization is, in the last analysis, underpinned by power, attempts
by lower participants to change it—or to resist changes proposed by
managers—require the mobilization of their minute individual en-
dowments of power into a unified countervailing force. The founders
establish a normative system and within this system invest the officers
with the right to rule. What exactly are they doing here? In effect,
they are constituting themselves into an army and surrendering their
freedom of action in certain defined spheres of behaviour by submitting to norms administered by leaders who are themselves constrained and structured in their behaviour. Why do they make this
surrender? For the same reason that a group of individuals under a
common threat of aggression might voluntarily place themselves
under the command of an agreed leader—because they believe they
have a better chance of countering their attackers if they combine
their efforts, pool their resources, fight as a unified body, and submit
to a discipline imposed by leaders that is necessary for the pursuit of
these objectives. On what terms do they make this surrender? On the
terms (i) that command is wielded only by those whom they have duly

authorized and (ii) that it is directed towards ends or means on which they place value.

A certain contrast would seem to emerge at once between the probable attitude of employees to management rule and their attitude to collectivity rule. The latter is likely to enjoy greater legitimacy since its membership elects the officers. Employees may well have been socialized to accept a legitimate entitlement of management to govern, but such a title is obviously more remote and abstract than that which they themselves extend to their own elected leader. However, this contrast can easily be exaggerated. Once the collectivity is established it becomes a partly independent force in the situation. Although the members surrender some freedom of action in order to pursue their goals more effectively, the collectivity will henceforth play an important part in determining what those goals are. Its leaders may interpret their role obligations in such ways as lead them to use collectivity control either to *raise* their members' aspirations or to *contain* them. Or they may use their position to pursue private goals to the same effects. They will undoubtedly have some scope for doing so. Of course the collectivity leader, like top management, must observe certain constraints to maintain his place. Members are conscious of some minimum level of return that they expect from their investment. Provided the leader fulfils the necessary obligations to his various environments, however, he has, like top management, an area of autonomy within which to pursue his own aspirations.

Even in pursuing the aspirations of his members the collectivity leader will be likely in some respects to set himself against them. His basic role is that of preserving and if possible strengthening the unity of the collectivity, for it is only through unity that the members' power can be mobilized. Deviants and rebels, by withdrawing in effect from the unity, reduce the power that is available to the collective. Even normally 'loyal' members may sometimes feel the pull of conflicting obligations and must therefore, for the sake of the collective, be kept in line. This explains the sanctity of the solidarity principle. If consensus on the legitimacy of union leadership breaks down, there is no power to exercise. One of the role-obligations of the union leader is therefore to maintain and strengthen consensus, and this obligation will be all the more vigorously pursued because it can be presumed to accord so closely with his own goals.

Insofar as leaders direct their motivation towards maintaining consensus, the authority which members vest in their leaders is then used against them to ensure that they continue to do so. To some extent this will be provided for in the normative system, which lays down sanctions against members who weaken unity by breaking norms, flouting collective decisions, defying collective authority, organizing factions, and promoting disaffection. The resources of the members will also be used to disseminate an ideology which stresses the value of solidarity, and to distribute propaganda which shows up collectivity policies in a good light. In addition to these activities, there are others to which leaders have looked for preservation of their own rule. Elections may be rigged (Rolph, 1962); norms introduced which impede the organizing of opposition (Roberts, 1956); and organizational resources employed in manoeuvres to weaken rivals (Allen, 1957). All such techniques have their limits of effectiveness. If the number of rebels becomes large enough, the withdrawal of authority from the common pool will reduce the ability of leaders to maintain the norms which seek to preserve unity and the collectivity will come under threat of dissolution. This is likely to be resisted to the utmost by the leaders, who face the destruction of the social organization through which they are pursuing their own aspirations. They are, in any case, likely to have internalized the collectivity ideology of solidarity and service to members. To interpret their responses as mere self-interest may under-estimate the complexity of the process. The fact remains, however, that the trade union often appears as another external constraint to the individual in his work situation. Its authority or power may be supplemented by a workplace collectivity in the form of the work group, which can bring its own informal sanctions to bear.

At this stage we have to make explicit the fact that to refer merely to the individual's membership of a trade union is greatly to over-simplify a complex pattern of affiliations. He relates himself to a number of collectivities structured into a hierarchy culminating in the national level of the union, which may indeed be related to the even higher collectivity of some central organization such as Britain's Trades Union Congress, or America's AFL–CIO.[2] The level of organization which proves effective for the pursuit of employee goals varies with the nature of the goal and the work situation (Chamberlain and Kuhn, 1965; Chamberlain, 1961). Some interests may be best pursued by a collectivity comprising the basic task group—for

[2] American Federation of Labor-Congress of Industrial Organizations.

example, the team on a machine or the crew of a steel furnace. For other interests the effective collectivity may be the larger work group of a department or a smelting shop. For still others, the common links may reach out to members of other departments, to all the departments of a plant, to all plants of a combine, to all firms of an industry, and even to a number of industries or, indeed, to all industries.[3]

At one level a collectivity may seek to act directly upon the social organization of one or more enterprises, aspiring either to change their norms in a direction which is more congruent for member's goals or to prevent incongruent changes sought by others. At another level, a collectivity may seek the same ends indirectly—perhaps through the exercise of political power. Terms and conditions of employment in a publicly-owned sector may be most effectively influenced by bringing pressure to bear on political representatives or government ministers (Humphreys, 1958). Another possibility is that one or more of the environments within which managements operate can be rendered more favourable to collectivity action by indirect political means—as when unions press for government action to maintain full employment and thus labour scarcity, or to bestow some favour on the product market from which the collectivity and its members expect to benefit, or to enlarge the legal rights of collectivities themselves. Maximum cooperation between collectivities at the highest level can be expected when their very survival and functions are threatened by legal or managerial attack. Their primary and urgent need will then be the creation of a social and legal environment within which they can prosper.

Thus the 'collectivity' may mean very different things according to the goal being pursued and the level at which action is appropriate. It may change as the collectivity at one level considers that effectiveness for the group concerned would be best served by upward—or downward—reference to a different level. The relevance and importance of these different levels of collective organization tends to fluctuate according to which goals are most immediately pressing and which level is perceived as most effective for their satisfaction.

[3] In British engineering, for example, all these levels have been relevant at different times for employee aspirations, though predominantly workers have 'found the appropriate institutions to represent their interests, not in one large organization, but at the points at which the assertion of skill, the impact of technical change and market variations have been most acutely felt—at workshop level'. They find that, 'for day-to-day purposes, the most effective features of their organization lie as near as possible to the point of production' (Marsh, 1965, p. 212).

The leaders of the different collectivity-levels operate within sharply differing constraint-sets. The range and type of their responsibilities are so markedly unlike that they may employ very divergent frames of reference and hence judgemental criteria. Shared culture and traditions may mitigate these differences, but nevertheless be unable to prevent significant divergencies in evaluation of workplace situations, problems, and policies. There is no space here to explore a whole field of enquiry concerning internal union conflict (Allen, 1957; Hoxie, 1920); nor the equally important subject of conflict *between* unions (Galenson, 1940; Webb, 1920). It must suffice to say that in some situations the individual may come to feel that his only real refuge is his immediate work group. Loyalty to that group and its leader may then rank as the prior obligation. Especially is this likely to be the case where the work group has proved the most effective instrumental level through which the individual's goals are pursued. If, at the same time, the group members find themselves in normative conflict not only with management, but also with some higher-level collectivity of their union, and unable therefore to legitimize the policies of either, the strength of their identification with the work group as their only source of legitimate leadership is likely to be very great.

The gap between the work group and the union hierarchy outside the enterprise is the most likely failure of articulation to develop within the union's structure. The group's members share a common work experience and a frame of reference which may well be strongly specific to their particular situation. The group's own leader, the shop steward, may be better placed in terms of the legitimacy and the immediacy of his leadership, his knowledge of the situation and its problems, and his facility for communicating with members, than is the salaried, professional union officer outside the plant. This would probably still be true even if unions typically directed the maximum possible effort and attention to cultivating their authority over, and communications with, members in the workplace, which they patently do not. Inadequacies in these respects may cause some members to see their union as just another bureaucracy, in relation to which they feel, as individuals, anonymous and powerless. Insofar as their resort to collective action against management norms may likewise derive from feelings of powerless anonymity, it could be their membership of the autonomous work group that provides relief from both enterprise and union.

Exploration of the possibilities at workplace level soon reveal the concept of the 'work group', however, to be a highly ambiguous one, since it can mean any one of four things. It may refer to a friendship clique whose members are bound by purely expressive ties in that they gain certain intrinsic satisfactions from their interactions within the group. Second, it may mean a subordinate group, defined by having a common supervisor. Third, there is the task group of employees who must collaborate if a given job is to be accomplished. Finally comes the interest group composed of employees (who may be geographically dispersed throughout the organization) who share common work interests and objectives. The interest group is a solidary group whose bonds are primarily instrumental in nature. The distinctions are, of course, analytical and there are many overlappings in practice. It is important to remember, however, that subordinate and task groups are not necessarily interest groups with solidary ties. Technology and aspirations divide men as well as bring them together. It is still true, however, that the subordinate or task group is a powerful influence on the individual's aspirations and goals. He may learn competitive individualism from his work group just as easily as he may learn solidarity and mutual support.

Leaders of higher-level collectivities are therefore profoundly affected in their task by the nature of the work-group culture, which we have seen to be shaped by structure and processes both internal and external to the organization. A highly active and cohesive workplace collectivity may prove embarrassing in its independence if it breaks union norms and behaves too disruptively. But unions could hardly exist were it not for the active minority among the rank and file at the workplace who, having fully internalized union ideology, perform unpaid services, uphold collective norms and values, and generally constitute a leadership nucleus among their fellows. For this active minority, the formation of the collectivity for the effective servicing of members' goals brings a secondary and derivative set of congruency considerations into play—namely those concerning the collectivity itself. The survival and effectiveness of the relevant collectivities may become terminal goals, and events and processes will be evaluated accordingly. Situations can arise in which officials or activists may call upon members to sacrifice purely personal goals to the collective interests. They may become so collectivity-oriented as to prejudice the individual interests which the collectivity was originally designed to serve (See Tagliacozzo and Seidman, 1956, for a full analysis of 'types' of union member).

For the mass membership, the collectivity is likely to rank as largely instrumental in nature and to be evaluated in terms of personal interests. The possibility of tensions within collectivities between officials, active minority and mass membership is thus plain to see. In principle, the union's social organization occupies a similar position in relation to these groups as does the social organization of the industrial enterprise in relation to its own stakeholders. In both cases, groups with differing goals seek to use an organization of power, resources and symbols in the service of their own interests. Such problems are, of course, specially marked where there are differences of industrial or occupational interest among the mass membership. The resulting strains and pressures can lead to changes in structure, with modifications, perhaps, in the system of government and representation, or to faction activities designed to sway union elections in favour of preferred candidates and policies.

On the whole, however, the goals of the groups within a union are better articulated than those of the enterprise. The pluralism of claimants which management cannot avoid—shareholders, consumers, suppliers, employees, government and public opinion—is less elaborate in the case of employee collectivities. Members have some control over the definition of leadership goals, the appointment of those directed to pursue them, and the policies that they employ. The appointment process results in the selection of those for whom leadership goals, as broadly defined by the members, offer adequate opportunities for realizing their personal goals, thus making some degree of identification possible between officers and members. The identification is far from complete, however. The exigencies of negotiations with the employers collectively may furnish union officers with a frame of reference significantly different from that of their members, as may also their involvement in national economic and social policy. This may lead their assessment of congruency for members to diverge from the subjective assessment made by the members themselves. Leaders may wish to cooperate with governments or employers in applying incomes policy, pursuing productivity campaigns, or hastening technological change. They may conclude agreements with employers which embody the most that can be gained but seem to the members a betrayal. They may support a government in unpopular measures that are demonstrably desirable in terms of long-run economic growth. In some of these actions they may be pursuing their own aspirations towards political preferment, state honours, or economic benefit.

Given that leaders may direct their efforts towards ends or means on which members place no value, a point may be reached at which members no longer accept their leadership as legitimate. The leaders may, however, be in a position to coerce them, and only beyond a certain point will this destroy the basis on which their power rests. Up to this point, coercion is quite possible within employee collectivities. A union which has managed, for example, to establish a 'closed shop' or control over promotion to better-paid jobs can effectively coerce quite sizeable groups of recalcitrants.

A group who cannot accept the official leadership as legitimate may transfer legitimacy, permanently or temporarily, to an unofficial leader. In the London docks, for example, the workers periodically followed the unofficial leader, Jack Dash. Popular journalists were apt to present this as 'the demagogue wielding power over the masses'. But for the dockers he offered a leadership which they legitimized. When the union, the Dock Labour Board, or the employer were behaving in ways which the dockers rejected, the dockers withdrew legitimacy and transferred it to Dash. He served to focus, to symbolize, and to express a mood and a purpose. When the mood had passed or the purpose was served, he fell back into obscurity. On issues where he did not speak the mind of the dockers, as on the subject of demonstrations against coloured immigrants, he was ignored in favour of other unofficial leaders.

2 EXTERNAL SOURCES OF COLLECTIVITY POWER

So far we have assumed that the power exercised by collectivity leaders derives solely from the members, i.e., from their constituting themselves into a collective body, with norms governing their own behaviour to ensure the unity of goal and action which is necessary for success. This assumption must now be modified. Collectivity leaders may draw power from external sources which they can use against their members. These include higher-level employee collectivities; management and employer collectivities; and the state.

The shop steward leader of a work group who seeks to discipline a deviant member may be able to call upon sanctions wielded by the branch, the district committee, or the national level of the union. He may also be able to call upon the sanctions of management or an employer collectivity. An agreement or even a tacit understanding with management that only workers in good standing with their union will continue to be employed will cause most individuals to hesitate before defying the collectivity's rule. In such a situation the collectivity and management jointly are imposing sanctions on the individual. Insofar, in fact, as the effective enforcement of all agreements and understandings is shared by both parties, the collectivity can call upon management sanctions to help in disciplining the individual. The state, too, may assist the collectivity. There is very little of this in Britain, but in other societies unions may lean heavily on state sanctions. In New Zealand, for example, union membership is legally enforced, and in the United States a majority vote among the employees of a plant secures to the favoured union a statutory right to be the exclusive bargaining agent.

The ability of collectivities to draw upon external sources of support for their control introduces a new factor into the relationships between leaders and their members. The former now have a degree of control in excess of what is granted to them by the latter. Their ability to use power against their members has therefore increased—which means that the maximum size of revolt which they can successfully contain has likewise increased. Against this, of course, must be set certain membership protections—delegate meetings, election of officers, appeals machinery, the possibilities of forming oppositional factions, the availability of alternative collectivities, the extent to which leaders have internalized an ideology of service to members' needs. The state may lend its weight to support the individual member against the collectivity by providing certain legal protections.

The control enjoyed by the collectivity, however, may remain great. When a collectivity is fully recognized, has a closed shop (McCarthy, 1964) and participates in joint agreements which successfully regulate terms and conditions of employment, it is in a very strong position in relation to the individual member. This means that any theoretical or empirical approach to union growth or character which proceeds from a micro-analysis focusing on individual rank and file attitudes is suspect, since it may overlook power relationships which determine behaviour. This also helps to explain ambivalences and paradoxes sometimes revealed in empirical research, when attitude surveys and observed behaviour appear to yield conflicting evidence.

3 COLLECTIVITIES AND THEIR EMERGENT PROPERTIES

It is clear from the foregoing that, with the formation of collectivities, there appears a new level of social structure with its own strategies and tactics (Bakke, 1946). Thus collectivity behaviour cannot wholly be explained in terms of the strategies and goals of the individual members. Those taking up leadership roles in the collective soon realise that their responsibility for maintaining and enhancing its strength obliges them to think in terms of its 'institutional' interests. These are by no means necessarily identical with the original individual interests which prompted the rank and file to form or join the collective (Perlman, 1928). These 'unintended' consequences illustrate the manner in which social structure is more than the sum of its parts. New properties emerge of which leaders must take account.

In doing so, however, leaders are never wholly determined in how they define and pursue the collective's institutional interests. Provided they achieve a certain minimum performance in meeting their members' expectations, they often enjoy a degree of autonomy in their exercise of the collective power and leadership opportunities vested in their office. To this extent their choices will reflect the values which inform their own aspirations. As Durkheim notes of 'chiefs' in general: 'Of course, it is from the group that they derive their power, but once power is organized, it becomes autonomous and makes them capable of personal activity. A source of initiative is thus opened which had not existed before then' (1964, p. 195).[4]

Appointed to preserve, strengthen, and in general nourish the interests of the collectivity as such, leaders thus interpret these role obligations in the light of their own goals and whatever leeway of autonomy they possess. The mobilization of power to strengthen the members of the group in their struggle; the pursuit of policies which maintain or strengthen the chances of institutional survival or growth; the devising of strategies for enhancing the collectivity's financial or organizational viability—all of these may be infused with leadership aspirations which include, perhaps, personal security, prestige, and the exercise of power and authority. Such tasks involve imposing behavioural uniformities upon members; socializing them in the values of solidarity and unity; structuring their perceptions in ways which minister to group unity; and drilling them in the requirements of effective collective action (Bakke, 1948). These strategies and goals are quite separate and distinct from the initial self-regarding strategies and goals of the individuals comprising the

---

[4] The power enjoyed by a leader may be directed not only towards the direct work interests and aspirations of his members, but also towards wider political issues about which the majority feel less strongly. Success in the former activity may endow him with considerable leeway in the latter.

collectivity. They create a new moral world of their own. In Durkheim's words: 'Everything which is a source of solidarity is moral, everything which forces man to take account of other men is moral, everything which forces him to regulate his conduct through something other than the striving of his ego is moral, and morality is as solid as these ties are numerous and strong' (1964, p. 398). This, then, is a moral order which develops out of the division of labour, the organization of collectivities, and the power relations to which they give rise. It was noted by Marx as early as 1847 that if the original aim of workers' combinations 'was that of maintaining wages, to the extent that the capitalists, in their turn, unite with the aim of repressive measures, the combinations, at first isolated, become organized into groups, and in the face of the unity of the capitalists, the maintenance of the combination becomes more important than upholding the level of wages' (Bottomore and Rubel, 1963, p. 194). Other examples may be given of strategies which arise from the institutional interests of collectivities. A group of members may be required to accept the hardships of open hostilities with management in order to protect a principle of vital importance for the wider collectivity. They may be required to share the burdens of a struggle which seems to have little or no relevance for them as individuals. They may be expected to acquiesce in a majority decision which benefits others at some relative or even absolute cost to themselves.

Rival collectivities may compete in a variety of ways for members, each using its power to entice or compel workers to join it rather than the competitor. Conflicts about role definitions (demarcation disputes), and about collectivity boundaries (jurisdictional disputes), would either not arise or be easier to resolve but for the existence of conflicting institutional interests. Within a collectivity, wide variations in earnings have sometimes been thought by collectivity leaders to threaten unity, and they have taken steps to restrain the excessive good fortune of some members. Management policies of a kind designed to wean the loyalty of the individual away from the collectivity and towards the company (e.g. profit-sharing) may well be opposed by collectivity leaders even though such policies may be in the interests of individual employees.

Leaders are likely to seek to close this potentially dangerous gap between individual and collectivity interests by trying to induce members to internalize collectivity interests and make them their own. If this identification can be achieved, then the individual's goals are also those of the collectivity. In some cases this identification is indeed carried to the extent that membership of, and participation in, the collectivity comes to have a terminal value. As already suggested it is doubtful if a collectivity could survive without a nucleus of members of this sort, for they play a considerable part at workplace level in socializing the large number for whom membership is primarily instrumental.

In the task of building up and maintaining the effectiveness of the collectivity, leaders must, as we have seen, have sanctions at their disposal. At all levels, positive sanctions consist in effectively servicing the needs of members. Negative sanctions at the level of formal union organization take the form of suspension from benefit or from office, fines, or expulsion. At the informal level of work-group collectivities, social pressures towards conformity range through a finely graded series from the almost imperceptible hint to the extreme severity of complete ostracism. It is these informal sanctions of approval and disapproval, popularity and isolation, which are the most pervasive and potent in buttressing group norms and values. When a mass meeting is in progress, for example, it is the group norms and values which are likely to be uppermost in shaping individual behaviour and responses. When commentators assert, in the name of 'individual freedom', that there should be a secret ballot on, say, a strike which is being proposed by shop stewards or union officials, they are really arguing that individuals should, as far as possible, be isolated from these group norms and values. Contrarily, the same observers are apt to argue, when men strike in *defiance* of their leaders, that the latter should 'assert their authority', i.e. that the strikers should be forced to submit to group leadership. These appeals to individual liberty often disguise the basic issue. The argument is usually not about the existence of social controls, but about the purposes towards which the controls are directed. Whether one approves of a particular instance of social control depends on one's view of the goals which it serves. Thus those who in general sympathize with the aims and social functions of trade unionism will tend to be unenthusiastic about measures designed to isolate the individual from group norms and values, while those who lack this sympathy will be quick to complain of 'the tyranny of the mob'.

The whole question of the interaction between the individual and the collectivity reminds us that, as in all other social contexts, the individual-in-society may figuratively be said to have two selves: the 'private' self and the 'social' self, which are sometimes in tension. The perspectives and interests of the private man may diverge from the perspectives and interests of the social man. This may pose methodological difficulties when attitude surveys are conducted within work organizations. Some respondents may reply to questions from a purely individual standpoint and others with group norms and values in mind. Others may move from one stance to the other without being aware of it. It is important to know which pattern of responses is being tapped.

This leads on to the fact of 'dual loyalties'. We have seen that when the individual takes stock of his location in the social organization he is likely to see some aspects as congruent for his aspirations and others as incongruent. He may join a collectivity directed towards removing or warding off incongruent aspects and enlarging the congruent. Thus the satisfactory pursuit of his aspirations owes something to the social organization as defined by management and something to the independent collectivity. In these circumstances we would expect a pattern of dual loyalties (Purcell, 1953).[5] We would also expect the proportions to vary as between situations—in some there would be a far greater consciousness of debt to the collectivity than in others. We might also expect that in a given situation the balance between the loyalties would vary through time—a crisis situation might produce a sharp shift towards collectivity-consciousness, with the balance moving back if confidence was restored. Such are the varying and shifting patterns of circumstances which help to determine how far at any given time employees are 'company-oriented' or 'union-oriented'; how far they perceive their work situation in 'harmony' terms and how far in 'conflict' terms.

Another important aspect of the emergent properties of collectivities is their effects on communications within the organization. The shop steward may try to prevent direct communication between management and individual worker, for this can separate the individual from group norms and values. He may assert that as the men's representative he should always mediate between management and men. His interest in this arrangement may derive not only from a concern with his own status and functions, but also from the fact that, in order to pursue his role obligation as leader and sustainer of group action and solidarity, he needs to screen all communication so that his

---

[5] Where trade unionism has spread up to supervisors and even middle managers who are conscious of being on a promotion ladder, some circumstances may produce sharply conflicting loyalties. In one large administrative undertaking in Britain where the union representatives were all supervisors, conflict was evident between the union role and the organizational role (Barlow, 1969).

members perceive it in terms of group norms. If management appears to be making a special effort to bypass him and communicate direct with employees he may react with suspicion, more especially where relationships are already bad. It may, nevertheless, seem to management in certain circumstances to be an indispensable part of their purpose. They are more likely to conduct the operation with success if they understand just what they are doing. Managers are often guilty of naiveté when they complain that shop stewards are wilfully failing to act as precise, accurate channels of communication. Such a complaint fails to understand the power relations which give rise to collectivities and the emergent properties which characterize them.

Yet another demonstration of these properties is the way in which each individual must be compelled to accept his share of the battle when collective action is decided on. Here again, the appeal to individual liberty often misunderstands the nature of the situation. Why, it is asked, should a person be obliged to join a strike, a go-slow, an overtime ban, a restriction on output, if he doesn't want to? Once again it can be shown how the formation of a collectivity brings into being patterns of behaviour which would not necessarily be the free choice of particular individual members. It is a natural tendency for the individual to desire some end which can only be secured by collective action, but to wish to evade the burdens and constraints which collective action requires.[6] Sanctions must therefore be employed to ensure discipline, for if one individual is permitted to break ranks the constraints on the others are weakened. In this as in other respects there is some parallel between management-labour relations and war between nation states. The predominant collective will of the members of the employee collectivity is to defeat the enemy, yet the private interest of the individual may be to leave the fighting to the others. All must therefore be constrained by a strict discipline.

Once the collectivity is established, therefore, with its norms, values, mechanisms of control, and its system of sanctions, it appears to the individual in some degree as an external constraint which stands against him. How far this is the case depends on the nature of his private goals and the extent of his effective control over, and participation in, the particular collectivity concerned (Hughes, 1968). But whether he is a willing or an unwilling participant, his work

---

[6] An example of tension between 'private' man and 'social' man.

group collectivity, especially, will have considerable control over what he wants from work and how he pursues those wants. Needless to say, the direction of control is not all one way. If enough members develop interests which are not currently being served, this fact is likely to be transmitted to the leadership. If the mediating mechanisms or the private goals of leaders impede this process a new collectivity or mode of action may emerge. Even so, the nature of members' interests and the manner in which they wish to see them pursued are likely to be strongly influenced by their membership of the collective and by its norms and values.

Much has been written about the mechanisms of democratic control within trade unions—delegate conferences, appeals machinery, periodic re-election of officers—and how far they can prevail against the preferences of established leaders (Tagliacozzo, 1956). Grass-roots movements can be frustrated in many different ways, and a number of difficult conditions have to be met if a breakaway organization is to be viable. Unofficial factions and activity patterns may spring up, with circumstances varying in the extent to which they structure opportunities for leaders to contain them (Martin, 1968, for discussion and further references).

In the earlier phases of large-scale industrialism, European socialists took a generally optimistic view of the problem of democratic control within workers' organizations. Marx and Engels saw oligarchy only as a possible early stage; workers would establish effective control of their own institutions as these took on a mass character and as a growing number of members acquired class consciousness and political sophistication. American political scientists took a similar view. But the optimism faded. 'As the trade-union and the socialist movement grew in size and power, members who came to disagree with the policies of incumbent leaders found, with rare exceptions, that it was impossible to dislodge those leaders from office. They discovered that officers whose authority originally and formally derived from the consent of the members gave officials power over the members' (Lipset, Trow and Coleman, 1956, p. 7).

Growing pessimism received theoretical support from the publication of Michels' *Political Parties* in 1911, with its 'iron law' of oligarchy. 'It is organization which gives birth to the dominion of the elected over the electors, of the mandatories over the mandators, of the delegates over the delegators. Who says organization, says oligarchy' (Michels, 1959, p. 401). Michels focused specially on the ways in which the professional orientations and private interests of officials and functionaries, combined with the apathy of the mass membership, leads to the attenuation of popular control. Technical specialization calls for expert leadership and 'the power of determination . . . is gradually withdrawn from the masses to be concentrated in the hands of the leaders alone' (p. 31). The intricacies and complexities of the wage struggle often lead union officials to 'deny that the mass of organized workers can possess a general view of the economic life of the country as a whole, and to deny, therefore, their capacity of judgement in such matters' (p. 32). Bureaucratic or specialist functions within the collectivity come to be viewed by incumbents as ends in themselves, and strategies shaped accordingly. Direct control by the rank and file is replaced by the increasing power of committees. Even in representative or delegate gatherings the superior knowledge, tactical position and skills of the leaders give them a great advantage over 'the incompetence of the masses'(p. 86). Leaders are apt to exploit this advantage for private ends. 'The apathy of the masses and their need for guidance has as its counterpart in the leaders a natural greed for power . . . What was initiated by the need for organization, administration, and strategy is completed by psychological determinism' (p. 205). The tendency of the holder of power is to 'consolidate it and to extend it, to multiply the ramparts which defend his position, and to withdraw himself from the control of the masses' (p. 207).

The classic study by Lipset, Trow and Coleman of the International Typographical Union, the only known substantial example of a formalized 'opposition' within a trade union, is at pains to stress the deviant nature of their subject. 'The experience of most people as well as the studies of social scientists concerned with the problem of organization would tend to confirm Michels' generalization' (1956, p. 4). But perhaps this is an over-endorsement. There is still the minimum of service which leaders must render to members' goals if they are to retain their authority. Cases are numerous where, in the absence of the minimum, members have withdrawn legitimacy and vested it in the unofficial leaders of lower-level collectivities. Grassroots power born of labour scarcity has greatly enhanced their ability to do so. Leaders must therefore not disappoint, offend or frustrate too many members at the same time. Should they appear to do so, younger and more militant aspirants to office will not be slow to make use of the fact in committees, elections and representative gatherings. Leaders may in any case have their own internal checks.

E

Insofar as they have internalized a spirit of service to what they feel to be a movement they will stop short of the excesses of cynical manipulation to which Michels assumes they will be prone. This internalization may even be strengthened by the general cultural values of the wider society. 'A culture oriented toward individual achievement still disapproves of the pursuit of self-interest in those areas in which individuals are expected to act in representative roles. The representative role sets a normative limit to the pursuit of self-interest even in a social system which is pervaded by an ethos of individual success' (Coser, 1956, p. 115).

One point can be made with certainty. It is a truism of organization theory that social processes cannot be understood simply by directing attention to the formally-prescribed structure (relevant aspects of union structure are examined in Edelstein, 1967). In relation to union democracy, certainly, no formalistic criterion of a kind which rested, say, on such principles as a high level of membership participation in the prescribed acts and procedures connected with union government would be adequate for judgement (Ross, 1969). A decision taken by a small minority, for example, may result from a complex of forces to which the 'silent majority' may have contributed in many different ways. Tiny 'ginger groups' may very effectively activate the checks and balances provided by the constitution, but in any case there are in practice many informal ways, direct and indirect, overt and subtle, localized and all-pervasive, which supplement formal provisions. For a fully adequate conceptual framework of union democracy, however, one must look beyond the organization to its environmental and historical setting—a setting which includes membership and societal values, economic and industrial environments, technology, and other constraints (Martin, 1968).

4 IDEOLOGIES OF MANAGEMENT AND COLLECTIVITIES

Ideology is a resource in the struggle for power, since it shapes the ways in which men perceive, think, feel, and act. Management seeks to propagate an ideology which justifies its behaviour, legitimizes its rule, evokes loyalty and commitment on the part of lower as well as higher participants, and serves as a support for those norms and values which are congruent for its goals. Collectivities likewise evolve an ideology to serve their own purposes, but its nature varies considerably according to situation and circumstance. Most collectivities need to have, if only in reserve, a set of doctrines which can be used if necessary to legitimize opposition to managerial rule, assert the desirability of independence, and create a group feeling which can provide the basis for collective action should it be required. But in certain types of situation the role of such doctrines may be minimal. Where collectivities are perceived by their leaders and members as depending heavily for their existence upon the grace and favour of management, or where, though not weak, they see their best interests in cooperating with management, ideologies of opposition, challenge, and hostility may be played down in favour of ideologies which promote the validity and desirability of collaboration. Some white-collar staff associations provide an example (Blackburn, 1967; Robinson, 1969). In general, however, ideologies of opposition are more to the fore. In extreme cases their emphasis on separateness, on loyalty to the norms and values of the group, on the absolute value of solidarity and willingness to accept the exigencies of the power struggle, may be so powerful as to constitute what is virtually a way of life.

On neither the management nor the collectivity side does the ideology take the form of a consistent and related body of ideas and values. Rather does it consist of a ragbag of assorted notions fashioned to suit varying exigencies, sometimes quite incompatible with each other. Managerial ideology, for example, includes aspects of self-orientation and group-orientation. On the one hand, value is attached to the notion of competitive striving for individual advancement as against the collectivist principles embodied in trade unions and organized work groups. On the other hand, there is likely to be a group-orientation stressing undivided loyalty to the organization and the value of team spirit and *esprit de corps*. Similarly, there may be an approving acceptance of the idea that high performance among managers can only be evoked by the appropriate financial reward, accompanied by a disdain for what is felt to be an excessive preoccupation among wage-earners with material gain. In the writings of many financial editors, what are described as 'incentives' for managers become 'bribes' when they have to be offered to wage-earners.

Employee ideologies likewise contain inconsistencies. The fact that collectivities have certain interests in common—such as the need to protect and enlarge their social, legal and political rights, or to stand together in an industrial struggle—requires that their ideology include universalist appeals to the solidarity of all workers and the brotherhood of man. The fact that they exist to promote the interests of particular groups, however, may require them to postulate exclusive rights of the craft, the occupation, or the industry. Thus the ideological ragbag must be able to serve both a general struggle when members stand shoulder to shoulder with other collectivities, and a purely self-regarding engagement when the collectivity may behave towards members of other groups with a ruthlessness and brutality which vie with their own legends about entrepreneurial behaviour in the dark historical past. Similarly, the ideology is apt to enshrine the virtues of government intervention when this seems likely to benefit the collectivity either directly or indirectly by creating a more favourable environment, such as a situation of labour scarcity, and to denounce it as a violation of freedom when it threatens collectivity functions by, for example, imposing restraints on wage and salary movements.

Managerial ideology often tends understandably to stress a unitary conception of the organization; to favour the view which sees it as having but one proper source of authority and one focus of loyalty (Fox, 1966). In this form the ideology serves three purposes. It is at once a method of self-reassurance, an instrument of persuasion, and a technique of seeking legitimation of authority. The reassurance function is not difficult to understand. For many managers, the full and complete acceptance of the idea that substantial sections of those whom they govern are in some measure disaffected is corrosive of self-confidence. This can be a powerful motivation towards believing that a basic harmony exists, and that any apparent demonstration to the contrary is due to faults among the governed—to stupidity, or short-sightedness, or out-dated class rancour, or an inability to grasp the basic principles of economics, or the activities of agitators who create mischief out of nothing. The ideology also serves as an instrument of persuasion. Managers seek to persuade their employees and the public at large that industry is a harmony of co-operation that only fools or knaves choose to disrupt. To the extent that they convince their employees their job is made easier; to the extent that they convince the public they gain sympathy whenever their policies are challenged by their workers. Finally, the propagation of the idea that the interests of the rulers and of the ruled are identical helps to confer legitimacy upon the regime.

These and other aspects of managerial ideology are most easily accepted by those who feel the social organization to be highly congruent with their aspirations. As one descends the hierarchy, with the growing possibility that employees will find the social organization in some respects incongruent, there may be an increasing tendency for the ideology, too, to appear incongruent. There will, of course, be no problem if employees lack the aspirations which promote perceptions of incongruency. Rival agencies of socialization may be absent or weak—as for example in totalitarian societies where organized challenges to management authority are not permitted, or where cultural values encourage submissiveness, or where technology and work organization create obstacles to the emergence of anti-management group feeling. Paternalistic family firms with a long-standing tradition of harmony may be able to create habitual modes of response among work groups which can last a long time provided habit is not disrupted by crisis or major change.

In situations where men are conscious of incongruency but are prevented from organizing themselves collectively by obstacles created by the technology, they sometimes seek to justify and rationalize self-seeking behaviour with an appropriate individualistic ideology. Philosophies which stress such maxims as 'Look after No. 1'; 'If you don't look after yourself in this life, nobody else will'; and 'You can't trust anyone around here', come into this category, and may be reinforced by local community or group values. The existence of technological and social obstacles to collective ideas and action explains why individualistic ideologies can sometimes persist among the least favoured members of an organization.

Strenuous efforts by top managers to propagate their ideology may delay collective action among employees, especially where sanctions are used against the occasional deviant. This is a situation in which those endowed with superior power may be able to induce the governed to internalize the ideology of the rulers. Again, they may be much assisted by the nature of the division of labour and other aspects of the social organization. Where subordinates are isolated from each other but in immediate contact with superiors they are in a position of personal dependency which may render them specially susceptible to the norms and values of management. Their internalization of these values may survive a major change in their structural position. Clerical staffs in the older type of 'counting-house' can often be found in this position of special vulnerability to management ideology. If the ideology is hostile to collective organization among white-collar staffs, as it often is in the private sector, unionism will be slow to spread.

Those among the governed who at some point aspire to organize their fellows into an independent collectivity are thus faced with a problem. Successful mobilization of their power depends upon their embracing values in opposition to those of management, yet until they can effectively counter management power with their own they may have difficulty in crystallizing and articulating their own independent values. For this reason, the formation of collectivities has often been at times of crisis, when a spontaneous gesture of revolt brings men together for an immediate, specific object. Part of the subsequent task of translating a movement into an organization lies in converting these temporary rebellious emotions into permanent autonomous values which legitimize the collectivity, structure its members' perceptions, and give them confidence for future claims and action.

The ideology tends to grow and gather accretions. Myths and martyrs strengthen it as a tool for the socialization of new members. Success breeds success. The importance, for employees wishing to challenge management, of having at their back a philosophy which shapes their perceptions and justifies their action, which they share with many others, and which has already been sanctioned by success, can hardly be exaggerated. A distinctive and deeply rooted ideology, such as that prevalent within long-established crafts, can give a handful of men the confidence to challenge a powerful management. The successful ideology therefore rests heavily on history. It assists the mechanisms of reinforcement through which grievances suffered by individuals gain credibility and conviction from being shared and compared. It assists the process by which discontent becomes institutionalized and built into the culture of the group. New recruits enter into a heritage of experience interpreted in a certain way, and learn the conventional wisdom distilled from those interpretations.

The significance of tradition is therefore manifest. It may prove, however, a source of weakness as well as of strength (Flanders, 1969). Tradition helps to socialize members in their obligations and to support the drooping spirits of activists at moments of doubt. It is likely to have been shaped, however, by calculations of means to ends which, though producing success in the past, may have less relevance in a present where ends, though remaining broadly the same, are receiving new practical interpretations, and where means too, therefore, call for adaptation to a changed environment. New interpretations and adaptations may prove difficult to achieve where tradition maintains habitual perceptions and responses generated in an earlier and different situation.

These characteristics and effects of ideology clearly illustrate the inadequacy of assuming 'that all the ideas and sentiments which motivate an individual have their origin in him alone, and can be adequately explained solely on the basis of his own life-experience'. Where an individual is a member of a cohesive work group he 'speaks the language of his group; he thinks in the manner in which his group thinks. He finds at his disposal only certain words and their meanings. These ... determine to a large extent the avenues of approach to the surrounding world ... Thus it is not men in general who think, or even isolated individuals ... but men in certain groups who have developed a particular style of thought in an endless series of responses to certain typical situations characterizing their common position' (Mannheim, 1960, pp. 2, 3).

As Mannheim says, the style varies with the situation. But Crozier, in describing the subculture of employees in a French industrial state monopoly, sketches a picture which could apply to many industrial workers in many advanced societies. 'The content of this subculture is in opposition to the goals of the organization and the aims of management. It implies an idealization of the past, some pessimism about the present, devaluation of the future, and distrust of management'. Even for workers who are favourably placed, 'the privileges they enjoy ... still seem insecure to them. They feel that they must exhibit an uncompromising attitude if they wish to escape the pressure for change that is working, they believe, against them. They view mechanization, for example, as a way of continually reopening the bargain they have struck. They suspect that the managerial groups are ... ready to utilize every loophole to manipulate the workers. A moderate aggressiveness may, in the final analysis, be the best means of protecting the group against any encroachment. Moreover, it provides a very good rationale for enforcing discipline within the ranks, and for resisting any attempt on the part of the higher-ups to divide and conquer' (1964, p. 80, 101–2).

The pessimism and short-run assessments characteristic of this perspective are 'in large part due', in the words of Jack Barbash, to the worker's 'lack of control—as he sees it—of the work situation ... The feeling of autonomy over the work situation varies roughly with the level occupied in the job hierarchy ... The managers, by contrast with ordinary workers, are likely to take a longer-run and more optimistic view, because they do have more security; they do have greater autonomy in their jobs ... At the high professional level the value which the employee puts on autonomy is the most important fact about his job; and the greater the extent to which job autonomy is realized, the more confident and long-run minded the employee will be' (1964, p. 70). Thus many important subcultural and ideological differences between workers and management derive from their varying evaluations of their own capacity to cope with change.

But of course collectivity ideologies consist of more than this. They need to support collectivities and their members in challenging the norms and values of employers and managers, and must therefore articulate and justify an alternative set of norms and values of their own. Employers and managers in Western countries have sometimes sought to legitimize their rule by reference to such common-law principles as individual freedom of contract and the unfettered prerogative of action conferred by property rights. Trade unions have played an important part in the construction of social and legal constraints on these freedoms and rights. Their very *raison d'être* involved them from the start in repudiating individual freedom of contract and denying the employer free discretion to conduct his business as he thought fit. Neither the worker who was prepared to accept sub-standard terms and conditions of employment, nor the employer who wished to offer them, could be allowed to do so if it could be prevented. Nor could the employer be deemed wholly free in the deployment of his labour and capital resources once he had hired them, for the assertion of union rights to participation in decision-making, in some cases to full decision-making itself, might extend to central issues of job organization, machine utilization, and discipline. To use the terms employed by Sir Henry Maine, who in his classic *Ancient Law* saw the development of progressive societies in terms of a movement from 'status' to 'contract', such tendencies as those just described imply a movement from contract back to new forms of status (Banks, 1964; Tannenbaum, 1951). Modern legal commentators see the current world very much in these terms (Friedmann, W., 1964).

As long ago as the turn of the century, Veblen saw the sociological significance of this. After noting the 'natural-rights principles that underlie modern business relations', he observed that the 'common-run of trade-union action is at variance with the natural-rights foundation of the common law'. The values and norms forced upon workers and their collectivities by the need for self-protection were 'extra-legal exigencies . . . which do not run in business terms and therefore are not amenable to the natural-rights principles of property and contract that underlie business relations'. The cultural significance of trade unionism was therefore that it sought a 'revision of the scheme . . . not in terms of natural liberty, individual property rights, individual discretion, but in terms of standardized livelihood and . . . standard relations'. The fact that the new aims, ideals and expedients did not accord with the 'received institutional structure' meant that the unions were, 'however crudely and blindly, endeavouring, under the compulsion of the machine process, to construct an institutional scheme on the lines imposed by the new exigencies given by the machine process' (Veblen, 1958, pp. 156–163).

The conflict between these institutional systems has of course been manifested in social, legal, and political struggles. The courts 'struck at the root of the matter in declaring trade-union regulations inimical to the natural rights of workman and employer alike, in that they hamper individual liberty and act in restraint of trade' (Veblen, 1958, p. 157). But the unions were instrumental in helping to spread social recognition of the 'gap between the formal equality of parties free to make contract as they wish, and the actual inequality and lack of freedom caused by stark differences of economic bargaining power' (Friedmann, 1964, p. 96). Under pressure of this social change, common-law courts have come gradually to extend judicial sanction to the establishment of a rough equality in economic and social conflicts by recognizing group pressure as legitimate. The unions have also helped to promote the concept of social accountability of private property in the means of production, a concept which has materially whittled away the bundle of rights of which property consists. In extreme cases, unions have found the exercise of power under private property so highly incongruent for their aspirations that they have taken as their banner its complete abolition, either throughout the whole society or in the particular sector in which they were interested. But responses often stop far short of this. Just as the individual's affiliations tend to be divided between the social organization and his independent collectivity, both of which may be varyingly congruent for his aspirations, so his value-orientations may similarly be of a dual nature, one set directed towards the norms and values of management, the other towards the norms and values of his collectivity. The balance may lie heavily towards one or the other, depending on circumstances, and may well fluctuate according to events.

The overall picture of collectivity ideologies, however, is of their significantly shaping the norms and values not only of their own members, but also of productive organizations and their social and

governmental environments. The essential circularity of social processes is thus made plain. Men's orientations to work are shaped by
social values and by cultural and subcultural traditions. Out of the
confrontation between these orientations and the social structure of
productive organizations, men develop their goals in work. In pursuing these goals, they generate new forms of social structure which
not only supplement or modify their goals, but also change the
institutional values of production and of the wider society itself.

It would be wrong, however, to emphasize only those aspects of
collectivity ideologies which challenge or reject the values of the
wider society or of certain social strata within it. Ideologies are
virtually certain to incorporate some of the attitudes and values of
the society in which they take their rise, and these may manifest
themselves in the choice of tactics, policies, basic objectives, and
leadership selection and behaviour. Lipset has contrasted the trade
union movement of America with those of north-western Europe and
Australasia in terms of the societal values which have helped to
shape them (1961, 1962). The fact that each society has its own
social configuration and historical development which is in some
respects unique enables us to make a related proposition about collectivity ideologies. These and the behavioural modes to which they
give rise are likely to differ as between societies for two distinct
reasons. First, the nature and manner of the collectivities' reaction
against, and rejection of, certain societal values is to some extent
uniquely determined by the particular configuration and history of
the society concerned. Second, the societal values and attitudes
which collectivities accept and embody in their functioning are
similarly likely to contain elements of uniqueness. The proportions
in which collectivities reject and accept wider social values vary as
between countries, and a study of the differences and their causes
might well generate useful questions in social dynamics.

5 COLLECTIVITY FUNCTIONS AND GROWTH

We have seen how collectivities may mobilize power, directly or
indirectly, to make the social organization more congruent with
members' aspirations, or to prevent other groups from changing it to
their disadvantage, or to change one or more of the organization's
environments in ways from which the collectivity or its members
expect to benefit. We have also noted that the benefits derived from
collectivities and their activities can be either instrumental or
terminal in nature. Among the early sociologists, Cooley showed

insight into the latter. 'Their function as spheres of fellowship and self-development is equally vital and less understood. To have a we-feeling, to live shoulder to shoulder with one's fellows, is the only human life . . . The union makes him feel that he is part of a whole, one of a fellowship, that there are those who will stand by him in trouble . . . Moreover, the life of labour unions and other class associations, through the training which it gives in democratic organization and discipline, is perhaps the chief guaranty of the healthy political development of the hand-working class. . . .' Cooley concludes that even 'if unions should never raise wages or shorten hours, they would yet be invaluable to the manhood of their members . . . Self-assertion through voluntary organization is of the essence of democracy . . .' (1962, pp. 287–88). In the last sentence Cooley is asserting the terminal value of participation in decision-making; a value that we have already noted as playing a part in employee aspirations.

Finally, we can use this analysis of collectivities to correct a common error. Trade union growth is often assumed to be simply and directly related to discontent. From a study of the properties of collectivities, however, we can see that it is not. Men may take up membership of a collectivity as a result of group pressures and group ideology. The collectivity may be in a good strategic position to impose it on them. Management goals become relevant here. These may include the belief that 100 per cent union membership must be accepted—or indeed, in some cases, positively sought. Agreements or tacit understandings to this effect may well result in management screening new recruits for their attitude on this issue, and putting pressure on existing employees to maintain union membership. But quite apart from management attitudes, the group structure of the social organization may facilitate large-scale recruitment into collectivities, as may local community structure and values. Legislation and state support may similarly favour union growth. None of these factors carries any necessary implication of discontent. Conversely, the existence of discontent may not be manifested in membership of unions. Structural obstacles or calculations of self-interest may intervene. Finally, as we have already seen, collectivities can be used not only to relieve positive discontents, but also to make a relatively satisfactory position even better. The appetite for self-enhancement is influenced by the opportunities for pursuing it, and men who are strategically placed for collective action may not only be driven on by the goad of discontent from behind but also drawn on by the beckoning fruits that lie ahead. It is for these reasons that no simple correlation exists between collectivity growth and discontent. Discontent may exist without trade union membership, and trade union membership may exist without discontent. Low-paid men with unfulfilling, monotonous work may remain outside unions; highly-paid men with satisfying work to which they are committed may join them.

CHAPTER V

Conflict and Joint Regulation

Having traced the sequence through which employee collectivities come into existence and develop their emergent properties, we turn now to examine their relationships with employers, employers' associations, and managements.

A point to recognize at the outset is that while the collectivity is generated out of manifest normative conflict, this conflict customarily extends only to a very small area of the total normative system of the enterprise. A large proportion of the system's norms are a matter of indifference to the collectivity's members insofar as they do not perceive themselves as affected by them.[1] They extend to them a low-key acquiescence that can be said to be legitimation of a passive kind. Other areas may command a somewhat stronger commitment. In Chapter II we examined a range of possible values which, if shared by management and employees, can provide the basis for positive normative agreement. Even the most casual observation offers evidence that shared values do in fact provide management with a considerable measure of active legitimation. This is demonstrated in such utterances by employees as: (i) 'It's his firm so I suppose he has some right to tell us what to do'; (ii) 'Someone's got to organize things and give orders'; (iii) 'He's so obviously an expert at the job that you feel you have to listen and take notice'; or (iv) 'They treat us reasonably well on the whole so we generally try to cooperate'. These sentiments indicate that the speaker is legitimizing

---

[1] This obviously leaves open the possibility that their perceptions may change. Decisions once accepted by unions and work groups as being outside their range of interest, such as those bearing on mergers, take-overs, investment and marketing strategy, and similar high policy issues, are coming to be perceived as relevant. There nevertheless remain large areas of the normative system, such as those regulating the minutiae of accounting, within which management's writ runs unchallenged simply because no collectivity perceives itself as affected. No area, of course, can be defined as permanently immune to challenge.

managerial rule on the basis of shared values in terms of (i) property rights (ii) the functional need for coordination and order-giving (iii) knowledge and expertise, or (iv) management's successful concern with employee aspirations.

Alongside these active and passive forms of normative agreement, however, we may find an area of normative conflict. In this area, the individual or the collectivity withdraws legitimacy from management rule. Consequent upon this breakdown of an authority relationship, power becomes the arbiter. Managers may be able to impose their norms upon subordinates, or subordinates theirs upon managers. If the collectivity is powerful and management complaisant enough, the collectivity may be able unilaterally to establish norms of its own either in the form of explicit rules or in the form of 'custom and practice'. In the absence of power or management complaisance sufficient for unilateral modifications of the normative system, the collectivity is likely to press for the right to participate in managerial decision-making procedures relevant to the norms with which it is concerned. In other words, in order to secure changes in substantive norms, the collectivity must secure changes in the procedural norms governing decision-making. It seeks to establish that henceforth all decisions about certain selected norms will be shared.

1   MANAGEMENT RESPONSES TO DEMANDS FOR JOINT REGULATION

What will be the response by management to this demand? Management may consider that it stands to benefit from the change, and may even initiate it. The structure of the industry and its market characteristics may, for example, give managements of different enterprises a common interest in allowing collectivities a voice in the norms governing terms and conditions of employment, provided identical terms can be imposed upon all competitors. In this way the rigours of competition are mitigated by some degree of market regulation. Provided the collectivity gives promise of being able to impose uniform terms upon all, management goals may be served by strengthening the collectivity sufficiently, through recognition and joint regulation, to enable it to do so. The existence of procedural agreement would not, of course, exclude the possibility of substantive disagreement and even manifest conflict over the nature of the terms themselves. It would not exclude, even, the possibility of substantive conflict coming to nullify, for management, the value of the procedural agreement. Nevertheless, situations of this kind have thrown up, in Western societies, many examples of collaborative patterns of relationships between collectivities and employers (Chamberlain and Kuhn, 1965; Fox, 1958; Walton and McKersie, 1965). It may be, though is not necessarily, on the basis of these collaborative procedural relationships that employers and unions feel able to engage in further joint action designed to change organizational environments in ways which both perceive as benefiting themselves. Union and employer representatives may join, for example, in lobbying for public subsidies or special legislation which handicaps competing products or competing nations, or in promoting consumer demand, or in colluding against the consumer interest.[2]

Management might also find a collectivity positively useful for maintaining industrial peace. Technologies which tend to throw up a constant succession of minor disputes—as in piecework trades with frequent minor changes of product or methods—may benefit from a union that is prepared, in return for management recognition and support, to discipline members into observing peaceful procedures of settlement. This would be a situation in which collectivity leaders might be valuable to managements as—to use Wright Mills' phrase—'managers of discontent' (1948, p. 9). Or again, perhaps the growing size and heterogeneity of the labour force leads management to believe that labour relations must now be systematized by means of standard pay scales and formal procedures of communication, and that this process of bureaucratization will be facilitated if engineered jointly with a trade union (Dubin, 1949).

But perhaps organized worker participation in decision-making does not commend itself to managers on any of these counts, or by any other criterion of their own interests. Management's perceptions of its position in terms of costs, markets, technology, planning norms or other environmental constraints may lead it towards unremitting resistance to the claims and aspirations of collectivities. Circumstances of this sort may shape the frames of reference of both sides along conflict lines, determining their perceptions of, and their

---

[2] This collaboration may bring the union concerned into conflict with other unions. In the United States, for example, construction and maintenance contractors joined with 'craft' unions (who organized their workers) in a marketing drive to persuade industrial companies of the advantages in contracting-out work of this kind. This quickly evoked a counter-blast from 'industrial' unions organizing construction and maintenance workers within the companies themselves, for the reason, of course, that work opportunities and union strength were being threatened. This conflict nearly broke up the central federal body of American unions, the AFL-CIO (Chandler, 1964).

behaviour towards, each other, including their strategy and tactics in the whole bargaining relationship. The collectivity's demand to participate may be condemned by management or its supporters (who may include the state) as—according to the society and its culture—an intolerable encroachment upon the prerogatives conferred by private property rights, or as a foolish and misguided obstruction to the beneficent operations of private enterprise and free markets, or as a selfish sectional interest blocking the aspirations of the people newly liberated from imperialism, or as a counterrevolutionary attempt to thwart the will of the masses.

This interaction between management's perceptions of its interests and its frame of reference towards collectivities may well be a two-way process. Management—and the state—may employ a frame of reference characterized by values which shape its perceptions. Those who, for example, are persuaded of the virtues of competitive individualism as against collective regulation may assume without evidence that no mutually-satisfactory accommodation is possible with unions on such subjects as technological change and other management interests; that unionism encourages mediocrity and holds back the able man; or that unions create conflict where all was once harmony. Those who are persuaded that in a communally-owned economy there can be no legitimate clash of interest between management and the managed will see independent collectivities as illegitimate assertions of purely sectional claims.

International comparisons reveal marked differences in structures and modes of joint regulation (Sturmthal, 1957; Ross and Hartmann, 1960), and employer attitudes are one of the important points of difference. Over the existing range of negotiable issues, bargaining relationships are marked in Britain and Scandinavia, for example, by relative mutual acceptance and respect, whereas in France employers with exceptions, resist effective wage bargaining and are adamant against impairment of their managerial authority (Meyers, 1965), and in Italy have never fully accepted unionism in the sense of becoming reconciled to permanent, stable, and close relationships (Ross and Hartmann, 1960), though there are signs of change (Giugni, 1965). Other factors besides employer attitudes, however, shape bargaining relationships, and the attitudes themselves are not constants but very much subject to the degree of strength which unions can deploy. Both in France and Italy, for example, the unions have been weak and divided by religious and other ideological differences, and in such circumstances joint regulation may lag simply because employers have not been forced to adapt their attitudes and practices to the fact of strong, stable unions, as they have in Britain, Scandinavia and America.

If unions are to stand any chance of forcing management to yield a share in decision-making, however, their struggle and the methods used must be tolerated by society and the state. In the last resort, it is the values and norms, legal and otherwise, of the wider society which determine whether or not the collectivity is able to impose itself upon the organization's procedural system. It may or may not enjoy the freedom to mobilize power and apply sanctions against management until management feels forced to accept it as a decision-making partner. Legislation may or may not eliminate the need for these procedural power struggles by expressly requiring managements to recognize collectivities in this role. Quite apart from statutory enactment to this end, national and local government authorities may employ many different forms of encouragement and discouragement to both parties. The pressures of so-called 'public opinion', too, are relevant, and may approve or disapprove management or collectivity behaviour, thereby possibly affecting the parties not only directly but also by weakening or strengthening governments in their ability or inclination to act.

In most Western societies, values and norms have of course favoured, within varying limits and on a somewhat fluctuating basis, the right of collectivities to form, mobilize power, and exercise it against management in the pursuit of their normative aspirations. In the Soviet Union, by contrast, a 'recent proclamation of the Central Committee of the Communist Party has declared that the "central tasks of the trade unions are to mobilize the masses in the struggle for the . . . further strengthening of the economic might and defensive power of the Soviet state . . . for technical progress, for continuous growth in labour productivity . . ." Only at the tail end of the proclamation was there mention of the goal of "further growth in the standard of living and culture of the workers". There are no anti-management overtones in this document, or in the many similar ones which have preceded it during the past three decades' (Granick, 1961, p. 193. See also Brown, E. C., 1958, 1960, 1963, 1965).

The willing acceptance of, or resigned submission to, procedural change by management leaves open the question of whether it will be followed by substantive agreement or conflict. These substantive outcomes may cause managements to revise their perceptions of joint regulation. Some who were previously amenable may regret it.

Others may come to perceive useful advantages after all. Still others may find their worst fears confirmed as conflict which had hitherto remained latent becomes overt.

Before we look closer at managerial relations with collectivities, however, we need to locate the study of conflict in organizations within a wider context. To refer to conflict and its regulation only in connection with collectivities would give a false impression, for it can also emerge on other levels and be regulated by other means.

2 TYPES OF CONFLICT SITUATION

Four basic types of conflict can be identified. The first involves only individuals. This is most likely to be found within the management hierarchy, and to arise out of struggles for power and status. The second involves management and a lower participant who is not a member of a collectivity. This arises typically from an individual seeking redress of a grievance or being punished for some infraction of a norm. The third is between a collectivity or one of its members and a manager or management group. The fourth involves conflict between collectivities over such issues as job rights, union member-ship, or union jurisdiction.[3]

The mechanisms evolved for handling these diverse patterns of conflict are not difficult to predict on the basis of the preceding analysis. For the first type there is no formal machinery at all. Whether the struggle takes place at the very top of the management structure or at some point lower down, the personal nature of the conflict cannot be admitted. To recognize, and thereby run the risk of seeming to legitimize, open struggles between individuals for status and power may be perceived as too destructive of cooperative effort, management ideology, and the notion of the unified team. The struggle must be civilized as far as possible by focusing it upon 'the organization's best interests'; by containing it within the constraints of policy discussions and debates on 'company strategy'. Thus 'in the event of a conflict between a junior or middle executive and his superior, there is no institutionalized procedure for impartially adjudicating the dispute. In the absence of an impersonal procedure which a set of norms provides for resolving conflicts the superior may exercise power or personal influence instead of legitimate authority' (Scott, 1965, p. 78). This is not to deny the nominal existence of such procedure in certain industrial organizations.

---

[3] Conflict of the third or fourth type may also involve a work group in conflict with some higher level of its own union outside the organization.

Some companies have unilaterally established appeal systems which give the employee the right to appeal through 'an upward channel of communication alternative to the chain of command', and nothing is usually stated which would exclude such categories of employees as professional, scientific, and executive. Nevertheless, 'just the operatives and clericals are expected to use them' (Scott, 1965, pp. 78–9).[4] Still less would such formal machinery be seen as relevant for resolving conflict between managers on the same hierarchical level. This is normally settled either by drawing in senior managers who decide the issue or, if the conflict is at the highest level, by involving the peers of the antagonists in what becomes a factional power struggle.[5]

Conflict of the second type, involving the individually-presented grievance by a lower participant, offers management the least challenge since the balance of power lies so heavily in their favour. The employee can bring little pressure to bear because the organization can impose severe penalties upon him—in the last resort, discharge—at a relatively much lower cost to itself. For this reason the individual is dependent on grace and favour. As we have seen, some organizations unilaterally establish a system which permits an employee to pursue his complaint through successively higher stages of the hierarchy. Even in these cases, however, there is nothing to prevent the system operating exclusively by reference to management goals and values. One study of these systems notes that: 'The difficulty with many formal programs of redress is that their values and the values of the organization ... are not perceived by participants as different. This is why a grin is often provoked when a person is told he can go over his superior's head if he has a problem' (Scott, 1965, p. 124). Escape from dependency upon management

[4] In Britain, a well-known example of a unilaterally established appeals system at the Glacier Metal Company is described by Jaques (1951). Nominally it covers all members of the company, but in an analysis of its operation Wilfred Brown, then chairman of the company, makes no reference to conflict between managers being handled by this formal machinery, and all his examples appear to relate to hourly-paid or low-level staff employees (1965, Chapter 18). References to the appeals system in a joint work (Brown and Jaques, 1965) give the same impression (See, for example, page 92).

[5] Some issues of dispute within the management system may bring in work groups and unions as allies of one or other of the factions. As already noted, research in the United States has shown that on the question of companies contracting-out maintenance or construction work, labour and management were as likely to be allies as enemies (Chandler, 1964). Managers with an interest in keeping such work within the company were supported by workers with a similar interest in opposing those managers and workers who stood to gain by contracting-out.

values in the resolution of conflict can best be assured by participation in an independent collectivity which cannot only define and articulate values and ideologies of its own that are congruent with members' aspirations, but can also muster the power to secure change in the normative system in the light of those values.

Thus the third type of conflict is between management and a collectivity. The collectivity may be in a position to impose severe penalties upon management through its ability to organize strikes, go-slows, working-to-rule, overtime bans, restriction of output, or withdrawal of goodwill (Eldridge, 1968; Knowles, 1952; Goodman, 1967; Ross and Hartmann, 1960). Through this exercise of power it can hope to compel management to accept modifications in the normative system. These may well be both substantive and procedural. The procedural changes will lie in the joint establishment of bilateral negotiating and dispute-settlement systems, through which the norms and values of the collectivity can be effectively brought to bear on decision-making.

The fourth type of conflict, that between employee collectivities, arises from attempts by a group to change the social organization in its own favour in ways which are perceived as being at the expense of some other group or groups. Industrial history reveals numerous examples, as when a powerful group seeks to enhance its own security by invading the job rights of a weaker group, or to maintain a privileged earnings differential by holding other groups in subjection. As with all the other situations described, manifest conflict need not materialize—management may see its best interests in allying itself with the assertive group and the victims may lack the will or the strength to resist. Assuming resistance, however, conflict will be manifested, with each group trying to compel management to act in its own favour. Management therefore has a strong interest in persuading the contesting groups to submit to orderly and peaceful procedures for the resolution of these conflicting claims.

Thus the four types of conflict are handled by management in very different ways. It inhibits the first by suppressing and refusing to legitimize any blatant assertion of personal interest, and it controls the second by its use of power-advantage to redress grievances in the light of managerial values and criteria. The third and fourth types are not open to treatment by either of these means. They involve collectivities which repudiate management ideology, which have freed themselves from dependence upon management grace and favour, and which have mobilized independent sources of power that they are prepared to pit against management in the open assertion of their own interests. Conflict with collectivities may be generated by either of two different sets of pressures upon management. Pressures by subordinates to change the normative system may be seen by management as threatening the organization's relationship with one or more of its environmental constraints, and therefore to be resisted. Alternatively, changes in one of the other constraints may be deemed by management to require changes in the normative system, thus generating conflict with subordinates if they see the changes as incongruent for themselves. Thus a rise in the level of aspirations of any interest group can produce conflict if it threatens changes in the normative system which would create incongruency for other groups.

3 CAUSES OF CONFLICT

It has become increasingly clear from the analysis, therefore, that the causes of conflict cannot be discovered simply by reference to the organization and what goes on within it. Managerial, employee and collectivity aspirations towards organizational norms mediate a wide diversity of structures, processes, values and norms outside the organization. Managerial action upon the normative system may be determined by external economic forces such as price and wage movements, technological change, market conditions or the industrial structure; by social forces such as rising public expectations of managerial performance; by membership of an employers' association; or by political factors such as legislation and government policy. Collectivity aspirations can be shaped by those of wider collectivities outside; by events in the social and economic system generally; by changes in other organizations or in other industries; by changes in the non-work lives and values of individuals; and by the shifting standards of the times as these are reflected in the views of whatever leadership and reference groups people turn to.

Within the organization, the translation of these external stimuli into effective action upon the social organization, via the perceptions and aspirations of individuals or collectivities, is differentially shaped by their location in the social organization and by access to power, individually or collectively applied. Thus aspirations constantly interact with the nature of the division of labour and the distribution of power to produce patterns of conflict. Much research has explored the effects of the work situation upon behaviour without adequately recognizing that these effects are mediated by the subjects' frame of reference which determines how they perceive and define the situation for themselves. Given the importance of the frame of reference, we need to know far more about the social and cultural forces which shape it. Meanwhile we have the numerous studies which draw attention to the links between grievance and conflict behaviour on the one hand, and the organization and design of work on the other (Devlin, 1965; Kuhn, 1961; Sayles, 1958; Scott *et al.*, 1963; Trist *et al.*, 1963; Woodward, 1965, Woodward, 1970). Others bring out the importance in this context of pay structures (Livernash, 1957; National Board for Prices and Incomes, Report No. 65; Turner, Clack and Roberts, 1967). Inequities, inconsistencies and anomalies of reward themselves throw up disputes. Thus organizations that are identical in their technology could show very different records of conflict simply by virtue of this factor alone.

4 THE SIGNIFICANCE AND MEANING OF CONFLICT

The significance and meaning of conflict in industrial society has received widely-differing interpretations. For Marx, of course, industrial conflict was at once the means of class self-realization and the expression of class struggle.[6] As such it was the instrument of revolutionary social change. Conflict rather than mutual accommodation was the historically-inevitable condition in capitalist society. Conflict was part of the progression in the levels of workers' consciousness from job to class to the ultimate victory of the working class over the bourgeoisie. It arose, of course, from the fact of private property which led to exploitation and the appropriation of surplus value by the capitalist.

The function of conflict in establishing and enhancing group identities received a major place in the work of Sorel (1961). '. . . the very content of the moral action lay for him in the aggressive affirmation of the group's integrity and solidarity against an outside group' (Shils, 1961, p. 14). No writer of intellectual stature has gone further in denying the validity of any consensual ethic. 'All attempts to reconcile differences between groups by compromise and negotiation, by the discovery of a common standard, through discussion or by joint renunciation were repugnant to Sorel and contrary to his ethical system' (Shils, 1961, p. 15). For Simmel, however, manifest conflict not only forged group identities and maintained group boundaries, but could also lead to institutions of regulation which might become a form of socialization. By permitting the resolution of

---

[6] For reasons of length it had to be decided, regretfully, that the present analysis could not be extended into the problems of class.

tensions between antagonists, these could have stabilizing and integrative functions for the relationship. In regulating the expression of rival claims, social structures could adapt and readjust to the norms and power relations of constituent sub-groups. These and many other propositions distilled from Simmel's classic work *Conflict* (1955) are re-formulated and examined critically in Coser (1956).

Early American sociologists thought along similar lines. For Cooley, Small, Ross and Veblen, conflict performed positive functions and provided a central explanatory category for the analysis of social change and of 'progress'. This did not mean that cooperation was excluded from their theorizing but rather that, as Cooley put it: 'conflict and cooperation are not separable things, but phases of one process which always involves something of both' (quoted in Coser, 1956, p. 18). A later generation, however, led by Talcott Parsons, has tended to replace analysis of conflict with the study of 'tensions', 'strains' and psychological malfunctioning. Focusing on the primary importance of social order, Parsons was led to view conflict as having primarily disruptive, dissociating and dysfunctional consequences. 'Parsons considers conflict primarily a "disease" ' (Coser, 1956, p. 21). This general orientation entered the field of industrial sociology through the medium of Elton Mayo and his disciples (Mayo, 1933; Mayo, 1945; Roethlisberger and Dickson, 1939; Roethlisberger, 1942. For critical evaluations, Baritz, 1965; Landsberger, 1958). Preoccupied with the Durkheimian problem of anomie, Mayo deplored the supposed destruction of the social bonds of traditional. society by competitive, individualistic, urban-industrialism. The industrial manager could help to save civilization by creating a system of collaboration at the workplace within which the individual could enjoy a sense of social function, responsibility, and cooperative fellowship (Bendix and Fisher, 1962). Conflict could hardly play anything but a disruptive, negative role in this view of the industrial scene. ·

From Marx to Mayo thus takes us from a point at which conflict is the dynamic of all constructive social change to a point at which it figures as the destruction of social hope. In recent years, the theoretical position of most industrial sociologists has swung back to the middle of the range. Manifest conflict is seen as having a constructive contribution to make towards what is defined as a 'healthy' social order. Given the appropriate institutions of regulation and control, the overt and active manifestation of conflict resolves discontents, reduces tensions, clarifies power relations and adjusts social structures accordingly, creates at least as many solidary groupings as it divides, and embodies the principles of self-determination essential to a free society (Dublin, 1954; Kerr, 1964; Harbison, 1954). As we shall see, however, there are still radical critics of the existing social order for whom these institutions of conflict regulation stand condemned by their very role as safety-valve. This perspective has no doubt been strengthened by such candid appraisals as that of Harbison (1954), who describes them as 'important bulwarks for the preservation of the private-enterprise system', and as 'very substantial support for our system of democratic capitalism' (pp. 274, 276). This issue will be examined more fully later. Meanwhile we need to examine the nature of these institutions more closely.

5 THE INSTITUTIONALIZATION OF CONFLICT

Whether managers believe that collectivity participation in decision-making can help them in market regulation or the maintenance of industrial peace, or feel compelled to submit to it under the use or threat of sanctions, it is common, in those societies where the state does not intervene to prevent or discourage it, for procedures of collective bargaining and dispute settlement to be jointly established.

The point has already been made that immeasurably the most important change in procedural norms so far as Western societies are concerned has been the almost universal spread of collective bargaining, otherwise referred to as joint regulation, bilateral regulation, joint negotiation and other variants. Collective bargaining between an employers' association and a union or group of unions, or between an enterprise—or one of its plants—and a union or group of unions, or between a plant management—or a particular manager—and one or more work groups, are all examples of a process which usually results in an agreement about substantive or procedural norms or both (Kahn-Freund, 1954b). Whether we call it a conflict-resolving or a norm-generating process is immaterial; it is in fact both. Slichter describes it as a system of industrial jurisprudence (1941).

The law may play an important part in the structuring and functioning of this process of norm creation and enforcement, and although all states impose some legal regulation they differ markedly in the extent and manner of their intervention. At one extreme, the Soviet Union reserves the major role to public planning agencies and leaves only a highly-circumscribed area of autonomy to managements and employee collectives. At the opposite extreme 'there is, perhaps, no major country in the world in which the law has played a less significant role in the shaping of these relations than in Great Britain and in which today the law and the legal profession have less to do with labour relations . . . British industrial relations have, in the main, developed by way of industrial autonomy . . . No one who has ever compared the situation [in Britain] with that, say, in the United States, in France or in Germany, can fail to see that we are dealing with a characteristic peculiar to the British industrial scene' (Kahn-Freund, 1954a, pp. 44, 45).

The law may seek to impose procedural or substantive norms or both. Whatever can be regulated by autonomous and voluntary joint processes can, by the same token, be regulated totally or partially by law. Thus on the procedural side employers may be required to recognize and negotiate with trade unions, or to set up representative workplace councils with their employees, or to share decision-making in some other way as with co-determination in West Germany. The state may also regulate the behaviour of the parties in other ways by, for example, restricting their use of coercive sanctions against each other, and by imposing procedures of mediation, conciliation, or arbitration in those situations where behaviour is thought seriously to threaten community interests. Substantively the role of law may be equally pervasive, imposing standard or minimum normative requirements covering, for example, wages, working hours, holidays, discipline, dismissals, the handling of redundancy, and other issues relating to health, safety, and welfare. As in the case of autonomous regulation, the legitimation of these legally-sponsored procedural and substantive norms by those subject to them is problematical, and the question of enforcement opens up a similar discussion concerning the nature and conditions of 'consent' and, in this case, the ethical and practical implications of attempting state coercion. These problems are becoming sharpened as societies tend increasingly to search for ways of registering the 'public interest' in the procedures of industrial relations and in their substantive outcomes (Kahn-Freund, 1969; Garbarino, 1969).

The wide diversity of legal intervention as between societies is equalled by the diversity of national systems of regulation, though of course many other factors besides the law produce these differences. Dahrendorf generalizes, however, that for effective regulation on an autonomous basis to be possible, three conditions must be fulfilled.

First, both parties 'have to recognize the necessity and reality of the conflict situation . . .'; that it is 'an inevitable outgrowth of the authority structure. . . .' Wherever the attempt is made to dispute the case of the opponent by calling it 'unrealistic', or to deny the opponent the right to make a case at all, or to put too great an emphasis on alleged 'common interests', effective regulation is not possible. 'The crucial factor for effectively regulating conflicts is recognition, and even emphasis, of systematic divergence and opposition'. The second condition is 'the organization of interest groups. So long as conflicting forces are diffuse, incoherent aggregates, regulation is virtually impossible'. Third, the opposing parties have to agree on certain formal rules of the game (1959, pp. 225–26).

The procedural agreements which embody these norms are often concluded between the higher-level collectivities—trade unions—and employers' associations or individual enterprises. Since they rule out the use of coercive action by either side until the procedure has been exhausted, the possibility exists that a lower-level collectivity, such as the union district or branch organization, or the work group, will see this constraint as disadvantageous on particular occasions and choose to ignore it. Britain is believed by some to have this problem in greater degree than any other advanced industrial society,[7] but the reasons for such international variations as do exist in the strength and independence of shop-floor union organization have not been explored, especially the cultural differences which are almost certainly an important factor. Explanations within the British context are, however, available (Flanders, 1965; Flanders, 1967; Donovan, 1968). Though there is not space here, these could easily be expounded in the terms of the present analysis. The relevant variables would include the shift of power away from management; the high aspirations of employees on such matters as earnings, security and job rights; the low aspirations of managers on such matters as manpower utilization; the anomalies and inequities within pay structures and labour relations generally; the failure of management and the higher collectivities to adapt the institutions of normative regulation to the rising aspirations of employees; and the differing assessments of congruency by the various levels of management and the various levels of collectivities (Fox and Flanders, 1969).

We have already noted the significance of 'disputes procedures' for the organization's decision-making structure, in that they permit the

[7] Although this is challenged by Turner (1969).

individual or group to appeal over the heads of successive levels of management until a satisfactory settlement is reached. If the agreement is with an employers' association, the stages extend to the top leadership of the association. But the institutions of joint normative regulation also include provisions for both sides to meet in ordered systematic ways and make decisions about *general* terms and conditions of employment, and other issues of mutual concern.

In establishing this procedural system, the two parties are jointly creating another social organization with its own division of labour, status relationships, and communications pattern. Insofar as this social organization is congruent with the aspirations of both sides, they will share certain values and norms relevant to it. The desirability of peaceful settlement; the importance of observing the other party's expectations in respect of procedure; the restraints and conventions of social interaction which maintain an environment favourable to compromise; these are at once the pre-conditions and the consequences of successful conflict-regulation. Insofar as there is normative agreement about these behaviours, it embodies a recognition by both sides that any immediate tactical advantage resulting from violation of shared expectations would be outweighed by damage to the system within which they had hitherto accomplished satisfactory results.

Failure on the part of either side, or of any collectivity level on either side, to achieve what they regard as speedy and just results may thereby create a strain upon the system, and possibly lead to withdrawal of support. The independent power enjoyed by many work-group collectivities in post-war Britain enables them not infrequently to challenge the social organization of conflict-regulation, more especially in certain industries. Impelled by rising aspirations; faced with the anomalies and inequities of pay systems distorted by managerial weakness and inflationary conditions; impatient with the cumbersome inefficiencies of the conflict procedures to which higher collectivities have committed them; work groups have increasingly violated institutional values and norms by using coercive action in defiance of procedure. This may create for some managements a downward spiral into disaster. Fearful of escalating the conflict with reprisals, they appease with concessions, hoping to draw the rebellious group back into the paths of institutional settlement. But this rewarding of coercion may simply add another motive for violating procedure.

Even in more favourable circumstances the institutions of conflict regulation may create problems. The norms and values shared by the representatives of both sides in this social organization may become almost as important in moulding their thought and behaviour as the requirements of their managerial or collectivity role. Simmel's proposition is 'that conflict usually takes place within a common universe of norms and rules, and that it leads to the establishment or extension of such norms and rules . . . Such rules contribute to the socialization of the contending parties by imposing restraints on both of them' (Coser, 1956, p. 123). Constituents, however, may neither understand nor approve these compulsions and restraints. The difficulty arises from the fact that there are three social organizations superimposed—the social organization of the enterprise itself; the social organization of the employee collectivity; and the social organization which regulates relations between the two. Some employees, such as shop stewards or branch officials, have roles in all three. Since they are subject as a consequence to pressures which may well on occasion conflict, they may sometimes need skill, sophistication and luck if they are to avoid severely disappointing certain expectations. For example, a shop-floor leader who is expected by the managerial and union hierarchies alike to observe the full protocol of the agreed procedure may be ignored by an impatient work group when he urges the appropriate restraints or considers their grievance insufficiently well-grounded to justify action. If he yields to work-group demands for coercive pressure which flouts the agreed procedure he takes the brunt of management, and perhaps union, condemnation. The management negotiator, too, may not be without his difficulties. Colleagues may become restless at the restraints and bargaining subtleties which he considers important to protect a satisfactory negotiating relationship. They may even ride rough-shod over them when they come to implement the agreement.

These considerations draw attention to the fact that the articulation and maintenance of full understanding and agreement between the negotiator and his constituents is essential if collective bargaining is to preserve its representative character. And if it loses this representative character it loses its value not only for the negotiating parties but also for the wider society which favours it as a conflict-resolving and norm-fixing method.

The reason for this emerges from the preceding analysis. Collective bargaining is a means of restoring authority relations when they have broken down as a result of normative conflict.[8] It restores 'consent'. In many Western societies it is perceived as superior in practical terms to a situation in which power is the arbiter, not least because subjection to power generates negative responses and guarantees instability as soon as counter-power can be mobilized. It may also be regarded as superior in moral terms in cultures which attach value to such principles as self-determination on the grounds that these are integral to human dignity.

All this is lost, however, if articulation between negotiator and constituents breaks down or is never established. The essential concept here is legitimacy. Unless subordinates themselves legitimize the norms to which their representatives are committing them, consent is not secured. Normative agreement is not established, and authority relations are not restored. This might seem too obvious to mention were it not for the fact that every day, somewhere, a manager or a union leader is trying to impose, on a group of employees or members, decisions which they are powerful enough to resist but on which he has not thought it necessary to secure their agreement based on full knowledge and understanding.

The fact of power is of course central to the argument. Whether we are concerned with relationships between top management and subordinate colleagues, or between management and lower participants, or between collectivity representatives and constituents, the greater the power enjoyed by the subordinates or constituents the more important it is for leaders to have their actions legitimized. Many instances of employees 'dishonouring' agreements, for example, can be explained by their never having 'honoured' them in the first place, as a result of leaders failing to understand, or choosing to ignore, the process of winning consent. The requirement of 'full knowledge and understanding' on the part of subordinates or constituents is therefore essential, for without it the stability of the authority relationship must always be in doubt. In behavioural terms, men are only committed to what they perceive themselves as committed to. Subsequent discovery that they have been deceived, misled, or denied the full facts at once threatens consent.

Even where decisions are being made at the point of action, this requirement raises practical difficulties. The more remote the

---

[8] This proposition also embodies the implication that where normative aspirations are constantly rising, in a context of normative confusion and flux, authority itself will be correspondingly unstable since the issue of legitimacy is constantly being re-opened.

decision-making process, and the greater the social and institutional distance between negotiator and constituents, the greater the problem. It reaches its maximum when the state seeks to intervene in industrial relations. Governments may find it possible to reach understandings with national union representatives through face-to-face consultations. There must be great uncertainty, however, as to how far work-group collectivities can be regarded as committed by these understandings, and corresponding uncertainty about the basis of authority in such situations. It is considerations like these which have led many observers and policy-makers in the past to conclude that joint regulation between the parties directly involved provides a more secure basis for order than regulation by the state. Legitimation and consent are less problematical.

In discussing the institutionalization of conflict we have been concerned with what some theorists refer to as the 'industrial relations system' (Dunlop, 1958; Flanders, 1965). The terms in which they define the concept of an industrial relations system articulate closely with the theoretical framework presented here. For Dunlop, 'the industrial-relations system involves three groups of actors: (1) workers and their organizations, (2) managers and their organizations, and (3) governmental agencies concerned with the workplace and the work community'. Every system creates a complex of norms to govern the workplace and its community and these take varied forms which include 'agreements, statutes, orders, decrees, regulations, awards, policies, and practices and customs'. The form of the rule does not alter its essential character, which is to define the status of the actors and govern their conduct. This conduct occurs within an environmental setting of three interrelated contexts: the technology, the market or budgetary constraints, and the power relations and statuses of the actors. 'The system is bound together by an ideology or understandings shared by all the actors' (Dunlop, p. viii). Dunlop compares the systems of a number of countries, while Flanders focuses specifically on the principles, structure and values of the system in Britain. Lipset (1961, 1962) suggests another line of analysis by which values implicit in trade union structure, policies and objectives can be related to the values of the wider society.

6 NORMATIVE REGULATION AND SOCIAL VALUES

Social values are relevant, however, in an even more fundamental sense in that they are manifested in the overall nature, structure and functioning of the industrial relations system itself. To bring out the issues it may be useful to think of two ideal-type situations (Fox and Flanders, 1969). But first we may remind ourselves of the nature of the problem. We are concerned with the role of normative systems in regulating the expectations, behaviour, and aspirations of a large number of occupational groups who are required to collaborate within a complex network of industries and organizations, all marked by extreme division of labour and hierarchical relations, and all subject to differing rates of technical and administrative change. How are these normative systems to be set up and constantly adjusted as occasion demands?

In the first of our ideal-types, the tasks of normative regulation and enforcement are wholly centralized. There is no free market in values and ideologies, and no freedom for interest groups to form independent associations and seek satisfaction of normative aspirations which they themselves formulate. In terms of employment relations, this implies one universal system which regulates normative relations on a unified and consistent basis within work establishments, between establishments in the same industry, and between industries. This comprehensive order is imposed (where necessary by coercion) through state or party agencies, but a unitary state ideology is disseminated which minimizes the need for power by promoting the legitimacy of the system as perceived by those whom it governs. Such a structure will display a high degree of social integration and predictability and a low degree of group self-determination and autonomy. A model of this kind might be useful for exploring the realities of highly centralized totalitarian regimes.

At the opposite extreme we have the pluralistic society in which state intervention is minimal. Through the mechanisms of freedom of contract, freedom of association, and a virtually unrestricted traffic in ideologies and values, combined with a strong preference for voluntary action and for a minimum of state coercion, there develops a wide variety of relatively autonomous but interacting norm-creating groups and agencies. Occupational groups are free to formulate and pursue their own normative aspirations. Given a situation in which groups lack the power to impose their own system on others, the group collaboration necessary for organizational action has to be achieved by the negotiation of compromise normative agreements.

A model of this sort, appropriately elaborated and refined, might be more relevant for analyzing societies of the Western type. Insofar as they do approximate to this pattern, they are trying to operate a method of defining the terms of economic collaboration which requires considerable skill, sophistication and tolerance. It also requires a great deal of luck, for social processes may generate normative divergence too wide to be susceptible to compromise. Perhaps luck tends to be under-estimated as one of the contributory factors to democratic virtue. It is true, too, that many qualifications need to surround the word 'free' in these propositions. The constraints of class, education and upbringing mould aspirations, and the distribution of power determines the ability of an individual or group to realize them. Nevertheless even an approximation to this model might be thought a considerable social achievement. To allow the constituent groups of a society even a limited degree of freedom to form their aspirations and rely on their capacity to produce the constant succession of legitimized compromises that thereby become necessary is to put that society under considerable test. Some degree of disorder is bound to result. It is a price that may be willingly paid, however, to avoid the authoritarian, centralized control that would be required for even an approximation to absolute order.

There is often a failure in Western societies, however, to grasp the nature of the values that underlie this strong preference for self-determination as against authoritarian control. Economists, for example, have tended to evaluate trade unionism and collective bargaining solely in terms of their substantive outcome. They exchange statistics about, say, the wage-earning share of the national income and similar indices, which, they feel, may some day settle once for all whether or not trade unionism is a gigantic hoax. Such considerations have their interest but are quite inadequate as a social assessment. Not only do they stress bargaining about financial rewards to the exclusion of other substantive issues like working hours, holidays, job security, redundancy and a whole range of matters relating to labour utilization, but more fundamentally they ignore the procedural aspect entirely. They focus on the question of *what* decisions are made to the exclusion of *how* they are made. Yet for many people in pluralistic societies it is the latter question that is crucial. Marshall has referred, for example, to collective bargaining in terms of citizenship. Having defined political citizenship as 'the right to participate in the exercise of political power', he suggests that trade unionism has 'created a secondary system of industrial citizenship parallel with and supplementary to the system of political citizenship' (1950, p. 44). It is for such reasons as these that collective bargaining is regarded by many of its champions as integral to the very nature of social functioning and social values characteristic of Western society.

The fact that the collective bargaining method of normative regulation has terminal value for many members of Western societies does not mean that it necessarily has terminal value for managements. Some, indeed, do hold such attitudes, and others may attach terminal value to procedural variants which they believe more fully embody the principles of 'responsible participation' than does collective bargaining (for one example, the John Lewis Partnership, see Flanders, Pomeranz, and Woodward, 1968). Many other managements, however, have come to regard collective bargaining as having instrumental usefulness in pursuing salient values of a very different kind. Their employees commit themselves thereby to the relevant norms and accept joint responsibility for them, thus providing the necessary basis of legitimacy for authority relations. There have emerged, over past decades, abundant reasons for managements to feel that legitimacy was becoming increasingly important and yet increasingly elusive. There are four relevant considerations here. Firstly, the growing size of work organizations and the increasing complexity of their social structure lead many managers to see cooperative and adaptive attitudes among lower participants as an increasingly important variable. Secondly, many advanced societies are witnessing a growing mistrust of hierarchical power domination, and it seems likely that this trend will continue. Thirdly, the accelerating pace of technological, administrative, and market change in a situation where lower participants have the power to resist puts a further premium on winning consent. The fourth point draws specific attention to this shift in the balance of power. Managements are driven to seek legitimacy because their ability to rely on power has greatly diminished as a result of the labour scarcity revolution created by government full employment policies. Marx's 'reserve army' of unemployed, a key notion in the concept of the power of the bourgeoisie, is a far less threatening shadow in the wings than it was. It still has its effects, but they are regional rather than national or international.

Faced with these pressures, those managements that are aware of the problem have sought ways of strengthening their legitimacy. The nature of their attempts has varied, of course, according to their evaluation of what employees wanted from their work—or, more importantly, what they could be brought to want. The emphasis in industrial societies upon material 'progress' and rising living standards has made these perhaps the chief test of managerial legitimacy. Increasingly authority is threatened if management is unable or unwilling to provide employees with the relative material standards to which it aspires, or if management imposes changes which threaten its employees' future position in these respects.

Within this context, collective bargaining has played a considerable part in maintaining a relatively high degree of social order during a period of rising substantive aspirations for goods and services and rising procedural aspirations for participative decision-making systems through which these substantive gains can be made and protected. Partial breakdowns have admittedly occurred, some of them far-reaching. When the industrial system seriously fails in these respects on any widespread scale, many of the other values which help to legitimize management rule come under rejection or the threat of it—acceptance of private property rights and the 'free enterprise' system; management's claim to leadership on grounds of expertise and success; the submission owed to a class, caste, or charismatic leader; or the respect due to a particular system of political or industrial decision-making. Insofar, therefore, as the values predominant in Western societies have been those suggested above, it can be said that the legitimation of managerial rule, in terms of the existence of shared values which provide a basis for normative agreement, has rested heavily on management demonstrating commitment to those values by conceding basic changes in procedural norms and, through these new procedures, making frequent adjustments in the substantive norms relating to rewards and other related issues. They have had literally to deliver the goods, and to share some of their decisions about the terms and methods by which the goods were to be produced.

7 MANAGERIAL PREROGATIVE

It could be argued, then, that collective bargaining, besides embodying in social action certain values integral to Western culture, has played a substantial part in restoring authority relations whenever they have been broken or threatened by normative conflict. This contribution will be approved by those who accept a need within the existing social and economic structure for upholding economic collaboration in circumstances which put it under strain. It will be condemned by those for whom the promotion of managerial legitimacy under private ownership or 'state capitalism' merely postpones the necessary day when the whole framework of economic collabora-tion will be reconstructed on different values.

Even so the acceptance of collective bargaining by management has only been partial. Some managements may not, for reasons already noted, value legitimacy even instrumentally. This preference may accurately reflect their objective situation, or it may not. In some cases it results from ignorance of events in their own organiza-tions. Basic to their misapprehension may be an assumption that the goals of middle and lower management are identical with their own. In fact their colleagues lower in the hierarchy may be accom-modating to new-found work-group power in ways which prejudice efficiency. Work groups may have found the prevailing norms incon-gruent with their rising aspirations and been able to enforce their own. Meanwhile top management, perhaps scarcely aware of the facts, reiterates the importance of managerial prerogative and assumes that prerogative is in fact succeeding in imposing the desired norms. Lacking effective leadership and guidance, what can middle manage-ment do in its own interests but accommodate to upper and nether millstones as best it can—sometimes giving way to work-group power but concealing these tactical retreats from superiors? Some-times, of course, top management perceives the facts about work-group power but lacks the right frame of reference, the analytical ability and the confidence in its own negotiating skills necessary for coping with the task of engineering normative agreement. In such situations the tendency may be to abuse work groups and unions for bringing power to bear; condemn governments for not taking on the task of 'controlling' them; declare itself helpless, and simply hope for the best, intermittently resorting, in the absence of any clear rational strategy, to the desperate expedient of a trial of strength which they usually lose.

In mentioning prerogative we have, of course, put our finger on what for management is the sensitive area of the debate (Chamber-lain, 1948; Chamberlain, *et al.,* 1963).[9] By accepting joint regulation, managers commit themselves to compromise and to abandoning some aspects of their claim to managerial prerogative. Neither may appeal to them. A fear may persist that once this claim is finally and formally abandoned their governance will be submerged beneath a

[9] Space limitations preclude all but the briefest references to international com-parisons (for which see Harbison and Myers, 1959, for analysis and further sources), and much of the discussion in this section has special relevance for the British situation.

chaos of incompatible pressures and demands. They may concede that the trend is against them and that collective bargaining is certain to extend its encroachments, but believe that meanwhile the concept of prerogative must be retained in order to serve them in a fighting retreat. Unless retreat is contested every inch of the way it will become a disorderly headlong flight productive only of confusion.

Accordingly, the predominant tendency has been for managements so far as possible to limit joint regulation to those issues in which they felt their prerogative to be least involved. We may usefully distinguish here between what has been called 'market' regulation—the determination of those norms which enter into the contract of employment, such as wage rates, working hours, overtime and holidays—and 'managerial' regulation—the determination of norms governing the utilization of the labour, capital and other resources brought together and coordinated by management (Flanders, 1965). In general, managements have been far readier to negotiate on 'employment contract' norms than on 'utilization' norms. In other words they have been readier to negotiate with employees about the terms on which they are to be hired than about how they are utilized and deployed once they have been hired.

There may seem to be a certain objective basis for this preference, on the grounds that the question of exactly what management does with a resource more closely touches its personal governance than the question of the terms of its hire. We need to note once again, however, the importance of attitudes and perceptions. Many employers in the nineteenth century regarded the fixing of wage rates as being as integral to their prerogative as any other aspect of their business. Time has wrought its changes until now the assertion by an employer of his absolute unilateral right to determine wage rates is perceived by fellow-employers as a distinctly old-world cause to whose loss they have become reconciled.

There has been no such general reconciliation, however, to the loss of prerogative in 'managerial' as distinct from 'market' regulation. Faced with the pressures mentioned earlier which are rendering legitimacy at once more necessary and more elusive, those managements who are aware of the problem have tended to seek ways of strengthening their legitimacy through devices which did not compromise a prerogative which was in fact vanishing but which they felt unable formally to relinquish. It is no accident that the past few decades have witnessed a succession of personnel panaceas most of which, on examination, show themselves to be attempts to convince employees that they have the substance of participation and influence while in fact giving them only the shadow.[10] Only comparatively rarely has management grasped that the only sure and stable way of maintaining its control was to share it.

There is no reason to assume, however, that this approach will not become more widespread. The shift away from the perceptions characteristic of many nineteenth-century employers was due to trade union pressure, changing social values, and modified assessments by employers of where their own best interests lay. We need not suppose that the present managerial stance on prerogative will be uniquely resistant to these agents of change. Indeed, as will be seen later, there are already signs of its crumbling.

Societies still differ greatly, as we have seen, in the degree to which managements find it possible to assert their prerogative successfully. In the United States and Britain, for example, labour has made some effective challenges, whereas French management has in general retained its control over utilization norms (Harbison and Myers, 1959). This difference does not arise from a greater manage-ment-labour value consensus in France, where it is far smaller than in the United States. It results from differences in power relations —from differences in the strength of employee collectivities at the organizational level—a factor determined by many variables, in-cluding of course the legal framework. The more favourable position of collectivities in the United States often enables them to contest management on those issues where value-consensus does not exist. Despite the far lower degree of legitimacy extended by French collectivities to their managements, they are less able to challenge managerial prerogative. The consequences are 'a potentially ex-plosive worker discontent' (Chandler, 1964, p. 21) and their resort to the mobilizing of political power through which managerial norm-fixing can be controlled by means of legal regulation.

8 THE DYNAMICS OF JOINT REGULATION

It remains now to explore briefly the nature of the joint-regulation or conflict-resolving process. There is space only for a passing glance

---

[10] Such situations therefore display what some theorists describe as 'inauthenticity', defined by Etzioni as prevailing 'when the underlying structure is unresponsive [to basic human needs] but an institutional or symbolic front of responsiveness is maintained' (1968, p. 881). He suggests, as of course do many others, that the prevalence of such shams is increasing in modern industrial society.

at some of its features, but even this can serve to illustrate the nature of the dynamics involved. The first point to be made is that we are concerned here not with normative consensus but with normative agreement, which usually involves negotiated compromise. Clearly the relative power of the negotiating parties has a considerable bearing on the sort of compromise that emerges. To the extent that one side enjoys superior power it will be able to impose terms upon the other. But the situation is far from being as simple as it is often assumed to be. It by no means follows, for example, that the stronger party will exercise its full power in this way. If managers, say, are seeking to strengthen authority relations through normative agreement, they certainly will not. If they do, their employees are likely to feel that the difference between a settlement by negotiation and a settlement by coercion has become too fine for them to appreciate. If they feel that they have, in fact, been coerced, the settlement may well have less legitimacy for them. They may feel less bound by it, and determined to escape from it as soon as they can, or even in extreme cases to ignore it altogether. This is why, for example, men striking for union recognition who were driven back to work by hunger after 'agreeing' to employers' terms that they renounce the union never felt morally bound to obey. Similarly, an employer or manager who finds himself in such market exigencies that he feels forced to 'negotiate' terms and conditions of employment that he considers outrageous may feel no keen moral obligation on the subject of these or future terms.

It is not, however, possible to draw a sharp dividing line between imposing a normative system by power and negotiating one by consent. Power and authority are not the terms of a dichotomy but, as was noted earlier, the opposite poles of a continuum. Negotiated agreements must therefore be expected to have varying degrees of legitimacy for either party depending on the extent to which they feel conscious of having been pressured into accepting its terms against their will. It is clear, therefore, why an experienced negotiator who values a bargaining relationship is unlikely to exert to the full any power advantage he may have. To do so may precipitate an escalating spiral of coercive sanctions which would threaten the whole relationship.

Does this mean, then, that although there are likely to be, by the nature of things, disparities of power—even major ones—between negotiating parties, normative settlements must, if they are to have legitimacy for both sides, emerge out of a roughly equal *exercise* of power? Again, this is too simple a view and overlooks the nature of bargaining dynamics.

A negotiator may, during the course of bargaining, threaten his opponents with sanctions in so blatant and ruthless a manner as to cause them to feel that they are being coerced. They will feel that power is being exercised against them, and may be compelled to submit because they cannot counter it in the same measure. If the agreement is concluded in this spirit, its legitimacy for them may well be minimal. But if, as bargaining proceeds, he seeks to persuade them that he and his constituents without exception hold sincere convictions about the justice of the case, the very extremity of his threats may cause them to become persuaded that this is indeed so. This, in turn, may bring about a shift in perceptions which leaves them less opposed to the claim than they were at the outset. They may feel that this emphatic use of sanctions is no mere cynical piece of power politics but a spontaneous expression of conviction to which they might be well advised to bend.[11] The very manifestation of such feeling may undermine their own conviction. As their perceptions move in the direction of normative accommodation towards the claim they will feel correspondingly less pressured by their opponent's sanctions. They will feel less as if they have been forced into acceptance against their will. The legitimacy of the agreement will therefore be that much greater. Power has thus played a part, not in coercing them to submit to the settlement, but in changing their perceptions so that they come to see the settlement as legitimate. It can be concluded, therefore, that the legitimacy of an agreement for both sides does not require a 'balanced' power relationship. Legitimacy is a function of perceptions, and perceptions can be affected by the use of sanctions in very different ways with very different consequences for the legitimizing process.

These considerations illuminate the importance of the way in which the negotiator marshals, presents, and supports his case. They

[11] There is a mediating social value of significance here. In many societies in the West, approval is given to the principle of groups fighting hard, within socially-sanctioned limits, for what they believe to be right. In its strong form this principle asserts that men *ought* to fight for what they regard as justice. Given a demonstration of deep conviction accompanied by a readiness to fight, the perceptions of an observer or of an opposing negotiator may be modified. No such effect is likely to be evoked when power is exercised in the apparent absence of moral conviction, as in the case of armed robbery by a man who is perceived as cynically exploiting the power of a gun. We can learn much, therefore, about perceptions and communications in a company much plagued by unofficial strikes when the senior executive describes his shop stewards, as one did recently, as highwaymen and bandits.

also cast light on the debate as to whether empirical data has any significant role in negotiations of this kind. It has often been questioned whether rational argument and the increasing use by negotiators of statistical data have any influence on the outcome. Is this not ritual shadow boxing, a procedural façade behind which negotiators weigh up how much power they and their opponents can apply? This question can be examined in the light of the preceding analysis. On the assumption that A's opponent, B, values their bargaining relationship, B may hesitate to reject completely a claim about which A clearly has strong and deeply-held convictions. It is therefore necessary for A to convince B that he does indeed feel this strongly about his claim. One way of doing so is to amass data and arguments which can plausibly be presented by A as having convinced him of the overwhelming justice of his own case. It may not be necessary for B himself to be convinced. The contribution of the data is not so much to convert B, but to persuade him that A feels so strongly about the validity of the claim that to reject it—or at least to reject it entirely—would threaten the stability of the joint regulation process, detract from the legitimacy of the settlement, and thereby weaken the whole purpose for which the exercise is designed. This will increase the likelihood that B will judge it prudent to give way. If, on the other hand, A's case is so flimsily supported as to convince B that no reasonable person—including A himself—could take it seriously, B may not only exercise his own power more confidently but also regard as cynical and provocative any exercise of power by A. If at the same time B succeeds in imparting the conviction that he believes profoundly in the justice of his own position, it may be A who considers it judicious to concede.

There are, of course, other dimensions and variables in the negotiating relationship, as Walton and McKersie demonstrate (1965. See also Dubin, 1960, 1965). Moreover, there are different types of bargaining relationships, of which this is only one example. Nevertheless, it illustrates the nature of the dynamics involved.

The outcome of the negotiation process, the collective agreement, is a revised normative system to which both parties commit themselves. It is one of the normative conventions of the procedural process that once agreement is reached, both sides suspend their aspirational pressures to change the normative system—sometimes the period of 'aspirational truce' is laid down in the agreement. Given the observance of this necessary convention, the reaching of agreement can be said to establish—given the necessary qualifications about the circumstances of its conclusion—the legitimacy of the norms that now come to prevail.

9 EVALUATIONS OF JOINT REGULATION

In discussing evaluations of collective bargaining we are concerned not only with the inherent nature of the institution itself but also with its present mode of functioning. Criticisms come both from those prepared to accept the existing structure, institutions and values of industrial society as a basis for reform and from those who condemn them root and branch.

In line with this distinction we have already briefly noted two sharply-contrasting perspectives. The first sees collective bargaining as one of the great social inventions of the West, embodying values which are integral to the very nature of social functioning and social institutions in these countries, while at the same time applying those values in ways which have issued in significant social change. The second includes several strands of radical criticism. Collective bargaining may be perceived as a form of compromise with the class enemy. The proletariat, instead of constantly seeking to test class relations to destruction, is agreeing to work within a system of the bourgeoisie's choosing which leaves the bourgeoisie itself still in control. As a result of indoctrination industrial man adheres to materialist, self-seeking values which have the effect of confirming and legitimizing the rulers in their domination. Since this induced value-consensus is sufficiently high to enable those in power to concede the subjected a minor voice in decision-making without danger of widespread disruption, the propertyless can be granted the right of collective bargaining. The ultimate irony is therefore that its victims are further confirmed in their attachment to the system by the delusion that they are playing a part in controlling it. Collective bargaining as at present practised therefore serves as a safety-valve which diverts the head of steam that would otherwise drive the engine of social change, and thereby distracts the working-class from its historic role. The values underlying the greater part of trade union and work-group behaviour show, it is said, how completely they have been assimilated to capitalist society. Their very structure and mode of operation are determined by the economic and social system to which they are a response. Limited as they inevitably are by their pragmatic orientations, they can never lead their members beyond the bounds of this pragmatism towards fundamental changes in

F*

power-structure and therefore in social relations. 'As institutions, trade unions do not *challenge* the existence of society based on a division of classes, they merely *express* it . . . They can bargain within the society, but not transform it' (Anderson, 1967, pp. 264–65, for a statement of this position). Viewed in this light, the institutions of conflict-regulation could be seen as part of the pattern of 'false consciousness'. They allow for marginal adjustments within what remains an exploitive set of power relations, and induce an illusion of 'progressive' social change. They compound their historical error by socializing each new generation into this false consciousness.

The alternative perspective concedes some of these points. The employee collectivities which arise from industrial organization, while professing in varying degrees a desire for a different type of social order, have in fact usually accommodated themselves to many of the values of Western capitalist society. The notion of a continuously rising material standard of life; the paramountcy of its demands over intrinsic values in work, over environmental amenity, over the values of stability, continuity, and often personal relationships; the indispensability of hierarchical organization with its massive inequalities in terms of status and functional privilege—none of these has been fundamentally challenged. But it could be argued that this is only one side of the picture. The other side reveals ways in which these new social structures have not incorporated the values prevalent in industry, business, and commerce, but have introduced their own. Managers have not been able, in fact, to manipulate value-consensus quite so conveniently as they would have preferred, as the examination of ideologies shows. Many ideas which are highly inconvenient for managerial prerogative—the concern for individual rights and the elimination of arbitrary rule; the importance of 'human' as well as 'market' values; the importance of maintaining secure legal foundations for employee collectivities—all show a trend towards greater strength. The fact is that in most Western countries the state apparatus has not given managerial prerogative the unqualified support that would have been necessary for the avoidance or suppression of these inconvenient values. As a result, management has not been able to build up ideological control to any considerable degree. The causes must be sought, of course, in the nature of the political decision-making system in these countries. The state has not extinguished all ideologies save those favourable to management. This is in contrast with, say, the Soviet Union, where state and party control over ideology and their support of management prerogative combine to ensure that management is less vulnerable to contrary or oppositional value orientations and normative aspirations among their employees.

The counter-values and ideologies of collectivities are brought to bear directly upon management through the joint regulation processes. This brings out another aspect of their significance. By insisting on a voice in the normative regulation of a widening range of issues, they have changed the procedures of conflict-regulation and decision-making and thereby the whole social nature of industrial organization. Whatever happens to the currently fashionable cry for 'participation', the employee collectivity will continue as one of its few practical manifestations in complex organizations, and will almost certainly continue to enlarge the area of decision-making in which it participates. Furthermore, employee collectivities have also played a part in seeing these rival values embodied in social policy outside industry as well as within it. The weakening of competitive individualism, for example, and its partial replacement by group and occupational solidarity has unquestionably contributed to the shift back from contract to status which lawyers note as a feature of recent times (Friedmann, W., 1964). These changes may be dismissed as trivial or illusory by those whose measuring devices are, so to speak, too cosmic in scale to record any earth tremor smaller than a major earthquake. The alternative view, however, can reasonably point out that to the men whose personal work experience may be transformed by them they may represent, as Marshall suggests, a new dimension of social citizenship. Clearly, then, each of these two perspectives is likely to be the consequence of a particular frame of reference which affects perhaps not only the selection of evidence but, more certainly, its interpretation and weighting. The observer's values concerning desirable and possible social change will affect, for example, his assessment of whether current social change is significant or trivial.

It by no means follows, however, that those who offer no basic challenge to the structure and values of industrial societies can find nothing of which to disapprove in collective bargaining. Economic liberals may deplore its interference with the operation of free markets. Planners may resent the obstacles it presents to their attempts at control. Both groups are alike in that they are really condemning the exercise of power by employee collectivities upon the process of normative regulation, that is to say, upon the decisions about which norms are to be used in conducting operations. The disciples of *laissez-faire* are arguing that management should be constrained only by the impersonal forces of unorganized markets when they decide which norms to apply to the conduct of their business. Those at the opposite extreme wish management to be normatively constrained by the priorities of the planners, and to be free from the power pressures which come from independent employee collectivities and which supposedly make planning difficult or impossible.

Which of the groups has the louder voice in any particular society depends, of course, on a number of factors, but obviously prominent among them is whether, and to what extent, the society in question has chosen, or has been pushed along, the path of government intervention in industrial, commercial, and financial affairs. Britain has been forced in this direction by, *inter alia,* major shifts in her position in the world economy and by political demands for government policies which maintain full employment. In this case, therefore, the predominant criticisms of the present modes of collective bargaining tend to come from the planning side. In the Soviet Union, as in many similar societies, near-total planning means the near-total exclusion of any independent norm-creating and norm-enforcing process which could disrupt state plans. In the United States, which neither by choice nor contingency is moving very rapidly along this path, the appeal of free markets still prompts some economists to expend considerable resources of time and intellectual energy in trying to assess what the effects of collective bargaining have been upon costs, prices, and the rate of change.[12]

The aspirations towards planning in Britain, insofar as they concern employment relations, derive from a two-fold social purpose. There is considerable agreement that steps should be taken to raise the income, relatively to others, of large numbers of people living on or near the standard currently defined as poverty. And secondly, the need—given current expenditures abroad on defence, foreign aid, and capital investment—to keep imports down and exports up forces governments to try to contain inflationary movements in costs, prices, and spendable income. This has involved them in attempts to restrain the general upward trend in wage and salary norms. Both these purposes have been partially or wholly frustrated by independent, sectional collective bargaining as at present practised. Experi-

---

[12] One expression of this haunting appeal of the 'non-union economy' can be found in Macdonald, (1963).

ence with the first teaches that collective bargaining is no tool of social justice insofar as this is defined as levelling up the very poor relative to others. The 'democratic' freedom of interest groups to formulate their own normative aspirations and fight for their own hand has the reverse side that groups which, through the accidents of social or technological circumstances, cannot mobilize the power to make their aspirations effective must remain subject to the power of others. When special efforts are made through collective bargaining to improve their position, those groups that are better off are likely to feel relatively deprived and to use their power to restore the original relationship. Thus social policy designed to change the rewards of one group relative to those of others cannot, in a society geared to competitive self-seeking, easily be exerted through the medium of collective bargaining. This leads on to consideration of the second social purpose. Securing restraint (i.e. the acceptance of a smaller wage or salary increase than would have been achieved in the absence of restraint policy) has not proved easy in a society characterized by pressure group activity in the competitive pursuit of income and status.

These problems can readily be expressed in the terms of the theoretical framework used here. For this purpose we take up again the notion of management making decisions within a set of constraints. When one of these constraints—organized labour—is powerful enough to oblige management to share its decision-making over a widening range of issues, the question posed in an earlier chapter appears to some to become even more pressing. Do the diverse mechanisms available to stakeholder groups for influencing management's decision-making favour some of these groups as against others? In many industrial societies, substantial bodies of opinion hold that, in full employment conditions, claims by powerful groups of organized labour asserted through the procedures of joint regulation prejudice national welfare by aggravating inflationary pressure, perpetuate social injustice among groups of employees who cannot assert themselves so effectively, hamper efficient utilization of resources, and help to raise prices against the consumer. Any assumption made, rightly or wrongly, in the past that the mechanisms of the market would effectively constrain the two negotiating parties and protect the interests of other stakeholders (weak employee groups included) is regarded as far less valid in an age of administered prices and managed markets. Even in the United States, 'there is a growing questioning of the usefulness of market forces in serving the public interest with respect to both wage and price determination' (Taylor, 1961, p. 351. See also Shonfield, 1965; Bakke *et al.,* 1963).

From these views has emerged the conclusion that the stability of national economies and currencies requires the intervention of government with some form or other of 'incomes policy', which may or may not include considerations of social justice (*British Journal of Industrial Relations,* November, 1964, and November, 1967, for symposia and international references). Joint regulation can no longer, it is said, be regarded as a private matter. Consumers, local community, national economic welfare; all have an interest in the outcome of joint regulation. Since these interests are no longer, if they ever were, protected by the market, other institutions must serve the need.

Under these pressures, many industrial countries have been engaged for some decades in a search for the appropriate mechanisms. This search, with its threat to the autonomy of negotiators, faces three types of opposition. First and foremost, of course, comes resistance from the deeply-rooted and powerful vested interests of joint regulation—the trade unions and their members, and even employers' associations and individual companies on those occasions when income restraint does not serve their immediate need. Second, there is uneasiness among some who fear that, unless great care is exercised, certain essential values of Western society may be compromised, leading perhaps to similar compromises in other fields of social action and thus to a gradual betrayal of its social and political philosophy. Third, there comes ideological attack from those who assert that ruling groups in Western society are too concerned about the threat to economic stability and social justice which allegedly comes from organized labour, and not concerned enough about the excessive privileges of other stakeholders such as shareholders and management itself. Given that the power structure of Western industrial society still favours these stakeholder groups, incomes policy must be seen, according to this view, as a means by which capitalist systems seek to solve their problems and contradictions at the expense of the working class (Rowthorn, 1967).

Controversies like these are not resolvable by 'evidence' since the contestants start out from totally opposed value systems. Meanwhile, however, countries continue their intermittent search attended by far more failure than success. Nevertheless, out of this increasing concern of governments with income movements, consequent upon their growing responsibility for national economic viability and growth, have come the beginnings of new emphases and modes in joint regulation which may grow and become permanent. They represent an extension in the area of joint decision-making, and thus a further change in procedural norms. To understand how this has come about we have to note that concern with national economic growth has led to a concern with managerial efficiency in the utilization of labour and capital. This, along with a quickening of domestic and international competition during the fifties, has stimulated in some countries, America and Britain among them, a significant rise in managerial aspirations in these respects. This heightened determination by top management to improve labour or capital utilization creates a considerable potential for conflict and disorder which can be explained in terms of the framework presented here. The explanation lies in seeing the normative system of the enterprise as in some sense the 'disputed ground'.

10 THE NORMATIVE SYSTEM AS THE 'DISPUTED GROUND'

From one point of view, when we examine the aspirations and goals of the different levels of management along with those of the other individuals and groups who make up the social organization, we derive a picture of the normative system as being subject to a complex pattern of manipulations, power pressures, and resistances. From this perspective, the normative system is the 'disputed ground' which individuals and groups seek to mould and manipulate in the service of their aspirations, striving either to introduce change that is congruent with them or resist change that is incongruent. This process can be illustrated in terms of a number of possibilities. In examining them it will be useful to reduce the complexity of the picture by means of an oversimplification. In place of the many-sided pluralism that has emerged from the analysis we may think in terms of the conventional two sides of management and workers; each side a homogeneous entity. A range of possibilities can then be postulated on the basis of certain assumptions about the level of aspirations on both sides and the distribution of power between them.

The lower the level of workers' aspirations, the less demands they make on the normative system, and this on the face of it would seem to enlarge the freedom enjoyed by management in the pursuit of their own aspirations. And so, in certain respects, it does. Certain kinds of change are easier to introduce to a docile, passive and undemanding labour force than to one that is keenly alert in pursuing an ever-enlarging set of aspirations. But in some circumstances the freedom of management may prove empty. Workers with low aspirations are weakly motivated. Yet some kinds of task, some kinds of pay system, and some kinds of group co-operation call for strong motivation if managerial purposes are to be achieved. Employees with high aspirations therefore offer management both a threat and a promise. Their energy may be turned against the normative system if it frustrates their aspirations, but alternatively it may be harnessed and directed towards managerial goals. Low aspirations, conversely, have a low potentiality for conflict, but may also have a low potentiality for what management would deem active, fruitful collaboration.

However, some employers and managers may welcome low aspirations among their employees not because this frees them to introduce change but because it relieves them of some of the *need* for change. In other words, if their own aspirations are low, the absence of demands by their employees upon the normative system will spare them the challenge of reconciling these demands with the requirements of the organization's environments. Such situations as these, where both managerial and employee aspirations are weak, can provide a formula for harmony and peace which derives from the fact that the interest groups comprising the organization make small demands upon the social framework of which they are a part. Provided that, with respect to both managerial and employee aspirations, the normative system provides the minimum congruency, such situations can persist for long periods.

Various factors may disturb the equilibrium. An adverse change in an environment may result in the organization no longer being able to supply even the minimum congruency with employee aspirations. They drift away and cannot be replaced. Changing social values or an enlargement of perceived opportunities consequent on increased power may quicken employee aspirations and lead to demands upon the normative system which management must reconcile with the demands of the environments. Management aspirations may similarly rise and lead them to act upon the normative system in ways which threaten to make it incongruent with employee aspirations.

We may link these various possibilities with their significance for the rate of organizational change. If management aspirations are high but employee aspirations low, the rate of change in the normative system may well be rapid as management pursues its modifications. Yet change will be peaceful because it is accepted passively by the other interest groups. Where employee aspirations are high but management aspirations low, the same result is likely—a rapid rate of change as work groups mould the normative system to their liking, not seriously challenged by management. Acquiescence and tacit acceptance of work-group 'custom and practice' becomes the normal managerial stance. The work group is changing norms in the light of its own aspirations with a considerable measure of management complaisance. There is general recognition that this describes the post-war situation in Britain with respect to the utilization of labour. Quickened by a consciousness of increased power, employee aspirations in the field of earnings, security, discipline and other aspects of job control have been rising,[13] while management aspirations towards efficiency of manpower utilization have been weak. The result has been the steady imposition of their own will by work groups upon the normative system, which has therefore undergone change as norms became modified in the interests of collectivity goals.

Since employee collectivities bear no responsibility for the organization's relationships with its environments, this process of steady encroachment in the service of collectivity goals is as likely as not to weaken rather than strengthen those relationships. Luck may postpone a reckoning if the environment becomes increasingly favourable and thus cushions declining effectiveness. Sooner or later, however, organizational deterioration is likely to reach a stage where it cannot meet the demands of its environments. The alternatives then become organizational extinction, a takeover by a powerful rival, or a rise in managerial aspirations—probably brought about by a change in top management.

Even where events do not reach this extreme stage, external or internal stimulus may raise management aspirations in ways that we have already noted. Whatever the cause, the scene is now set for conflict. As management takes hold of the normative system to strengthen the organization's relationships with its environments, it comes up against the high aspirations of employee interest groups who are seeking to mould the system for different ends. The maximum potentiality for conflict therefore exists when all the

---

[13] For a full study of the effects of high instrumental aspirations among sections of British manual wage-earners upon their attitudes to work, management, the union, politics, and the class structure, see Goldthorpe *et al.*, (1968a); Goldthorpe *et al.*, (1968b); and Goldthorpe *et al.*, (1969a).

relevant interest groups, including management, have a high level of aspirations, for it is in these circumstances that the normative system is most keenly contested. The situation is, after all, one in which management is trying to regain lost control. It seeks to wrest back an initiative which it has lost to the work group. But with work groups now enjoying a measure of power along with management, all the organized interests comprising the organization are now able to contend effectively for control of the normative system, which becomes more widely than ever before the subject of a struggle for mastery.[14]

11 NEW MODES OF JOINT REGULATION

This situation taxes managers' skills and sophistication to the utmost. They may attempt to fall back on legalistic definitions of managerial prerogative, seeking to impose change in the teeth of opposition and mistrust. This stance is open to the criticism that it ignores the facts of the organization's social structure. It fails to acknowledge the existence of rival bases of power, rival focuses of loyalty, and rival ideologies within the organization. The onset of conflict does not necessarily, however, indicate this kind of management response. A history of managerial weakness and low aspirations tends to create a set of expectations among employees upon which their strategies become based. A new regime may see as its first task the establishment of a different set of expectations. Rational discussion may not be sufficient to convince collectivity leaders that management is resolved on a new policy, and conflict may be necessary to establish this conviction. This illustrates the fundamental importance of expectations and explains why history is an indispensable dimension in the analysis of industrial situations. Conflict can be followed, however, by creative negotiation designed to achieve agreed changes in the normative system which give both sides something of what they want. Under modern conditions, when the returns from coercion become increasingly doubtful, it is upon the promotion of this joint 'problem-solving' approach that management's freedom to innovate largely rests. We thus reach the paradox that only by fully recognizing and accepting the constraints imposed by the aspirations of its subordinates, and working through these constraints towards a new synthesis, can

[14] Discussion and documentation of situations of this kind in the United States, for example, can be found in Healy, (1965); Miernyk, (1962); and Somers *et al.*, (1963); all of which include further references.

management now enjoy any creative role in its handling of the social organization.

But in what way does this approach represent a new mode of collective bargaining? The conventional practice customarily involves management and employee representatives in negotiating the norms which regulate the contract of employment, without reference to the norms which regulate production methods and the utilization of capital and labour. And in the type of situation under examination it is the latter norms—norms which have been informally and often unilaterally moulded by work groups solely in the light of their own goals—which management is interested in changing. The answer evolved by a growing number of managements has been to link the negotiation of changes sought by work groups in employment norms with the negotiation of changes sought by management in production norms. Work groups find themselves able to accept changes in the latter in order to secure desired changes in the former, and management vice versa. Management and employee collectivities may in this way be able to achieve a major reconstruction of the normative system which leaves all the parties conscious of having improved their position. In Britain this approach has understandably been strongly encouraged by the principal institution of incomes policy, the National Board for Prices and Incomes (1967), since wage improvements are accompanied by production improvements which wholly or partly finance them. The practice has gained considerable ground under the name of 'productivity bargaining' (Flanders, 1964). A similar trend in the United States, deriving from pressures on management caused by rapid technological change and intensified competition, has been described as 'creative collective bargaining' (Healy, 1965).

We are here concerned with the reverse side of the proposition that low aspirations among management and employees offer low potentiality for conflict but also low potentiality for maximizing the fruits of collaboration. When aspirations on both sides are high there is high potentiality for conflict but also high potentiality for maximal collaboration. Not only are the employees strongly motivated, but the managers also are equally motivated to seek ways of directing this energy into normative patterns which serve their interests as well as those of employees.

The significance of the new bargaining style should therefore not be underestimated. In a situation where the rising aspirations of different stakeholders cause them to contest increasingly strongly for control over the normative system, so-called productivity bargaining secures agreement on a 'package deal' of changes which between them offer something to the aspirations of all the parties involved. It represents a joint struggle to accommodate conflicting demands to the survival or growth needs of the coalition. The distinction between this mode of bargaining and the more conventional pattern has been explored by Chamberlain and Kuhn (1965), in terms of 'cooperative' and 'conjunctive' bargaining, and by Walton and McKersie (1965) in terms of 'integrative' and 'distributive' bargaining.

Distributive bargaining is the 'joint-decision process for resolving conflicts of interest . . . The term itself refers to the activity of dividing limited resources. It occurs in situations in which one party wins what the other party loses' (Walton and McKersie, 1965, p. 11). Integrative bargaining implies a joint problem-solving search process which results in the normative system being changed in such ways as to enable both management and work groups to feel they have benefited. In the language of game theory, it is a positive-sum rather than a zero-sum game. It implies 'that intelligent union and management officials will observe that the mutual relationship can be improved, to the advantage of each, by holding out the promise of benefit to the other party too' (Chamberlain and Kuhn, 1965, pp. 424–35).

What underlies this shift from a win-lose power struggle over dividing a given stock of resources towards a joint problem-solving effort to enlarge the stock? Basically it represents a shift in frames of reference and perceptions on both sides. In conventional distributive or conjunctive bargaining, management clings to the notion that it must retain its formal prerogative over the norms governing the utilization of resources, fearing that to submit these issues to the negotiating table would result in a cumulative dissolution of their rule by openly acknowledging the employees' right to participate in an ever-widening range of decision-making. Joint regulation is therefore limited to the norms governing the employment contract. Meanwhile, work groups informally establish 'custom and practice' which in fact does encroach, in a manner formally unacknowledged but tacitly acquiesced in by management, on their prerogative. This managerial frame of reference may be complemented by a counterpart on the union or work-group side which equally manifests a win-lose perspective. This is the view by which anything that is in management's interests must, by definition, be opposed to the interests of the work group. This is, of course, a product of the type of situation where normative conflict has eroded value-consensus and generated a sub-culture informed by values and norms hostile to management's. Perceived in these terms, events and propositions which favour management's cause will automatically be defined as prejudicial to the employees'.

Integrative or cooperative bargaining cannot be pursued between parties who employ these frames of reference. On the management side, the joint problem-solving approach requires formal acknowledgement of the relinquishing of vital areas of prerogative. Work groups are invited to participate in a joint reconstruction of the normative system as it affects not only employment-contract norms but also utilization norms. On the work-group side, there has to be acceptance and trust that while the joint search is designed to reduce costs, this search will not be exploited by management to serve their ends at the expense of the employees. In the words of Walton and McKersie, 'One test of the extent to which the search process is really functioning is the extent to which the union and management abandon their respective offensive and defensive postures' (1965, p. 152).

It is also clear that the principal initiative has to come from management. Only management can acknowledge that its prerogative has become a procedural façade behind which its control is slipping away. Only management can bring about a relaxation of the anti-management culture evoked by past managerial behaviour.

Finally, one would predict that the new modes of regulation, involving as they do a closer collaborative pattern of relationships, would be condemned by those whose anti-management stance is ideological and total. The perspectives and behaviours required for integrative bargaining are incompatible with the class war. Viewed in these terms, integrative bargaining inveigles the working class into 'a new and subtler form of subservience at the very point in history when it is powerful enough to meet and reject the challenge' (Topham, 1967, p. 137). The correct response for collectivity leaders, however, according to this standpoint, is not flatly to oppose the new capitalist strategies but to use them as a vehicle for mounting an offensive campaign for 'workers' control'—i.e. for fundamental changes in procedural norms.

Even given collaborative attitudes there will remain an extent to which normative agreement is problematical. To suggest otherwise would be to imply that a normative system which adequately meets employees' aspirations is invariably the optimum one in the eyes of managers for coping successfully with all the constraints through which they have to pursue their own aspirations. This is demonstrably not so. In many cases, however able and skilful the management, its reconciliation of environmental with internal demands, and indeed its reconciliation of conflicting internal demands, can only be partial and this must limit the extent of normative agreement. In the short run, a point is reached when no further change can be agreed. In the medium and long term, perhaps, goals or material technology or environmental constraints may change in ways which reintroduce possibilities of trading. But at any one time there is a limit. In the unresolved area that remains, power is the arbiter, exercised either by management over work groups or work groups over management.

12 CIRCUMSTANCES PROMOTING CUMULATIVE DISORDER

The new modes of bargaining, with their 'joint problem-solving' approach along with the appropriate frames of reference, may also increasingly come to be seen by management as the best strategy for coping with another possible outcome of situations which combine strong shop-floor group solidarity with full-employment conditions. This is the emergence, in certain kinds of social and cultural context, of symptoms of cumulative disorder focusing mainly on earnings (Fox and Flanders, 1969). A joint search for a mutually-beneficial package deal of normative change in work methods may lead to a wholesale reconstruction of workplace relations which includes an attempt to re-design crumbling payment systems on a new and stable basis. What is the nature and cause of these symptoms?

Given rising aspirations, a plurality of separate, independently-minded, and internally unified work groups within the organization's labour force, a normative system that fails to hold the consent of one or more of these groups, and a situation of relative labour scarcity which gives them power to act, the scene may be set for progressive fragmentation of whatever degree of normative order exists.

Britain shows symptoms of moving in this direction. Essentially the process can be described as one in which lower-level collectivities break through the normative systems established by higher-level collectivities, and impose or negotiate their own. In the typical situation, a normative system covering a number of different groups comes under increasing tensions for a variety of possible reasons. Perhaps certain groups wish to challenge some of the norms on which they have developed new aspirations. Perhaps anomalies and inconsistencies of regulation between groups within the system, or in relation to groups in other systems, are not resolved. In response to these failures of the system, which is now perceived as illegitimate and lacking in authority, those groups with sufficient power break through it and impose their own norms. Insofar as they serve as reference points for other groups, either in the same system or in others, their example is followed. Extreme frustration builds up among those groups who come under the same tensions but who lack power. Meanwhile, each normative system becomes either replaced or supplemented by a number of smaller systems. This increases the likelihood of disorder, since groups governed by different normative systems are clearly likely to behave in ways which frustrate each other's expectations. Besides making predictability and integration of action difficult this may create mutual frustration, jealousy, and rivalry, leading to severe inter-group conflict. Moreover, this fragmentation of normative systems is itself a factor making for tension between norms and aspirations. Disorder feeds upon disorder. When the progressive and arbitrary fragmentation of normative systems has passed a certain point, nothing short of their wholesale reconstruction on a basis of legitimacy can remove the source of disorder. In general it can be argued that the more numerous the normative systems regulating employment relations, the greater the problem of social order, since the task of finding the requisite measure of integration among the various systems becomes increasingly difficult to solve. In other words, the more regulation is fragmented, the greater the likelihood of disorder when the different groups have their expectations formed and their actions guided by unrelated and divergent sets of norms.

No assumption should be read into this analysis that social order is the greatest good. The aim is simply to indicate the dynamics of certain social processes under certain conditions. In this case the social consequences could be far-reaching. The proliferation of norm-fixing groups and the resulting multiplicity of normative systems may produce a degree of disorder which is felt by substantial sections of society to impede and imperil vital functions of social life and government. In industrial relations the economic consequences are not confined to strikes and other dislocations of the productive process. The loss of integration and predictability is also expressed in such features as chaotic pay differentials and uncontrolled movements of earnings and labour costs. And the political consequences are decidedly no less important. Growing disorder may threaten the government's ability to govern and start to generate strong popular demands for authoritarian state intervention to restore order.

An excessive proliferation of normative systems can therefore produce social consequences that are similar to those resulting from the absence of any norms to regulate conflict. Both situations can be seen as a breakdown of social regulation. Both can be described in the terms of Durkheim's characterization of anomie. It is the cause, as he said:

> '... of the incessantly recurrent conflicts, and the multifarious disorders of which the economic world exhibits so sad a spectacle. For, as nothing restrains the active forces and assigns them limits they are bound to respect, they tend to develop haphazardly and come into collision with one another, battling and weakening themselves. To be sure, the strongest succeed in completely demolishing the weakest, or in subordinating them. But if the conquered, for a time, must suffer subordination under compulsion, they do not consent to it, and consequently this cannot constitute a stable equilibrium. Truces, arrived at after violence, are never anything but provisional, and satisfy no one. Human passions stop only before a moral power they respect. If all authority of this kind is wanting, the law of the strongest prevails, and latent or active, the state of war is necessarily chronic' (1964, p. 3).

Again, in another passage, Durkheim notes what happens when 'an abrupt growth of power and wealth' creates unstable conditions by upsetting the established scale of values:

> 'The scale is upset, but a new scale cannot be immediately improvised. Time is required for the public conscience to reclassify men and things. So long as the social forces thus freed have not regained equilibrium, their respective values are unknown and so all regulation is lacking for a time. The limits are unknown between the possible and the impossible, what is just and what is unjust, legitimate claims and hopes and those which are immoderate. Consequently there is no restraint upon aspirations' (1952, p. 253).

The process may also be described in terms of its impact upon the institutions of collective bargaining. The normative systems fashioned by the evolution of bargaining in Britain, particularly in the structure of industry-wide agreements, can no longer cope with the increased input of conflict which has been generated in postwar circumstances. That is why the systems are weakened and, to some extent, in a state of collapse.

Thus we see the fundamental problem of societies that aspire to be democratic in the sense in which this word is usually understood in the Western world. They seek a balance that is notoriously difficult to maintain. They eschew such a degree of social order and integration that would require for its achievement a centralization of normative regulation repugnant to their social values. On the other hand, the degree of permitted decentralization of normative regulation may produce social disorder too threatening for society to tolerate, precipitating a retreat to the safety of state regulation.

In a situation marked by shop-floor power, rising aspirations, and normative fragmentation, the task of reconstructing normative systems which, by knitting together groups previously governed by different systems, reduce the threat of disorder, is of course enormous (See also Goldthorpe, 1969b). Success requires that all the groups concerned perceive the larger normative framework—whether it covers a plant, a company, or an industry—as legitimate. Yet the very experience of normative independence and initiative may generate group expectations which cannot co-exist within one all-embracing system. If so, the alternatives are, as we have noted, the tolerance of a possibly high degree of organizational disorder or a widespread demand for the use of state power to impose normative systems which would not have legitimacy for those whose working lives they regulated. The degree of power required to enforce them in the circumstances postulated would unquestionably result in fundamental changes in the nature and institutions of the society concerned. It remains to be seen whether industrial societies do, in fact, move into this kind of situation or some milder form of it. If they do not then questions of equal interest will arise concerning the social and cultural characteristics, processes and mechanisms which have enabled them to avoid it.

There are two schools of thought which would wish at the very least to supplement this analysis of possible cumulative disorder. Some left-wing theorists see, to some extent in Western Europe generally but particularly in Britain, a resurgence of militancy which is of major significance in that it reveals collective action at the shop-floor level taking up the avant-garde position of leadership in the class struggle. The role of the left must be to focus this 'scattering of isolated local demands' into a unified class-conscious national struggle for fundamental economic and social change (Anderson, 1967). The empirical basis for any hopes in this direction might appear to be slender. There is little sign that the groups taking part in these fragmented assertions of rising aspirations are ready to allow their efforts to be channelled into the pursuit of revolutionary change. Most industrial societies have experienced phases during which hopeful revolutionaries adorned grass-roots movements with their own slogans only to find the banners abandoned on the field once certain immediate bread-and-butter demands had been won. Nevertheless, the attention of a number of European theorists has been caught by the current trends (e.g. Gorz, 1964; Mallet, 1963).

Paradoxically, one of the factors seen by some of these theorists as progressively enhancing rank-and-file power—to be used perhaps in a progressive encroachment upon management's rule until 'workers' control' is achieved—is adduced by the other very different school of thought as part of an argument that 'worker protest' is destined to diminish in significance in advanced industrial societies. This factor is the new science-based technology characterized by automation, continuous-process production, the investing of even low-level jobs with some degree of responsibility and autonomy, and a tendency to upgrade manual-work roles towards white-collar status. For some Marxists, these trends appear to bring to the organized work group a power which can and eventually will be used in a calculated advance towards ultimate control. In the opposing view, they contribute to a complex of influences which are integrating employees more fully into the company's corporate community, causing them to identify more readily with top management goals, and transforming the union role, if it continues to have one at all, into virtually that of an auxiliary to management which, far from presenting any serious challenge, contributes to the increasingly important functions of regulation, planning, and control (Galbraith, 1969). Viewed from this perspective, any apparent resurgence of militancy is a short-term phenomenon of no great significance. These opinions are often associated with the 'convergence' thesis that, once countries enter into the advanced stages of industrialization, they tend to become increasingly comparable in their major institutional arrangements and in their social systems generally (Kerr, *et al.,* 1962, for a statement of this view; Goldthorpe, 1964, and Wolin, 1960, for a critique; Aron, 1967a and 1967b for further discussion). Galbraith, for example (1969), analyses the functions of unions in the West and in the Soviet Union in a manner clearly meant to suggest their similarities and which expresses his belief in 'the convergent tendencies of industrial societies, however different their popular or ideological billing' (p. 390).

Whatever changes are wrought in the very long term, however, certain specific problems will certainly remain to be grappled with in the short and medium run. The institutions of joint regulation that

· have developed within industrial societies of the Western pattern have revealed, in varying degrees, a failure to cope with certain emergent problems which seem likely to become more rather than less pressing. Sectional and autonomous collective bargaining has not only thrown up considerable inflationary difficulties for governments seeking to maintain economic stability and steady growth, but has also demonstrated its unfitness as a medium for the pursuit of what is widely defined within these societies as social justice. Both these characteristics it shares, needless to say, with many other institutions in these societies. It remains to be seen whether social inventiveness and cohesion are adequate to generate modifications which meet the problems while still respecting the values on which joint regulation is based.

CHAPTER VI

Summary and Conclusions

In summarizing the principal ideas of the theoretical framework suggested in the preceding chapters we must begin with the crucial importance of substantive and procedural aspirations. Cultural and subcultural variations within and between societies are apparent, but so is a widespread and growing tendency for men to expect their governments to create the conditions for economic growth and a continuously rising standard of life. So, too, in some advanced industrial countries, is an increasing inclination to ignore, evade, or openly challenge hierarchical rule and leadership; a development which is affecting not only management and trade unions but also politics and other institutions such as universities and the Roman Catholic Church. Whether or not this proves to be a temporary phase in the case of non-work institutions, it may well, so far as industry is concerned, be a permanent development which is, perhaps, only to be expected as employees become better educated, more articulate and self-aware, and increasingly disposed to challenge limits to their normative aspirations. Cultural differences will certainly affect the speed and nature of change, but we cannot ignore the tendency for even groups in less 'developed' societies to accept, by emulation, the values and aspirations of those societies which they perceive as 'modern' or 'advanced'.

Of major significance in the discussion of orientations and aspirations is the general ethos surrounding the notion of scientific and technological 'advance'; the notion which has shaped Western society, virtually dominates it today, and shows signs of extending its dynamic to the whole of human society. One of the cant phrases of our times, rarely challenged with any success, is: 'You cannot stop progress', when progress is defined as 'more', 'bigger', 'newer', or 'faster'. An important component of this general ethos is, of course, the value attached to ever-rising standards of consumption. The widespread acceptance of this ethos by management and managed alike has given a characteristic shape to the normative systems of work organizations,

182

a shape much influenced by what has been perceived as necessary for 'efficiency', 'competitiveness', 'growth', and 'technological change'. These perceived 'necessities' have often taken the form of hierarchical structures marked by extreme inequalities of reward, status, control, and job interest. Shared values, disseminated and maintained by many diverse means, have enabled management to retain considerable legitimacy and therefore authority in the face of these inequalities. But some aspects of even shared values may generate conflict, as when the method of production or distribution of a finite quantity of wealth is perceived as a win-lose or 'zero-sum' game. Moreover, the ethos of economic growth and material progress is not the only source of values in any society. Employee collectivities have helped to promote managerial recognition of individual and group rights to certain modes of normative treatment which acknowledge the importance of dignity, respect, and other so-called 'human' as opposed to 'market' values.

There has nevertheless been little concern even by employee collectivities with values associated with the question of what work does 'to' us, as opposed to what it does 'for' us; with the intrinsic or expressive as opposed to the extrinsic or instrumental rewards. This might be explained by supposing that until men achieve a certain level of physical comfort and security they are unlikely to give high priority to the 'needs' of 'personality development' as culturally defined. But this 'certain level' is itself open to cultural definition, and if social influences ensure that this level constantly rises then the intrinsic values in work may continue to take relatively low priority. There are some grounds for believing that this is in fact happening, and that work organizations and conflict within them will continue to be shaped mainly by values arising directly or indirectly out of a concern with extrinsic rewards. As the members of advanced in-dustrial societies become increasingly affluent they show little sign of wishing to trade extrinsic rewards in work for intrinsic. This instru-mentalism is often attributed simply to the influence of advertising agencies—an attribution viewed sceptically by those who consider this influence to be greatly exaggerated. But advertising is only one manifestation of an ethos which pervades the life of modern society and is all the more potent for being taken so much for granted. Quite apart from the conditioning consequences of work itself, structured as it normally is to induce the assumption that extrinsic considera-tions must be considered paramount, much of the content of social communication and most of the decisions, policies, and demonstrated preferences of governments and public authorities, industries and services manifest, directly or indirectly, the same preoccupation. Figuratively speaking, we absorb the ethos with the air we breathe.

Given that the ethos becomes embodied in social institutions, which in turn socialize successive generations of men in the relevant values and assumptions, the system may appear to possess a dynamic of its own independent of the wills of those who operate it. This dangerous acceptance of what can prove to be a self-fulfilling prophecy may be checked, however, by remembering that there are alternative philosophies of the social role of work and industry. This is not to underrate the very powerful forces making for continuation—indeed for progressive reinforcement—of currently-prevailing values. Certainly the individual who occupies a humble role may feel helpless to change the values which inform the institutions of his society. Collectively with his fellows, however, he may be able to act, as the history of 'social reform' clearly demonstrates. Much depends here, of course, on leadership. If, as material needs become increasingly well served, men are to broaden and deepen the rewards they gain from work, they must first be convinced that such rewards are worth the pursuing. Since many of us are not yet so persuaded, it may only be under the leadership of those in whom we have confidence that we modify the claims we make on work. The attitudes and values, and the stature and courage, of trade union and political leaders as well as of managers themselves must therefore be seen as significant variables in the situation.

Sceptics who assert that values which relate to the maximization of economic growth have now become so powerful as to be irresistible by leadership of this sort may of course be proved right—and their scepticism may be among the factors producing this result. But we can note one type of challenge to unrestrained economic growth which seems as if it may achieve some success in coming decades—the growing concern with environmental amenity and conservation. This could prove no more than a fashion, but we cannot dismiss the possibility that the mass media may help to popularize this concern and thereby create a mood which encourages further discussion and eventually action. If the values underlying the maximization of economic growth can receive scrutiny and check from this perspective, it becomes conceivable that they could receive a similar critical appraisal from another.

In this context it is important to remain alert to national differences which may contain the seeds of divergent development.

Hayward notes, for example, that in France 'the ideological presuppositions of a pecuniary culture' are not accepted without demur. 'The economic planning process has been deliberately used as a means of preventing France drifting into an imitation of the pecuniary culture of the U.S.A. . . .' (1969, p. 84).

Paradoxically, technological advance could itself help to promote stronger appreciation of, and even appetite for, intrinsic rewards from work. Some forms of modern technology, such as the continuous-process system characteristic of the chemical industry, increase 'the worker's control over his work process' and check 'the further division of labour and growth of large factories. The result is meaningful work in a more cohesive, integrated industrial climate. The alienation curve begins to decline . . . as employees in automated industries gain a new dignity from responsibility and a sense of individual function . . .' (Blauner, 1964, p. 182). Other automated work patterns suggest a less felicitous picture (Mann, 1962), but the possibility remains that the exigencies of economic 'progress' may create work situations which socialize men into new expectations.

An additional possibility is a quickening concern among rank and file employees with the terminal values of participation in decision-making. Although empirically this is difficult to disentangle from the instrumental concern it could nevertheless represent a growing interest in the intrinsic work values. In some situations it could be fully compatible with measures aimed at maximizing economic growth; in others it would not. Collectivity leaders may well enjoy some degree of choice between encouraging and discouraging an aspiration of this sort.

The assertion with which this chapter began concerning the crucial importance of aspirations applies as much, of course, to management as to rank and file employees. The aspirations of managers interact with the constraints confronting them to produce their work goals. These, as we have seen, usually lead them towards hierarchical structures and an emphasis on the instrumental function of work. Given these goals, they seek to shape the organization's normative system accordingly. But the other interest groups also have their work goals. These may be such that a normative system which is congruent with management goals is congruent also with theirs. Insofar as this is so, normative agreement will secure the managerial legitimacy on which can rest authority relations characterized by willing compliance. Insofar as the normative system sought by management is perceived by, say, a rank and file group as incongruent with their goals, the norms concerned will not have legitimacy for the subordinates and authority relations suffer accordingly. Power may then become the arbiter. Whether the resulting norms are imposed by management on subordinates or vice versa, forced compliance typically limits the extent and quality of collaboration. This may or may not be perceived as important by the participants. If it is, or if the power struggle itself threatens to involve more cost than benefit, negotiated compromise on the relevant norms may be pursued through diplomacy conducted on agreed lines within a jointly-established normative structure of bilateral regulation. To the extent that the resultant settlement is perceived by both parties as legitimate it can establish, or re-establish, authority relations. To the extent that either party feels coerced by an exercise of power from the other, legitimacy and authority will be absent. As we saw, however, this is not to say that an exercise of power by one side necessarily results in the other feeling coerced. It may contribute to a shift in perceptions which results in a fully-legitimized normative agreement.

The employee collectivities instrumental in these processes introduce social change into the organization inasmuch as they are concentrations of power which set up their own leaders, challenge managerial rule, create new patterns of interaction between organizational members, and establish new centres of authority and loyalty which compete with those offered by management. To support and legitimize these forms of behaviour they evolve their own ideologies which challenge those of management. Insofar as management ideology and practice draw upon norms and values favoured and disseminated by ruling groups in the wider society, employee collectivities find themselves, perhaps, drawn into ideological and power contests of major social significance.

In acting upon the normative system of the organization they seek to change it in directions congruent with their aspirations and to prevent other individuals or groups rendering it incongruent. Such action may be exerted upon financial rewards, opportunities of control over the work situation, the status system, or any other organizational variable perceived as relevant. Assessments of congruency become more complex by virtue of the fact that collectivity leaders and members may evaluate situations in terms of what they perceive as congruent with the survival, cohesiveness or growth of the collectivity itself, as well as in terms of the direct interest of members as individuals.

Managerial responses to employee collectivities vary according to their own goals which, as we have seen, are likewise shaped through the interaction of aspirations and environmental constraints. In some circumstances collectivities may be congruent with those goals. Manifest conflict develops, however, when management challenges attempts by a collectivity to modify some element or elements of the normative system, or when a collectivity resists changes proposed by management. Whether management finds collectivity action congruent and supports it, or finds it incongruent and resists it, the eventual outcome in many cases is further social change, taking the form of new joint procedures of normative regulation. This involves management in formally relinquishing unilateral prerogative over the norms at issue, but offers what may be seen as an advantage by restoring authority relations.

In the process of these struggles collectivities seek to enlarge their power by uniting with others. Managements may follow suit. Alliances born of common situations may combine with other social forces to produce class consciousness and class hostilities. Modifying these hostilities may be the spread of the jointly-operated institutions of normative regulation as they move beyond the organization to cover localities, regions and industries; developing meanwhile their own norms of compromise, restraint, and mutual respect. Congruency assessments continue to increase in complexity, for each higher level of collectivity organization has leaders who must evaluate these joint institutions, along with the other aspects of their environments, in terms of congruency for their goals.

But social change does not stop there. The assessments of congruency made by collectivities and management alike may extend to the organization's environments. The state of markets, the state of the law, the state of public opinion; these and other variables may lead the contending groups to reach out to the widest possible spheres of action. The search for power may lead to political action at the highest level. Confrontations at every stage can change social structures at the local, regional or national level by modifying authority relations, creating new patterns of interaction and new modes of decision-making. Meanwhile ideologies become further elaborated and new social norms and values are opposed to the old. Disseminated now by new centres of collectivity power at many different levels of social interaction, the new values add their weight to other forces which may produce significant shifts in social priorities and social criteria. These concentrations of collectivity power may come to exert themselves in areas of decision-

G

making far removed from the original concerns of the individual members. Just as managers may enjoy a certain autonomy of goals once they have satisfied the many diverse claimants who bring expectations to bear upon them, so may collectivity leaders. Provided that leaders are fulfilling their primary task of serving the perceived interests of members, they may be free to use collectivity power in very different fields of social policy.

This sequential argument indicates the manner in which interactions between employee aspirations and the hierarchical structures of work organizations can generate concentrations of power, which in turn produce social change. We need, however, to supplement this sequential view with the recognition that as a result of these changes the new entrant goes into a system vastly different from the notional one presented at the earlier stages of our analysis, for it is a system which has already gathered accretions and modifications as a result of the forces at work. The social and political role of top-level collectivities may, for example, have contributed to governmental full-employment policies which, by promoting labour scarcity, have transformed power relations within the organization in favour of lower participants. They may also have contributed to changes in the legal environment. Collectivities outside and inside the organization may have moulded it nearer to their heart's desire, modifying the processes of decision-making and through them the norms governing wage rates, hiring, promotion, dismissal, and many other aspects of the system. Collectivity power may bear upon the new entrant to bring him into membership and define his goals and the means by which they are to be pursued without giving him much, or indeed any, choice in the matter. His whole relationship to the organization may be regulated in this way. Class, community and work-group norms and values, already historically formed, may mould his orientations to work and leisure, shaping his perceptions and thereby his behaviour.

We have now worked our way back to the point at which we began, with the individual entering the work organization. The analysis helps us, however, to understand how the organization and its environments have been modified by past responses which have generated new structures, new bases of power, and new values. It is these modified situations with which the individual now interacts. Just as in our earlier notional picture, the individual makes congruency assessments in relation to all the changes and accretions which have overtaken the organization. The norms now governing payment systems, wage rates, working hours, promotion, dismissal and any other relevant issues may or may not be congruent with his aspirations. The existing pattern of collectivities and their modes of action may or may not appear appropriate for pursuing changes in those norms. The jointly-maintained procedures for settling disputes may or may not operate to his satisfaction. Collectivity ideologies may or may not express the values he wishes to articulate. His responses to these changes and accretions will be drawn from the same Mertonian paradigm of conformity, innovation, ritualism, retreatism and rebellion, directed now towards the various collectivity levels to which he is related. These will determine, for example, whether he is a passive conformist, an active loyalist, or a rebel. If perceptions of incongruency are shared by sufficient others, combined action may be directed against the collectivity; i.e. attempts made to change its norms, its leaders, or its policies. Alternatively, rival collectivities-within-collectivities may develop, leading to 'unofficial' or breakaway movements of various kinds.

These possibilities are suggested in order to illustrate the unceasing dynamics of change. A complete analysis of these dynamics would have to consider in detail the many additional sources from which impulses come to bear upon the social organization—changes in domestic and international market conditions; technological innovations; rising standards of managerial professionalism; the rising aspirations of men everywhere; changes in the law or public expectations. All these pressures may bring management and subordinate groups into sharper confrontations, promoting on the one hand conflict, on the other hand new social forms of mutual accommodation; each with its own values and ideology, each with its wider implications reaching perhaps far beyond the organization's boundaries.

Thus there emerges a view of the social organization as the 'disputed ground' which individuals and groups seek to capture for their own purposes. Order is preserved, however, by shared values which support normative agreement, or which enable normative conflict to be regulated and resolved with the minimum of disruption to the collaborative process. The frame of reference through which the parties perceive normative conflict is, nevertheless, crucial in determining behaviour and its outcome. Management may deny the validity of other perceptions and attribute conflict to failures of communication or to the machinations of ill-disposed agitators. They may insist on a unitary view of the enterprise which takes no account of possibly-divergent sectional goals but assumes instead a community of interests pursued through the unchallenged exercise of managerial prerogative. A union may occupy the opposite extreme, perceiving the situation as a zero-sum game in which a gain for management must automatically be defined as a loss for itself or its members. A third possibility is that both parties see the organization as a pluralistic structure within which there may be divergent interests that can be reconciled by a joint problem-solving approach. The frame of reference required for this may involve management in changing its perceptions of normative conflict and managerial prerogative, and employee collectivities in accepting that normative change can be a positive-sum game benefiting both parties.

What also emerges from the analysis is that industrial managers would derive great advantage from being able to mould men's values so as to ensure authority relations without having to relinquish some of their prerogative in the pursuit of negotiated normative compromises, creative or otherwise. This requires control over the market in ideas and the suppression of those independent organizations which might promote and disseminate specially inconvenient opinions and attitudes. For these purposes management needs the active support of the state and its coercive apparatus. In many Western countries the development of political ideas and institutions and the distribution of political power have been such as to rule out this possibility except in periods of national crisis or acute internal upheaval. In Britain even the emergency conditions created by two wars of national survival generated only very limited moves in this direction. Other Western countries such as Germany, Italy and Spain have had a very different history, and totalitarian regimes within the Eastern bloc continue, as does Spain, to offer industrial management this kind of support. The question of how long they can maintain it involves many variables, prominent among them being state power over communications and combination both within and across national frontiers.

But the question of how long the system can be maintained can be directed not only to unitary, closed societies but also to pluralistic, open ones. It cannot be assumed that such mechanisms, planned and unplanned, as make for social cohesion, value consensus, and normative agreement in these societies will necessarily continue permanently to provide a sufficient basis for economic collaboration while permitting highly decentralized and independent normative regulation. Events may bring about normative divergencies and conflict too wide to be bridged by negotiated compromise. Power would then become the arbiter. But whose power? The disorder created by the use of 'private' power is apt, beyond a certain point, to evoke a demand for the restoration of order by 'public' power, a demand which may well, incidentally, cut across class lines. There are symptoms of strain in Britain, as we have seen, which may be explicable in terms of this analysis. Aspirations on all sides are ever quickening with respect to living standards, and management's ability to meet them is increasingly the basis on which its legitimacy rests. Since these are appetites which grow by what they feed upon, they provide a particularly unstable basis for managerial authority. Meanwhile the shift of power away from management to organized labour means that when employees withdraw legitimacy from managerial rule for any reason they are apt to make conflict manifest and visible by bringing collective sanctions to bear. This has already stimulated demands for authoritarian solutions. Given the narrow economic safety margin within which the British economy operates, a continuing increase in disorder could arouse a reaction sufficient to evoke state attempts to impose order.

Such speculation generates many questions. Are these apparently centrifugal and dispersive symptoms of normative divergence within Britain's industrial society merely a phase of temporary difficulty or are they the early signs of powerful forces which will gradually overtake all advanced industrial societies of the Western type? Could the answer be that they will overtake some societies and not others? If so, what social characteristics and mechanisms protect those that escape the problem? In those that do not escape, will sufficient creativeness and resilience be available to enable them to adapt in ways which preserve their essential values?

At this stage we are brought back to a point urged in the earlier part of this chapter. Ultimately the answers to questions like these will be found in the choices men make and in the leadership they offer or receive in making those choices. Leadership carries responsibilities here, for we have noted that there is a margin of autonomy which leaders can use to further the values they choose. In this sense the situation is open for all the institutions and organizations of work and industry. This is to say no more than that it is not organizations as such, but individual men who aspire, will, and act. They must therefore be fastened inescapably with the ultimate responsibility for their own fate.

Annotated Bibliography

In contrast to a study which explores intensively a narrowly-defined and limited field, this book seeks to link a wide range and diversity of phenomena within a common theoretical framework. This means that the bibliography cannot realistically attempt the same task as is appropriate to the former exercise. An intensive working of a limited field makes possible a more-or-less exhaustive survey and evaluation of the relevant literature. To attempt the same for an extensively-ranging perspective would make the bibliography itself a major work. What is presented here, therefore, is unavoidably a selection from which many valuable references have had to be excluded. So far as possible, however, reference has been made to some of the early classics in each particular field along with up-to-date sources which draw attention to current problems and issues. The 'extensive' nature of this book also has implications for the annotations, which serve a purpose somewhat different from that appropriate to an intensive study. They could never hope to cover between them all the facets of every debate, controversy, or disputed interpretation touched on in this book. They are directed mainly, therefore, to indicating in what field or aspect the particular item makes its contribution (where this is not obvious from the title), and, in certain cases, its special value. All works cited in the text have been listed, together with many additional titles. Some articles can be found reproduced, in whole or part, in subsequent collections of 'readings', and the appropriate details are included in the reference. Given the range covered by this book and the impracticability of full bibliographical coverage, a number of other lists are included among the references.

ABEGGLEN, J. G. (1958). *The Japanese Factory*. Glencoe (Illinois): The Free Press. Of special interest, in this context, in showing how the social structure and cultural norms of the wider society shape industrial organization, attitudes to authority, and other aspects of behaviour.

AIKEN, M.; HAGE, J. (1966). 'Organizational Alienation: A Comparative Analysis.' *American Sociological Review*, 31 (4): 497–507. A comparative study of sixteen welfare organizations which examines the relationship between two types of alienation—alienation from work, and alienation from expressive relations.

ALLEN, V. L. (1957). *Trade Union Leadership*. London: Longmans Green.

ANDERSON, N. (1961). *Work and Leisure*. London: Routledge and Kegan Paul. One of the first efforts at examining the relationships between work and leisure.

ANDERSON, N. (1964). *Dimensions of Work: The Sociology of a Work Culture*. New York: David McKay. Includes comparisons between philosophies of work in developing countries.

ANDERSON, P. (1967). 'The Limits and Possibilities of Trade Union Action' in BLACKBURN and COCKBURN (1967), pp. 263–280.

ANSHEN, M.; BACH, G. L. (eds.) (1960). *Management and Corporation 1985*. New York: McGraw-Hill.

ANSOFF, H. I. (ed.) (1969). *Business Strategy*. Harmondsworth: Penguin.

ARENSBERG, C. M. (ed.) (1957). *Research in Industrial Human Relations: A Critical Appraisal*. New York: Harper and Row. A useful collection of thirteen studies by R. Bendix, J. C. Worthy, H. L. Wilensky, C. M. Arensberg, D. Riesman and W. Bloomberg, A. J. Siegel, H. A. Simon, W. Moore, L. R. Sayles, F. C. Mann, W. F. Whyte, M. Haire and S. Barkin. Many are relevant to one or other of the themes of this essay; all are interesting surveys of their various fields; all have useful lists of further references.

ARGYRIS, C. (1957). *Personality and Organization*. New York: Harper and Row. Contains a detailed analysis of the so-called 'mature' 'self-actualizing' personality as against the 'immature' one.

ARGYRIS, C. (1964). *Integrating the Individual and the Organization*. New York: Wiley & Sons. An elaboration and development of his earlier work. Of special relevance is his concept of the personality and the organizational conditions necessary for its fulfilment.

ARON, R. (1967a). *18 Lectures on Industrial Society*. London: Weidenfeld and Nicholson.

ARON, R. (1967b). *The Industrial Society*. London: Weidenfeld and Nicholson.

ARON, R. (1968). *Main Currents of Sociological Thought*, Vol. I. Harmondsworth: Penguin. Contains a useful section on Marx, including his concept of alienation.

AUBERT, V. (ed.) (1969). *Sociology of Law*. Harmondsworth: Penguin. A collection of readings which includes several valuable selections relevant to this essay.

BABCHUK, N.; GOODE, W. J. (1951). 'Work Incentives in a Self-Determined Group'. *American Sociological Review*, 16 (5): 679–687. Examining the causes of low morale in a large department store, the authors show how a group of employees changed the organization and planning of work, the division of labour, and the rewards system.

BAIN, G. S. (1967). *Trade Union Growth and Recognition; With Special Reference to White-Collar Unions in Private Industry*. Research Paper 6, Royal Commission on Trade Unions and Employers' Associations. London: H.M.S.O. Particularly useful for its review of the situation in Britain with regard to white-collar unionism. Has many useful references.

BAIN, G. S. (1970). *The Growth of White-Collar Unionism*. Oxford: Clarendon Press. Through an examination of the situation in Britain, seeks to identify the major factors which determine the growth of white-collar unionism.

BAKKE, E. W. (1946). *Mutual Survival: The Goal of Unions and Management*. New York: Harper and Row.

BAKKE, E. W. (1948). 'Why Workers Join Unions' in BAKKE and KERR (1948), pp. 41–49.

BAKKE, E. W.; KERR, C. (eds.) (1948). *Unions, Management and the Public*. New York:

Harcourt Brace. A valuable collection of several hundred selections, many of them classic pieces, covering every aspect of industrial relations. Only the broadest categories can be sketched here; they include development of unions, response of management, collective bargaining, terms of agreement, the interest of the community. Selected authors range from Marx, Engels and Durkheim to the Webbs, J. T. Dunlop and G. D. H. Cole.

BAKKE, E. W. (1953). *The Fusion Process: A Map for the Exploration of the Relationships of People and Organizations*. New Haven: Yale University Press. The fusion process is defined as the simultaneous operation of a 'socializing' process by the organization and a 'personalizing' process by the individual.

BAKKE, E. W. *et al.* (1963). 'Public Policy and the Public Interest—Problems of the American Industrial Relations System: A Symposium'. *Industrial and Labor Relations Review*, 16 (4): 511–556.

BAKKE, E. W. (1966). *Bonds of Organization: An Appraisal of Corporate Human Relations*. Connecticut: Archon Books. Offers a system model of the organization which, unusually, includes the trade union.

BALDAMUS, W. (1951). 'Types of Work and Motivation'. *British Journal of Sociology*, 2 (1): 44–58.

BALDAMUS, W. (1961). *Efficiency and Effort*. London: Tavistock. Of special interest here is Chapter 8, which discusses the normative element in attitudes towards work.

BANKS, J. A. (1963). *Industrial Participation: Theory and Practice*. Liverpool: Liverpool University Press. Workers in a factory were studied from the point of view of their readiness to 'participate' by seeking promotion to supervisory rank, or election to the offices of joint-consultation representative or shop steward.

BANKS, J. A. (1964). 'The Structure of Industrial Enterprise in Industrial Society' in HALMOS (1964), pp. 43–61.

BANKS, O. (1960). *The Attitudes of Steelworkers to Technical Change*. Liverpool: Liverpool University Press.

BARBASH, J. (1964). 'The Elements of Industrial Relations'. *British Journal of Industrial Relations*, 2 (1): 66–78.

BARITZ, L. (1965). *The Servants of Power: A History of the Use of Social Science in American Industry*. New York: Wiley & Sons. Makes special reference to the Hawthorne investigations and their consequences.

BARLOW, G. (1969). 'Some Latent Influences in a Pay Claim: An Examination of a White Collar Dispute'. *British Journal of Industrial Relations*, VII (2): 200–210.

BARNARD, C. I. (1956). *The Functions of the Executive*. Cambridge (Mass.): Harvard University Press. First published in 1938, this is one of the classic theoretical analyses of formal organizations, still necessary reading for those interested in this field. It includes a specially interesting section on the theory of authority.

BARNES, L. B. (1960). *Organizational Systems and Engineering Groups*. Boston: Harvard Business School. Extract also in WALKER (1962), pp. 214–221.

BAUMOL, W. J. (1959). *Business Behavior, Value and Growth*. New York: Macmillan.

BECKER, H. S. (ed.) (1966). *Social Problems: A Modern Approach*. New York: Wiley & Sons.

BEHREND, H. (1953). 'Absence and Labour Turnover in a Changing Economic Climate'. *Occupational Psychology*, 27 (2): 69–79.

BEHREND, H. (1957). 'The Effort Bargain'. *Industrial and Labor Relations Review*, 10 (4): 503–515.

BELL, D. (1961). *The End of Ideology*. New York: Collier. Chapter 11, 'Work and its Discontents', discusses changing aspirations and the 'cult of efficiency' against the historical background of previous attitudes to work. In Chapter 15, 'Two Roads from Marx: The Themes of Alienation and Exploitation and Workers' Control in Socialist Thought', Bell argues that 'the fullness of life must be found in the nature of work itself'.

BENDIX, R. (1956). *Work and Authority in Industry: Ideologies of Management in the Course of Industrialization*. New York: Wiley & Sons. A tour-de-force of historical sociology which analyses the ideological methods by which the entrepreneurial classes in

England, America and Russia set about creating and managing a disciplined industrial labour force.

BENDIX, R. (1963). *Work and Authority in Industry: Ideologies of Management in the Course of Industrialization*. New York: Harper and Row. This paperback version includes a new essay, 'Industrialization, Ideologies, and Social Structure', which replaces the original Conclusion.

BENDIX, R. (1966). *Max Weber: An Intellectual Portrait*. London: Methuen. Of special relevance here—Chapter III discusses Weber's ideas relating to 'Aspects of Economic Rationality in the West'.

BENDIX, R.; FISHER, L. H. (1962). 'The Perspectives of Elton Mayo' in ETZIONI (1962), pp. 113-126.

BENDIX, R.; LIPSET, S. M. (eds.) (1967). *Class, Status, and Power*, 2nd ed. London: Routledge and Kegan Paul.

BENSMAN, J.; GERVER, I. (1963). 'Crime and Punishment in the Factory'. *American Sociological Review*, 28 (4): 588–598. Arguing that deviant behaviour is the result of a plurality of ends as well as of the conflict between ends and means, this paper presents an interesting study of the complex social nature of one particular form of 'crime' in an aircraft factory working on government contracts.

BERGER, P. L. (ed.) (1964). *The Human Shape of Work: Studies in the Sociology of Occupations*. New York: Macmillan. Contains chapters on the assembly-line worker (Chinoy); the business executive (Underwood); and the general sociology of work (Berger).

BIERSTEDT, R. (1950). 'An Analysis of Social Power'. *American Sociological Review*, 15 (6): 730–738. Also in COSER and ROSENBERG (1966), pp. 143–156; DUBIN, 1961, pp. 238–246. Argues, *inter alia*, the importance of distinguishing power from prestige, influence, dominance, rights, force, and authority.

BLACKBURN, R.; COCKBURN, A. (eds.) (1967). *The Incompatibles: Trade Union Militancy and the Consensus*. Harmondsworth: Penguin.

BLACKBURN, R. M. (1967). *Union Character and Social Class*. London: Batsford. Includes a well-documented account of the development of combination among bank employees in Britain.

BLAU, P. M. (1956). *Bureaucracy in Modern Society*. New York: Random House. A short introduction to the study of bureaucracy, its strengths and weaknesses, and the internal responses to which it gives rise.

BLAU, P.; SCOTT, W. R. (1963). *Formal Organizations: A Comparative Approach*. London: Routledge and Kegan Paul. Offers an analytical framework for viewing formal organizations. It examines the social structure of work groups, communications, supervisory and management roles, the social environment, and organizational dynamics. There is ample discussion of the literature and a useful 45-page bibliography.

BLAU, P. (1964). *Exchange and Power in Social Life*. New York: Wiley & Sons.

BLAUNER, R. (1964). *Alienation and Freedom: The Factory Worker and His Industry*. Chicago: University of Chicago Press. In what has become a widely-read, standard text, Blauner adapts Marx's theory of alienation in terms of Seeman's analysis (1959), and applies it to a range of industrial settings—a print shop, a textile mill, a car-assembly factory, and an automated chemical plant.

BLAUNER, R. (1967). 'Work Satisfaction and Industrial Trends in Modern Society' in BENDIX and LIPSET (1967), pp. 473–487. Also in GALENSON and LIPSET (1960), pp. 339–360; ETZIONI (1969), pp. 223–249. Discusses the concept of job satisfaction in relation to occupation and variations in job structure, and concludes with a valuable note on methodological problems in job satisfaction research.

BLUMBERG, P. (1968). *Industrial Democracy: The Sociology of Participation*. London: Constable.

BLUMENTHAL, W. M. (1956). *Codetermination in the German Steel Industry*. Princeton (N.J.): Princeton University Press.

BOTTOMORE, T. B. (1965). *Classes in Modern Society*. London: Allen and Unwin.

BOTTOMORE, T. B.; RUBEL, M. (eds.) (1963). *Karl Marx: Selected Writings in Sociology and*

Social Philosophy. Harmondsworth: Penguin. Includes selections on the sociology of capitalism—origins and development, social system, ideology, alienation, and class conflict.

BOX, S.; COTGROVE, S. (1966). 'Scientific Identity, Occupational Selection and Role Strain'. *British Journal of Sociology,* XVII (1): 20–28.

BRIGGS, A. (ed.) (1962). *William Morris: Selected Writings and Designs.* Harmondsworth: Penguin. Morris's pamphlet, 'Useful Work versus Useless Toil' (1885), is included, pp. 117–136.

BROWN, E. C. (1958). 'Labor Relations in Soviet Factories'. *Industrial and Labor Relations Review,* II (2): 183–202.

BROWN, E. C. (1960). 'The Local Union in Soviet Industry: Its Relations with Members, Party, and Management'. *Industrial and Labor Relations Review,* 13 (2): 192–215.

BROWN, E. C. (1963). 'Interests and Rights of Soviet Industrial Workers and the Resolution of Conflicts'. *Industrial and Labor Relations Review,* 16 (2): 254–278.

BROWN, E. C. (1965). *Soviet Trade Unions and Labour Relations.* Cambridge (Mass.): Harvard University Press.

BROWN, W. (1965). *Exploration in Management.* Harmondsworth: Penguin.

BROWN, W., JAQUES, E. (1965). *Glacier Project Papers.* London: Heinemann.

BUCKINGHAM, W. (1961). *Automation: Its Impact on Business and People.* New York: Harper and Row.

BUCKLEY, W. (1967). *Sociology and Modern Systems Theory.* Englewood Cliffs (N.J.): Prentice-Hall.

BURNS, T., STALKER, G. M. (1961). *The Management of Innovation.* London: Tavistock. Essential reading for its conceptual distinction between 'mechanistic' and 'organic' types of management structure; a distinction drawn also by other writers (see SPENCER and SOFER, 1964) and proving to be of considerable importance for theory and research.

BURNS, T. (1962). 'The Sociology of Industry' in WELFORD *et al.* (1962), pp. 185–215. A useful introduction to the scope of industrial sociology, giving a good summary of problems and issues.

BURNS, T. (ed.) (1969). *Industrial Man.* Harmondsworth: Penguin. A useful collection of readings designed to illustrate the broad scope of industrial sociology as the subject needs to be defined.

CAPLOW, T. (1954). *The Sociology of Work.* New York: McGraw-Hill. A good general introduction to the subject. Specially relevant chapters include 'The Assignment of Work', 'The Measurement of Occupational Status', 'Occupational Institutions' and 'Occupational Ideologies'.

CAREY, A. (1967). 'The Hawthorne Studies: A Radical Criticism'. *American Sociological Review,* 32 (3): 403–416. A trenchant critique of the famous Hawthorne experiments, often regarded as a milestone in social research. Carey argues that the conclusions are wholly unsupported by the evidence.

CASTLE, P. F. C. (1956). 'Accidents, Absence and Withdrawal from the Work Situation'. *Human Relations,* 9 (2): 223–233.

CHAMBERLAIN, N. (1948). *Union Challenge to Management Control.* New York: Harper and Row. A classic contribution on the subject of managerial prerogative.

CHAMBERLAIN, N. W. (1961). 'Determinants of Collective Bargaining Structures' in WEBER (1961), pp. 3–19.

CHAMBERLAIN, N. *et al.* (1963). 'Management Rights and Labor Arbitration: A Symposium'. *Industrial and Labor Relations Review,* 16 (2): 183–253.

CHAMBERLAIN, N. W.; KUHN, J. W. (1965). *Collective Bargaining,* 2nd ed. New York: McGraw-Hill. A powerful piece of theorizing on its subject.

CHANDLER, M. K. (1964). *Management Rights and Union Interests.* New York: McGraw-Hill. An important contribution to the study of managerial prerogative.

CHEIT, E. (ed.) (1964). *The Business Establishment.* New York: Wiley & Sons. A valuable collection of essays on business ideologies and the social and political environment of business.

CHILD, J. (1969a). *British Management Thought*. London: Allen and Unwin.

CHILD, J. (1969b). *The Business Enterprise in Modern Industrial Society*. London: Collier-Macmillan.

CHINOY, ELY. (1955). *Automobile Workers and the American Dream*. New York: Doubleday. One of the classic sociological studies of that much-researched symbol of alienation, the car worker. Chinoy examines his work, his aspirations, and his current adaptations of traditional American values.

CLARKE, A. C. (1956). 'The Use of Leisure and its Relation to Levels of Occupational Prestige'. *American Sociological Review*, 21 (3): 301–307.

CLEGG, H. A. (1951). *Industrial Democracy and Nationalization*. Oxford: Blackwell. Presents an interpretation of 'democracy' in industry recently challenged by BLUMBERG (1968).

CLEGG, H. A. (1960). *A New Approach to Industrial Democracy*. Oxford: Blackwell. Compares differing national interpretations of 'industrial democracy' and from these seeks to present a general theory: a theory assailed by BLUMBERG (1968).

CLEGG, H. A. (1970) *The System of Industrial Relations in Great Britain*. Oxford: Blackwell. The standard text on its subject.

CLEGG, H. A.; KILLICK, A. J.; ADAMS, R. (1961). *Trade Union Officers: A Study of Full-Time Officers, Branch Secretaries and Shop Stewards in British Trade Unions*. Oxford: Blackwell.

COOLEY, C. H. (1962). *Social Organization*. New York: Schocken. In Chapters XXIII and XXIV, especially, Cooley offers insight into ways by which the wealthy and powerful can secure acceptance of their norms and values.

COSER, L. A. (1956). *The Functions of Social Conflict*. London: Routledge and Kegan Paul. An essential item in any study of cooperation-conflict theory. Coser, distilling propositions from the work of Georg Simmel, argues that certain forms of conflict may be a precondition for the orderly functioning of society. There is an introductory review and appraisal of historical and current perspectives of American sociologists towards conflict.

COSER, L. A.; ROSENBERG, B. (eds.) (1966). *Sociological Theory: A Book of Readings,* 2nd. ed. New York: Macmillan. A useful collection which includes sections on social control, power and authority, cohesion and conflict, role-taking and reference group, status, class, bureaucracy, and alienation and anomie. Many standard references are brought together (e.g. Goldhamer and Shils, and Bierstedt, on power; Marx and Seeman on alienation).

COTGROVE, S. (1965). 'The Relations Between Work and Non-Work Among Technicians.' *Sociological Review,* 13 (2): 121–129. Confirms that the work situation is a significant variable for the sociological analysis of occupations, and goes on to suggest that 'involvement' in work depends also on the needs and expectations which the worker brings with him. Further education appears to be one of the factors promoting the expectation and enjoyment of intrinsic satisfactions in work.

CROZIER, M. (1964). *The Bureaucratic Phenomenon*. London: Tavistock.

CUNNISON, S. (1966). *Wages and Work Allocation*. London: Tavistock. Stresses the relationship between the social processes of the work situation and the social structure and processes of change in the wider society.

CYERT, R. M.; MARCH, J. G. (1959). 'A Behavioral Theory of Organizational Objectives' in HAIRE (1959), pp. 76–90.

DAHL, R. (1957). 'The Concept of Power'. *Behavioral Science*, Vol. 2: 201–215.

DAHRENDORF, R. (1958). 'Out of Utopia: Toward a Reorientation of Sociological Analysis'. *American Journal of Sociology*, LXIV (1): 115–127. Also in COSER and ROSENBERG (1966), pp. 209–227. Attacking the 'universal consensus' view of the social system, Dahrendorf argues that society has two faces of equal reality: one of stability, harmony, and consensus, and one of change, conflict, and constraint.

DAHRENDORF, R. (1959). *Class and Class Conflict in an Industrial Society*. London: Routledge and Kegan Paul. A critical examination of Marxist and subsequent class theories, viewed in the context of changes in the structure of industrial societies; followed by the presentation of an alternative theory of class and class conflict.

DALTON, M. (1950a). 'Conflicts between Staff and Line Managerial Officers'. *American Sociological Review*, 15 (3): 342–351. Also in ETZIONI (1962), pp. 212–221, ETZIONI (1969), pp. 266–274; DUBIN (1961), pp. 196–207; LITTERER (1969), Vol. I, pp. 397–406. Research in three industrial plants revealed conflict between managerial staff and line groups that hindered the attainment of 'organizational' goals.

DALTON, M. (1950b). 'Unofficial Union-Management Relations'. *American Sociological Review*, 15 (5): 611–619.

DALTON, M. (1959). *Men Who Manage*. New York: Wiley & Sons. A vivid documentation of the manipulations, manoeuvres, feuds and power struggles which managers may bring to bear upon the social organization of the enterprise.

DALTON, M. (1962). 'Cooperative Evasions to support Labor-Management Contracts' in ROSE (1962), pp. 267–284.

DANIEL, W. W. (1969). 'Industrial Behaviour and Orientation to Work—A Critique'. *Journal of Management Studies*, 6 (3): 366–375.

DAVIS, L. E. (1966). 'The Design of Jobs'. *Industrial Relations*, 6 (1): 21–45.

DAVISON, J. P.; FLORENCE, P. S.; GRAY, B.; ROSS, N. S. (1958). *Productivity and Economic Incentives*. London: Allen and Unwin.

DENNIS, N.; HENRIQUES, F.; SLAUGHTER, C. (1957). *Coal is Our Life*. London: Eyre and Spottiswoode. A study of a Yorkshire mining village which examines attitudes to work, leisure, family and sex patterns, and relations between the social structure of work and the social structure of the community.

DERBER, M.; CHALMERS, W. E.; EDELMAN, M. T. (1961). 'Union Participation in Plant Decision-Making'. *Industrial and Labor Relations Review*, 15 (1): 83–101.

DEUTSCHER, I. (1950). *Soviet Trade Unions*. London: Royal Institute of International Affairs. A historical study of the evolution of Soviet state attitudes towards the functions of trade unions. Needs supplementing with the studies of MCAULEY (1969) and BROWN (1958, 1960, 1963, 1965).

DEVLIN, RT. HON. LORD. (1965). *Final Report of the Committee of Inquiry under the Rt. Hon. Lord Devlin into certain matters concerning the Port Transport Industry*. London: H.M.S.O., Cmnd. 2734.

DOBB, M. (1942). *Soviet Planning and Labour in Peace and War*. London: Routledge and Kegan Paul. Includes a sympathetic account of the methods and achievements of Stakhanovism.

DONOVAN, LORD. (1968). *Report*, Royal Commission on Trade Unions and Employers' Associations 1965–1968. London: H.M.S.O.

DUBIN, R. (1949). 'Decision-Making by Management in Industrial Relations'. *American Journal of Sociology*, LIV (4): 292–297. Also in MERTON *et al.*, 1952, pp. 233–240.

DUBIN, R. (1954). 'Constructive Aspects of Industrial Conflict' in KORNHAUSER, DUBIN and ROSS (1954), pp. 37–47.

DUBIN, R. (1956). 'Industrial Workers' Worlds: A Study of the Central Life Interests of Industrial Workers'. *Social Problems*, 3 (1): 131–142. Also in ROSE (1962), pp. 247–266. A frequently-quoted paper in which Dubin reported that three out of four in a sample of 491 workers do not perceive their jobs and work places as central life interests for themselves, but find the real centre of life in family, leisure, recreation, or other voluntary activities.

DUBIN, R. (1958). *The World of Work: Industrial Society and Human Relations*. Englewood Cliffs (N.J.): Prentice-Hall.

DUBIN, R. (1958). *Working Union-Management Relations: The Sociology of Industrial Relations*. Englewood Cliffs (N.J.): Prentice-Hall. One of the few attempts to locate industrial relations phenomena within a sociological framework. Besides many useful references in the text, it has a 22-page bibliography.

DUBIN, R. (1959). 'Industrial Research and the Discipline of Sociology'. *Proceedings of the 11th Annual Meeting*, Industrial Relations Research Association. Includes an elaboration of Dubin's arguments against those of the 'self-actualization' school who believe that work should be a central life interest.

DUBIN, R. (1960). 'A Theory of Conflict and Power in Union-Management Relations'. *Industrial and Labor Relations Review*, 13 (4): 501–518.

DUBIN, R. (ed.) (1961). *Human Relations in Administration*, 2nd ed. Englewood Cliffs (N.J.): Prentice-Hall. An excellent collection of readings linked by a commentary by Dubin. The contents are too elaborately structured to permit of easy summarization, but they cover many aspects of organizational behaviour and include many standard references by such writers as Barnard, March and Simon, Harbison, Argyris, Strauss, Mayo, Sayles, Shils, Merton, Roethlisberger, Dalton, Etzioni, Burns, Tannenbaum, Selznick, Bendix, and Dubin himself.

DUBIN, R. (1965). 'Industrial Conflict: The Power of Prediction'. *Industrial and Labor Relations Review*, 18 (3): 352–363.

DUBIN, R. (1968). 'Control Evasion at the Management Level' in DUBIN (ed.) (1968), pp. 433–436. A brief but useful discussion of ways in which managers, in pursuing their own work goals, may evade or distort control mechanisms and manipulate communication systems.

DUBIN, R. (ed.) (1968). *Human Relations in Administration*, 3rd ed. Englewood Cliffs (N.J.): Prentice-Hall. This edition drops some selections included in the 1961 edition and introduces some new ones.

DUMAZEDIER, J. (1967). *Towards a Society of Leisure*. New York: The Free Press.

DUNLOP, J. T. (1950). *Wage Determination Under Trade Unions*. New York: Kelley.

DUNLOP, J. T. (ed.) (1957). *The Theory of Wage Determination*. London: Macmillan. Includes papers on the forces determining wage levels; the impact of trade unions; wage structure; the nature of bargaining; and the labour market.

DUNLOP, J. T. (1958). *Industrial Relations Systems*. New York: Holt. In this important book, Dunlop offers a definition of an 'industrial relations system' and goes on to compare a number of national systems.

DUNLOP, J. T. (ed.) (1962). *Automation and Technological Change*. Englewood Cliffs (N.J.): Prentice-Hall.

DURKHEIM, E. (1952). *Suicide*. London: Routledge and Kegan Paul.

DURKHEIM, E. (1964). *The Division of Labour in Society*. New York: The Free Press.

EDELSTEIN, J. D. (1967). 'An Organizational Theory of Union Democracy'. *American Sociological Review*, 32 (1): 19–31.

EISENSTADT, S. N. (1958). *Bureaucracy and Bureaucratization: A Trend Report and Bibliography*. Oxford: Blackwell. (*Current Sociology*, Vol. VII, No. 2, 1958). A 26-page trend report (but note date of publication), and 33 pages of annotated bibliography.

ELDRIDGE, J. E. T. (1968). *Industrial Disputes: Essays in the Sociology of Industrial Relations*. London: Routledge and Kegan Paul.

EMERSON, R. M. (1962). 'Power-Dependence Relationships'. *American Sociological Review*, 27 (1): 31–41. An important paper which argues that power resides in relationships of dependence.

ETZIONI, A. (1961). *A Comparative Analysis of Complex Organizations*. New York: The Free Press. Presents a systematic theoretical apparatus which employs 'the pattern of compliance' as a variable for classifying and comparing organizations. Compliance combines a structural variable (type of power) with a motivational one (type of involvement), and is related to other important variables. There are many references to the literature and 37 pages of bibliography.

ETZIONI, A. (ed.) (1962). *Complex Organizations: A Sociological Reader*. New York: Holt.

ETZIONI, A. (1964). *Modern Organizations*. Englewood Cliffs (N.J.): Prentice-Hall. A useful introduction to organization theory.

ETZIONI, A. (1968). 'Basic Human Needs, Alienation, and Inauthenticity'. *American Sociological Review*, 33 (6): 870–883.

ETZIONI, A. (ed.) (1969). *A Sociological Reader on Complex Organizations*, 2nd Ed. London: Holt. Twenty-two of the thirty-nine papers included are new to this edition. Both this and the 1962 edition are valuable collections which bring together much useful and widely-scattered material.

EVAN, W. M. (1961). 'Organization Man and Due Process of Law'. *American Sociological Review*, 26 (4): 540–547.

FAUNCE, W. A. (1958). 'Automation in the Automobile Industry: Some Consequences for In-Plant Social Structure'. *American Sociological Review*, 23 (4): 401–407. Studies the effects of automation upon interactions between workers. In general, the data suggest that many workers are virtually isolated socially.

FEUER, L. (1962). 'What is Alienation? The Career of a Concept'. *New Politics*, 1 (3): 116–134. Also in STEIN and VIDICH, 1963, pp. 127–147.

FLANDERS, A. (1964). *The Fawley Productivity Agreements*. London: Faber and Faber. A detailed and influential study of the first major exercise in comprehensive productivity bargaining.

FLANDERS, A. (1965). *Industrial Relations: What is Wrong With the System?* London: Faber and Faber. Contains an analysis of what is meant by an 'industrial relations system'; and analyses the British system and the challenges with which it is confronted.

FLANDERS, A. (1967). *Collective Bargaining: Prescription for Change*. London: Faber and Faber. Based on his written evidence to the Royal Commission on Trade Unions and Employers' Associations, this book forms a companion piece and a practical sequel to the 1965 essay.

FLANDERS, A. (1968). 'Collective Bargaining: A Theoretical Analysis'. *British Journal of Industrial Relations*, VI (1): 1–26. Examines critically the classical model of collective bargaining first advanced by the Webbs.

FLANDERS, A. (1969). *Trade Unions and the Force of Tradition*. The Sixteenth Fawley Foundation Lecture, University of Southampton.

FLANDERS, A. (ed.) (1969). *Collective Bargaining: Selected Readings*. Harmondsworth: Penguin.

FLANDERS, A. (1970). Commission on Industrial Relations, *Report No. 4*. London: H.M.S.O., Cmnd. 4264.

FLANDERS, A.; CLEGG, H. A. (eds.) (1954). *The System of Industrial Relations in Great Britain*. Oxford: Blackwell.

FLANDERS, A.; POMERANZ, R.; WOODWARD, J. (1968). *Experiment in Industrial Democracy*. London: Faber and Faber.

FOX, ALAN. (1958). *A History of the National Union of Boot and Shoe Operatives*. Oxford: Blackwell. An example of an industry in which union and employers developed (as well as conflict relations), collaborative relationships on the basis of market regulation.

FOX, ALAN. (1966). *Industrial Sociology and Industrial Relations*. Research Paper 3, Royal Commission on Trade Unions and Employers' Associations. London: H.M.S.O. Also in FLANDERS (ed.) (1969), pp. 390–409. Suggests ways in which management behaviour in the field of labour relations may be affected by ideological perspectives which see the organization in 'unitary' terms. It is suggested that a 'pluralistic' perspective is more congruent with modern reality and would make for more rational decisions.

FOX, ALAN. (1968). 'Labour Utilization and Industrial Relations' in PYM (1968), pp. 41–64. Examines the origins and nature of 'restrictive practices'; the work-goals which inspire them; responses of management; and the various measures proposed by those who seek to eliminate them.

FOX, ALAN.; FLANDERS, A. (1969). 'The Reform of Collective Bargaining: From Donovan to Durkheim'. *British Journal of Industrial Relations*, VII (2): 151–180.

FRASER, R. (ed.) (1968). *Work: Twenty Personal Accounts*. Harmondsworth: Penguin. Vivid, impressionistic accounts of personal experience in a wide range of jobs. They include contributions from factory workers, a printer, a research scientist, and a technician. Raymond Williams reviews the whole collection with a concluding chapter on 'The Meanings of Work'.

FRASER, R. (ed.) (1969). *Work 2: Twenty Personal Accounts*. Harmondsworth: Penguin. A second series, nearly half of them drawn from industry. Alvin Gouldner contributes a concluding chapter on 'The Unemployed Self'—the parts of the self often rejected by modern work technologies and structures.

FRIEDMANN, E. A.; HAVIGHURST, R. (1954). *The Meaning of Work and Retirement.* Chicago: University of Chicago Press. Examines the meanings that people in several different occupations find in their work—steel workers, coalminers, skilled craftsmen, salespeople, and physicians. Workers of lower skill and socio-economic status were more likely to see their work as having no other than financial meaning. Non-financial meanings become increasingly important as one ascended occupational and skill ladders.

FRIEDMANN, G. (1961). *The Anatomy of Work.* London: Heinemann. An eloquent critique of modern, sub-divided, de-personalized labour and its implications for leisure, mental health, and future social developments. Friedmann urges the elimination of 'atomized' jobs and the extension of 'job enlargement'—a cry receiving renewed emphasis today under the name of 'job enrichment'.

FRIEDMANN, G. (1964). *Industrial Society: The Emergence of the Human Problems of Automation.* New York: The Free Press. A valuable study which traces the rationalization and increasing sub-division of labour from Taylorism onward. Themes covered include fatigue, work environment, accidents, monotony, and the Human Relations movement.

FRIEDMANN, W. (1964). *Law in a Changing Society.* Harmondsworth: Penguin. A useful introduction to the impact of social change on law—mainly English, though there are comparative observations. Particularly relevant is the chapter on 'Contract', which shows how this legal concept embodies social ideologies of some significance for power relations.

GALBRAITH, J. K. (1962). *The Affluent Society.* Harmondsworth: Penguin. Valuable in presenting a perceptive and highly critical view of the post-war society within which the industrial organization operates—its dominant values and preferences and the interests that support them and help to shape men's attitudes to work and production.

GALBRAITH, J. K. (1969). *The New Industrial State.* Harmondsworth: Penguin.

GALENSON, W. (1940). *Rival Unionism in the United States.* New York: American Council on Public Affairs.

GALENSON, W.; LIPSET, S. M. (eds.) (1960). *Labor and Trade Unionism: An Interdisciplinary Reader.* New York: Wiley & Sons.

GARBARINO, J. W. (1969). 'Managing Conflict in Industrial Relations: U.S. Experience and Current Issues in Britain'. *British Journal of Industrial Relations,* VII (3): 317-335.

GERTH, H. H.; MILLS, C. W. (eds.) (1946). *From Max Weber: Essays in Sociology.* New York: Oxford University Press. Contains the classic essays on discipline, power and authority.

GIDDENS, A. (1968). 'Power in the Recent Writings of Talcott Parsons'. *Sociology,* 2 (3): 257-272. A description and a critique.

GINSBERG, M. (ed.) (1959). *Law and Opinion in England in the Twentieth Century.* London: Stevens.

GINZBERG, E.; BERG, I. E. (1963). *Democratic Values and the Rights of Management.* New York: Columbia University Press. An important contribution to the debate on managerial prerogative.

GIUGNI, G. (1965). 'Recent developments in collective bargaining in Italy' in *International Labour Review,* 91 (4): 273-291. Also in FLANDERS (ed.) (1969): pp. 267-285.

GLASER, B. G. (1963). 'The Local-Cosmopolitan Scientists'. *American Journal of Sociology,* LXIX (3): 249-259.

GOLDHAMER, H.; SHILS, E. A. (1939). 'Types of Power and Status'. *American Journal of Sociology,* XLV (2): 171-182. Also in COSER and ROSENBERG (1966), pp. 134-143; DUBIN (1961), pp. 247-252. A classic paper that has proved influential in the debate on the nature of power.

GOLDTHORPE, J. H. (1964). 'Social Stratification in Industrial Society' in HALMOS (1964), pp. 97–122. Also in BENDIX and LIPSET (1967), pp. 648–659.

GOLDTHORPE, J. H. (1966). 'Attitudes and Behaviour of Car Assembly Workers: A Deviant Case and a Theoretical Critique'. *British Journal of Sociology,* XVII (3): 227–244. Argues that previous attempts to explain work behaviour focused exclusively on the exigencies of the technology and the organizational structure, and left out of account the orientations that men bring to their employment and how these determined their 'definition of the situation'.

GOLDTHORPE, J. H.; LOCKWOOD, D.; BECHHOFER, F.; PLATT, J. (1968a). *The Affluent Worker: Industrial Attitudes and Behaviour.* Cambridge: Cambridge University Press. By-product of a larger project aimed at testing empirically the idea that manual workers and their families are being assimilated into a middle-class pattern of life. Employees of three major industrial concerns in Luton are studied in the light of their work experience and their relations with workmates, with company, and with trade unions. The findings stress their largely instrumental orientations to work, and emphasize a 'social action' approach which recognizes the importance of work orientations as against 'technological determinism' in explaining industrial behaviour. Certain implications for industrial sociology are considered.

GOLDTHORPE, J. H.; LOCKWOOD, D.; BECHHOFER, F.; PLATT, J. (1968b). *The Affluent Worker: Political Attitudes and Behaviour.* Cambridge: Cambridge University Press.

GOLDTHORPE, J. H.; LOCKWOOD, D.; BECHHOFER, F.; PLATT, J. (1969a). *The Affluent Worker in the Class Structure.* Cambridge: Cambridge University Press.

GOLDTHORPE, J. H. (1969b). 'Social Inequality and Social Integration in Modern Britain'. *Advancement of Science,* December, 1969: 190–202.

GOODMAN, J. F. B. (1967). 'Strikes in the United Kingdom: recent statistics and trends'. *International Labour Review,* 95 (5) 465–481.

GORZ, A. (1964). 'Trade Unionism on the Attack'. *International Socialist Journal.* April, 1964.

GOTTSCHALK, A. W.; WHITTINGHAM, T. G.; WILLIAMS, N. (1969). *British Industrial Relations: An Annotated Bibliography.* University of Nottingham, Department of Adult Education. A most useful compilation which, despite its title, includes a section on 'Comparative Industrial Relations'.

GOULDNER, A. W. (1955). *Patterns of Industrial Bureaucracy.* London, Routledge and Kegan Paul. A classic of the literature which (a) offers a case study of a management change leading to increased bureaucratization, and (b) presents a theoretical framework which elaborates certain Weberian ideas on bureaucracy; postulating the three types of 'representative', 'punishment centred', and 'mock' bureaucracy and applying them to the data.

GOULDNER, A. W. (1957). 'Cosmopolitans and Locals'. *Administrative Science Quarterly,* 2 (3): 281–306. Also in LITTERER (1969), Vol. 1, pp. 223–238.

GRANICK, D. (1961). *The Red Executive: A Study of the Organization Man in Russian Industry.* New York: Doubleday. A readily-available study of considerable interest as one perspective on its subject. It covers the Russian manager, his education and background; the nature of Russian industrial bureaucracy and business control; the position of labour and the trade unions; and a study of management techniques in the factory. Comparisons are drawn with America and similarities are seen to be numerous—and to include, for example, restrictive practices by workers. A short reading of works in English is added.

GREENBERG, C. (1958). 'Work and Leisure under Industrialism' in LARRABEE and MEYERSOHN (1958). Also in *Commentary,* 16 (1): 57–61; WALKER (1962), pp. 437–442.

GROSS, E. (1958). *Work and Society.* New York: Cromwell. A considerable study covering the professions and professional styles of life.

GUEST, R. H. (1962). *Organizational Change: The Effect of Successful Leadership.* London: Tavistock. Study of a large industrial plant which, over a period of three years, measurably improved its performance following the appointment of a new manager, who initiated changes in interaction and communication patterns.

Techniques of participation and consultation brought about greater satisfaction among subordinates in a complex hierarchy.

HABER, s. (1964). *Efficiency and Uplift: Scientific Management in the Progressive Era 1890–1920*. Chicago: University of Chicago Press. A useful study of one aspect of the secularized gospel of work and efficiency—its expression in the form of scientific management.

HABER, w. (ed.) (1966). *Labor in a Changing America*. New York: Basic Books.

HAGEN, EVERETT E. (1965). 'Some Implications of Personality Theory for the Theory of Industrial Relations'. *Industrial and Labor Relations Review*, 18 (3): 339–351.

HAIRE, M. (ed.) (1959). *Modern Organization Theory*. New York: Wiley & Sons.

HAIRE, M.; GHISELLI, E. E.; PORTER, L. W. (1963). 'Cultural Patterns in the Role of the Manager'. *Industrial Relations*, 2 (2): 95–117. Also in WEBBER (1969), pp. 325–341. See also HAIRE *et al.* (1966).

HAIRE, M.; GHISELLI, E. E.; PORTER, L. W. (1966). *Managerial Thinking: An International Study*. New York: Wiley & Sons. An elaboration of HAIRE *et al.* (1963).

HALMOS, P. (ed.) (1964). *The Development of Industrial Societies*. Sociological Review Monograph No. 8, University of Keele.

HANDYSIDE, J. D.; SPEAK, M. (1964). 'Job Satisfaction: Myths and Realities'. *British Journal of Industrial Relations*, 11 (1): 57–68.

HARBISON, F. H. (1954). 'Collective Bargaining and American Capitalism' in KORN-HAUSER, DUBIN and ROSS, 1954, pp. 270–279.

HARBISON, F.; MYERS, C. A. (eds.) (1959). *Management in the Industrial World: An International Analysis*. New York: McGraw-Hill. Management in twelve countries examined as an economic resource, as an elite, and as a system of authority. Useful in illustrating the influence of cultural values and norms on management philosophies and work relations.

HARRINGTON, M. (1962). *The Other America*. New York: Macmillan. The book that 'rediscovered' poverty in America.

HARRIS, A. I.; CLAUSEN, R. (1966). *Labour Mobility in Great Britain*. Government Social Survey, London: H.M.S.O.

HAYEK, F. A. (1960). 'The Corporation in a Democratic Society: In Whose Interest Ought it and Will it be Run?' in ANSHEN and BACH (1960), pp. 99–117. Also in ANSOFF (1969), pp. 225–239.

HAYWARD, J. E. S. (1969). 'The Reduction of Working Hours and France's Fifth Plan'. *British Journal of Industrial Relations*, VII (1): 84–112.

HEALY, J. J. (ed.) (1965). *Creative Collective Bargaining: Meeting Today's Challenges to Labor-Management Relations*. Englewood Cliffs (N.J.): Prentice-Hall. An account of labour-management situations in which the negotiating parties have attempted to be institutionally inventive. The nature of 'traditional' bargaining is described; the challenges being presented are analysed; and an attempt is made to define the essential features of some of the more creative efforts at meeting those challenges.

HEARNSHAW, L. S. (1954). 'Attitudes to Work'. *Occupational Psychology*, 28 (3): 129–139. General survey with a useful bibliography.

HENEMAN, H. G. *et al.* (1960). *Employment Relations Research: A Summary and Appraisal*. New York: Harper and Row. A valuable survey of the issues and the literature.

HENNING, D. (1968). 'A Theory of Non-Financial Controls' in DUBIN (ed.) (1968), pp. 425–427.

HERZBERG, F.; MAUSNER, B.; PETERSON, R.; CAPWELL, D. (1957). *Job Attitudes: Review of Research and Opinion*. Psychological Service of Pittsburgh. A useful critical analysis of many books and articles about job attitudes and their relationships to productivity.

HERZBERG, F.; MAUSNER, B.; SNYDERMAN, B. (1959). *The Motivation to Work*. New York: Wiley & Sons. Puts forward the 'motivation-hygiene' concept of job attitudes and tests it empirically on 200 engineers and accountants.

HERZBERG, F. (1968). *Work and the Nature of Man*. London: Staples Press. An elaboration in both theoretical and empirical terms (documenting replications from many countries) of the motivation-hygiene concept of job attitudes. Despite being somewhat fancifully deployed in biblical dress, the essential notion has proved a stimulating contribution to the debate.

HILL, J. M. M.; TRIST, E. L. (1962). *Industrial Accidents, Sickness and Other Absences*. London: Tavistock. Suggests that absence phenomena, including accidents, reflect the quality of the relationship between the individual and the organization.

HOBHOUSE, L. T. (1911). *Liberalism*. London: Oxford University Press. A classic statement of liberal ideals, useful in this context as identifying the cultural tradition which stresses full development of the individual personality—a key notion in 'self-actualization'.

HOLLANDER, E. P.; HUNT, R. G. (eds.) (1967). *Current Perspectives in Social Psychology*. New York: Oxford University Press.

HOLLOWELL, P. G. (1968). *The Lorry Driver*. London: Routledge and Kegan Paul. In the course of exploring the life of the lorry-driver, puts forward a theoretical framework for examining alienation in work.

HOPPOCK, R. (1935). *Job Satisfaction*. New York: Harper and Row. The first full-length book on job satisfaction. More subtle in its perceptions than many of the empirical studies which followed it.

HOROWITZ, I. L. (ed.) (1965). *The New Sociology*. New York: Oxford University Press.

HOXIE, R. F. (1920). *Trade Unionism in the United States*. New York: Appleton-Century. A classic of the early literature which can still offer much insight.

HUGHES, E. C. (1959). 'The Study of Occupations' in MERTON, BROOM and COTTRELL (1959), pp. 442–458.

HUGHES, J. (1968). *Membership Participation and Trade Union Government*. Research Paper 5, Part 2, Royal Commission on Trade Unions and Employers' Associations. London: H.M.S:O.

HUMPHREYS, B. V. (1958). *Clerical Unions in the Civil Service*. Oxford: Blackwell. The index of this historical study offers examples (under 'Political activity') of the use of political pressures in the interests of job regulation.

HUNTER, L. C.; REID, G. L. (1968). *Urban Worker Mobility*. Paris: O.E.C.D.

HYMAN, H. H. (1967). 'The Value Systems of Different Classes' in BENDIX and LIPSET (1967), pp. 488–499. A social-psychological perspective, with many useful references, on the analysis of stratification and class aspirations.

INGHAM, G. K. (1967). 'Organizational Size, Orientation to Work and Industrial Behaviour'. *Sociology,* 1 (3): 239–258. Another exploration into the importance of orientations to work. A high level of attachment to the organization (measured by absenteeism and turnover) is seen as a result of congruence between orientations and organizational control structure.

INKELES, A.; BAUER, R. A. (1959). *The Soviet Citizen: Daily Life in a Totalitarian Society*. Cambridge (Mass.): Harvard University Press.

INTERNATIONAL LABOUR OFFICE (1962). *Workers' Management in Yugoslavia*. Geneva. The most thorough and conscientious account available in English, with a detailed examination of the literature supplemented by field research.

JASINSKI, F. J. (1968). 'Use and Misuse of Efficiency Controls' in DUBIN (ed.) (1968), pp. 437–442.

JAQUES, E. (1951). *The Changing Culture of a Factory*. London: Tavistock.

KAHN-FREUND, O. (1954a). 'Legal Framework' in FLANDERS and CLEGG (1954), pp. 42–127. This describes the legal setting of industrial relations in Britain as it was in 1954. Although to some extent overtaken by subsequent developments, it still offers great insight into the place of law in the British system.

KAHN-FREUND, O. (1954b). 'Intergroup Conflicts and Their Settlement'. *British Journal of Sociology,* V (3): 193–227. Also in FLANDERS (ed.) (1969), pp. 59–85. An important and stimulating paper.

KAHN-FREUND, O. (1959). 'Labour Law' in GINSBERG (1959), pp. 215–227. Also in AUBERT (1969), pp. 80–89.

KAHN-FREUND, O. (ed.) (1965). *Labour Relations and the Law—A Comparative Study*. London: Stevens.

KAHN-FREUND, O. (1969). 'Industrial Relations and the Law—Retrospect and Prospect'. *British Journal of Industrial Relations*, VII (3): 301–316. A powerful piece of analysis prompted by the Report of the Royal Commission on Trade Unions and Employers' Association, of which the author was a member.

KASSALOW, E. M. *et al.* (1965). 'A Symposium: Professional and White-Collar Unionism: An International Comparison'. *Industrial Relations*, 5 (1): 37–150.

KATZ, D. (1954). 'Satisfactions and Deprivations in Industrial Life' in KORNHAUSER, DUBIN and ROSS (1954), pp. 86–106. A useful survey of the themes and issues involved.

KATZ, D.; KAHN, R. L. (1966). *The Social Psychology of Organizations*. New York: Wiley & Sons. Offers a theoretical framework based on 'open-system' theory which emphasizes the close relationship between a structure and its supporting environment. This requires a concern with 'inputs', 'through-put' and 'outputs'. The conceptual categories and general approach owe much to Parsons. Among the important themes dealt with are organizational effectiveness, organizational roles, power and authority, communications, decision-making, leadership, and organizational change.

KERR, C. (1954). 'Industrial Conflict and its Mediation'. *American Journal of Sociology*, LX (3): 230–245. Also in KERR (1964), pp. 167–200. Explores the nature of industrial conflict; argues that it serves important social functions; analyses responses to conflict; and distinguishes between, and evaluates, two different types of mediation, 'tactical' and 'strategic'.

KERR, C. (1964). *Labour and Management in Industrial Society*. New York: Doubleday. A useful collection which brings together some of his best-known papers.

KERR, C.; DUNLOP, J. T.; HARBISON, F. H.; MYERS, C. A. (1962). *Industrialism and Industrial Man*. London: Heinemann.

KERR, C.; FISHER, L. H. (1957). 'Plant Sociology: The Elite and the Aborigines' in KOMAROVSKY (1957), pp. 281–309. Also in KERR (1964), pp. 43–82. A valuable discussion (a) of the dangers of limiting inquiry to the work organization and ignoring the external environment, and (b) of the values of the 'plant sociology' school (Mayo, Whitehead, Whyte, and Homans being prominently treated). This is an important contribution towards enlarging the horizons and perceptions of students of industrial sociology.

KILBRIDGE, M. D. (1961). 'Turnover, Absence, and Transfer Rates as Indicators of Employee Dissatisfaction with Repetitive Work'. *Industrial and Labor Relations Review*, 15 (1): 21–32.

KLEIN, L. (1964). *Multiproducts Ltd: A Case Study on the Social Effects of Rationalized Production*. London: H.M.S.O. The application of work study and other 'scientific management' techniques in an engineering factory is analysed in terms of their impact on operators and management—'two societies', each with its own norms of behaviour, preoccupations, interests and values.

KLEINGARTNER, A. (1968). 'The Organization of White-Collar Workers'. *British Journal of Industrial Relations*, VI (1): 79–93.

KNOWLES, K. G. J. C. (1952). *Strikes—A Study of Industrial Conflict*. Oxford: Blackwell. A standard text on its subject.

KOMAROVSKY, M. (ed.) (1957). *Common Frontiers of the Social Sciences*. Glencoe (Illinois): The Free Press.

KORNHAUSER, A.; DUBIN, R.; ROSS, A. M. (eds.) (1954). *Industrial Conflict*. New York: McGraw-Hill. An invaluable source comprising 40 original contributions by prominent writers, under five major heads—Basic Issues; Roots of Industrial Conflict; Dealing with Industrial Conflict; Industrial Conflict in Other Societies (Britain, Germany, Russia and Sweden); and Industrial Conflict: Present and Future. Many of the contributions are on the societal rather than the organizational level, and are specially useful in this context for that very reason.

KORNHAUSER, A. (1954). 'Human Motivations Underlying Industrial Conflict' in KORN-HAUSER, DUBIN and ROSS (1954), pp. 62–85. A valuable statement which fully locates the organization within its social and cultural setting, and views employee aspirations from both a psychological and a sociological perspective.

KORNHAUSER, A. (1965). *Mental Health of the Industrial Worker*. New York: Wiley & Sons. An important study based on industry in Detroit, which brings mental health criteria to bear upon the psychological effects of machine industry on workers at all skill levels. The outstanding finding is that mental health varies consistently with the level of jobs the men hold. Kornhauser claims to demonstrate that this relationship cannot be explained away as due to self-selection or other extraneous factors. This is but one facet, however, of a large body of findings on the worker's orientations to his job, to his union, to his leisure, and to social and political issues of many kinds.

KORNHAUSER, W.; HAGSTROM, W. O. (1962). *Scientists in Industry*. Berkeley (Cal.): California University Press.

KUHN, J. W. (1961). *Bargaining in Grievance Settlement: The Power of Industrial Work Groups*. New York: Columbia University Press. A perceptive study in American work-group bargaining behaviour, focusing on the 'fractional' shop-floor bargaining of the sort now also widespread in many sections of British industry. It also analyses the pressures of conflicting goals upon the different levels of management, showing how 'collusion' with work groups may take place to the detriment of top management goals.

LANDSBERGER, H. A. (1958). *Hawthorne Revisited*. Ithaca (New York): Cornell University Press. Along with CAREY (1967), KERR and FISHER (1957), and BARITZ (1965), indispensable for forming a judgement on the Hawthorne investigations and their conclusions about worker motivations.

LARRABEE, E.; MEYERSOHN, R. (eds.) (1958). *Mass Leisure*. Glencoe (Illinois): The Free Press.

LASLETT, P.; RUNCIMAN, W. G. (eds.) (1967). *Philosophy, Politics and Society,* Third Series. Oxford: Blackwell.

LAWRENCE, P. R.; LORSCH, J. (1967). *Organization and Environment*. Cambridge (Mass.): Harvard University. An important book which shows how the characteristics of an organization's various sub-environments affect internal structure and behaviour.

LEAVITT, H. (ed.) (1963). *The Social Science of Organizations*. Englewood Cliffs (N.J.): Prentice-Hall.

LEVINSON, H. M. (1966). *Determining Forces in Collective Wage Bargaining*. New York: Wiley & Sons.

LIKERT, R. (1961). *New Patterns of Management*. New York: McGraw-Hill.

LIPSET, S. M. (1961). 'Trade Unions and the Social Structure: I'. *Industrial Relations,* 1 (1): 75–89.

LIPSET, S. M. (1962). 'Trade Unions and the Social Structure: II'. *Industrial Relations,* 1 (2): 89–110.

LIPSET, S. M.; BENDIX, R. (1959). *Social Mobility in Industrial Society*. London: Heinemann.

LIPSET, S. M.; TROW, M. A.; COLEMAN, J. S. (1956). *Union Democracy: The Internal Politics of the International Typographical Union*. Glencoe (Illinois): Free Press. A classic of the literature which, in the process of exploring the reasons for the well-known I.T.U. exception to Michels' 'Iron Law of Oligarchy', offers great insight into many other aspects of the printer's role that are relevant to this essay—orientations to work, craft norms and values, the influences of industrial and job structure etc.

LIPSET, S. M.; TROW, M. (1957). 'Reference Group Theory and Trade Union Wage Policy' in KOMAROVSKY (1957).

LITTERER, J. A. (ed.) (1969). *Organizations,* Second Edition. Vol. 1, *Structure and Behavior;* Vol. 2, *Systems, Control, and Adaptation*. New York: Wiley & Sons. A valuable collection of readings.

LIVERNASH, E. R. (1957). 'The Internal Wage Structure' in TAYLOR and PIERSON (1957), pp. 140–172.

LOCKWOOD, D. (1958). *The Blackcoated Worker: A Study in Class Consciousness.* London: Allen and Unwin. Argues that the development of class consciousness and trade unionism among clerks has reflected the major changes in their economic position, social status, and total work situation.

LUKES, S. (1967). 'Alienation and Anomie' in LASLETT and RUNCIMAN (1967), pp. 134–156. An incisive analysis of Marx's concept of alienation and Durkheim's of anomie. Indispensable for anyone seeking order out of conceptual chaos.

LUPTON, T. (1963). *On the Shop Floor.* Oxford: Pergamon Press. Compares two widely-differing work situations in terms of job structure and work flow, the social relationships which they create, and the opportunities and incentives they give to the growth of collective control. These structures and processes are seen in the context of such external factors as industrial structure, cost structure, and the characteristics of product and labour markets.

LYMAN, E. (1955). 'Occupational Differences and the Value Attached to Work'. *American Journal of Sociology,* 61 (2): 138–144.

MCAULEY, M. (1969). *Labour Disputes in Soviet Russia, 1957–1965.* Oxford: Clarendon Press.

MCCARTHY, W. E. J. (1964). *The Closed Shop in Britain.* Oxford: Blackwell.

MCCARTHY, W. E. J. (1966). *The Role of Shop Stewards in British Industrial Relations.* Research Paper 1, Royal Commission on Trade Unions and Employers' Associations. London, H.M.S.O.

MCCARTHY, W. E. J. (1967). *A Survey of Employers' Association Officials.* Research Paper 7, Royal Commission on Trade Unions and Employers' Associations. London: H.M.S.O.

MCCARTHY, W. E. J.; PARKER, S. R. (1968). *Shop Stewards and Workshop Relations.* Research Paper 10, Royal Commission on Trade Unions and Employers' Associations. London: H.M.S.O.

MCCORMICK, B. J. (1969). *Wages.* Harmondsworth: Penguin.

MCCORMICK, B. J.; SMITH, E. O. (eds.) (1968). *The Labour Market.* Harmondsworth: Penguin. A useful collection of readings covering the demand, supply and allocation of labour, trade unions, bargaining theory, unemployment, full employment and inflation, and labour's share in the national income.

MACDONALD, R. M. (1963). *Collective Bargaining in the Automobile Industry: A Study of Wage Structure and Competitive Relations.* New Haven: Yale University Press.

MCGREGOR, D. (1960). *The Human Side of Enterprise.* New York: McGraw-Hill. Contains his exposition of 'Theory X' and 'Theory Y' assumptions about men's orientations to work. Has an influential place in the self-actualization literature.

MALLET, S. (1963) *La Nouvelle Classe Ouvrière.* Paris: Editions du Seuil.

MANN, F. C. (1962). 'Psychological and Organizational Impacts' in DUNLOP (1962), pp. 43–65.

MANNHEIM, K. (1960). *Ideology and Utopia.* New York: Harcourt Brace. Chapters 1 and 2 offer particularly useful insight into the nature of ideology.

MARCH, J. G. (ed.) (1965). *Handbook of Organizations.* Chicago: Rand McNally. A mammoth work in which thirty-one distinguished contributors bring to the study of organizations the disciplines of sociology, economics, psychology, political science, and industrial administration. This comprehensive reference source covers structure, influence, growth, and development, exploring theories and methodologies relating to all aspects of organizational and interpersonal behaviour.

MARCH, J. G.; SIMON, H. A. (1958). *Organizations.* New York: Wiley & Sons. A widely-read and influential work based on a 'behavioural' approach: i.e. that propositions about organizations are statements about human behaviour. A wide range of published material is distilled into a series of inter-related propositions.

MARRIS, R. (1964). *The Economic Theory of Managerial Capitalism.* New York: The Free Press.

MARSH, A. (1965). *Industrial Relations in Engineering.* Oxford: Pergamon Press.

MARSH, A. I. (1966). *Disputes Procedures in British Industry.* Research Paper 2 (Part 1), Royal Commission on Trade Unions and Employers' Associations. London: H.M.S.O.

MARSH, A. I.; MCCARTHY, W. E. J. (1968). *Disputes Procedures in Britain.* Research Paper 2 (Part 2), Royal Commission on Trade Unions and Employers' Associations. London: H.M.S.O.

MARSHALL, T. H. (1950). *Citizenship and Social Class.* Cambridge: Cambridge University Press.

MARTIN, R. (1968). 'Union Democracy: an explanatory framework'. *Sociology,* 2 (2): 205–220.

MASLOW, A. H. (1954). *Motivation and Personality.* New York: Harper and Row. Contains his theory of the 'hierarchy of needs', which has played an important part in the arguments of the self-actualization school.

MASLOW, A. H. (1965). *Eupsychian Management.* Homewood (Illinois): Irwin and The Dorsey Press. Philosophical jottings which elaborate the concept of self-actualization and at the same time qualify its applicability.

MAYNTZ, R. (1966). *The Study of Organizations: A Trend Report and Bibliography.* Oxford: Blackwell (*Current Sociology,* Vol. XIII, No. 3, 1964). An extremely useful trend report of 25 pages, followed by 30 pages of bibliography.

MAYO, E. (1933). *The Human Problems of an Industrial Civilization.* New York: Macmillan.

MAYO, E. (1945). *The Social Problems of an Industrial Civilization.* Cambridge (Mass.): Harvard University Press.

MEIJ, J. L. (ed.) (1963). *Internal Wage Structure.* Amsterdam: North-Holland Publishing Co.

MERTON, R. K. (1957). *Social Theory and Social Structure.* Glencoe (Illinois): Free Press.

MERTON, R. K. (1966). 'Social Problems and Sociological Theory' in MERTON and NISBET, (1966), pp. 775–823.

MERTON, R. K.; BROOM, L.; COTTRELL, S. L (eds.) (1959). *Sociology Today: Problems and Prospects.* New York: Basic Books.

MERTON, R. K.; GRAY, A. P.; HOCKEY, B.; SELVIN, H. C. (eds.) (1952). *Reader in Bureaucracy.* Glencoe (Illinois): Free Press. A collection of 54 papers culled from the literature, grouped under the following heads: Theoretical Conceptions, Bases for the Growth of Bureaucracy, Bureaucracy and Power Relations, The Structure of Bureaucracy, Recruitment and Advancement, The Bureaucrat, Social Pathologies of Bureaucracy, and Field Methods for Studying Bureaucracy. Writers include Weber, Gouldner, Simon, Veblen, Michels, Bendix, Selznick, Mills, Dubin, Lipset, Merton, and Mannheim. There is a 14 page bibliography.

MERTON, R. K.; NISBET, R. A. (eds.) (1966). *Contemporary Social Problems,* 2nd ed. New York: Harcourt Brace.

MEYERS, F. (1965). 'The Role of Collective Bargaining in France: The Case of Unemployment Insurance'. *British Journal of Industrial Relations,* 3 (3): 363–391.

MICHELS, R. (1959). *Political Parties.* New York: Dover Publications.

MIERNYK, W. H. (1962). *Trade Unions in the Age of Affluence.* New York: Random House.

MILLER, E. J.; RICE, A. K. (1967). *Systems of Organization.* London: Tavistock. Tavistock researchers have looked for forms of work organization which provide a closer match between 'task' and 'human need'. Miller and Rice now suggest that this approach has limitations, and explore the implications for organizational theory and practice, using case-studies in sales-force organizations, a dry-cleaning enterprise, a family production business, a steel works, a research unit, and an airline.

MILLS, C. W. (1948). *New Men of Power: America's Labor Leaders.* New York: Harcourt Brace.

MILLS, C. W. (1956). *White Collar.* New York: Oxford University Press. A sociological analysis of the new middle classes in America, with sections on work, status, values and ideologies.

MISHAN, E. J. (1969a). *The Costs of Economic Growth.* Harmondsworth: Penguin. Indispensable reading for anyone wishing to understand modern industrial society.

MISHAN, E. J. (1969b). *Growth: The Price We Pay*. London: Staples Press. A popular version of MISHAN (1969a).

MIZRUCHI, E. H. (1965). 'Alienation and Anomie: Theoretical and Empirical Perspectives' in HOROWITZ (1965), pp. 253–267.

MOORE, W. E. (1951). *Industrial Relations and the Social Order*, rev. ed. New York: Macmillan.

MORSE, N. G.; WEISS, R. S. (1955). 'The Function and Meaning of Work and the Job'. *American Sociological Review*, 20 (2): 191–198. A useful study of a national sample of 401 employed men at all socio-economic and occupational levels.

MOUZELIS, N. P. (1967). *Organization and Bureaucracy*. London: Routledge and Kegan Paul. Given the chaotic state of organization theory, this book could help students considerably in establishing their bearings, especially if read in conjunction with MAYNTZ (1966).

MUNNS, V. G. (1967). *The Functions and Organization of Employers' Associations in Selected Industries*. Research Paper 7, Royal Commission on Trade Unions and Employers' Associations. London: H.M.S.O.

NAGEL, J. H. (1968). 'Some Questions about the Concept of Power'. *Behavioural Science*, Vol. 13 (2), March.

NATIONAL BOARD FOR PRICES AND INCOMES. (1967). Report No. 36: *Productivity Agreements*. London: H.M.S.O., Cmnd. 3311.

NATIONAL BOARD FOR PRICES AND INCOMES. (1968). Report No. 65 and Supplement: *Payment by Results Systems*. London: H.M.S.O., Cmnd 3627 and Cmnd 3627–1. The first of these two valuable reports concerns itself with payment-by-results systems of wage payment and their influence on productivity and earnings. The second reviews the literature on the subject; reports the views of professional bodies; and offers twelve case studies.

NEAL, A. G.; RETTIG, S. (1963). 'Dimensions of Alienation among Manual and Non-Manual Workers'. *American Sociological Review*, 28 (4): 599–608. A postal questionnaire produced support for the argument put forward by SEEMAN (1959) for separation of alternative meanings of alienation.

NICHOLS, T. (1969). *Ownership, Control and Ideology*. London: Allen and Unwin.

NISBET, R. A. (1967). *The Sociological Tradition*. London: Heinemann.

NOSOW, S.; FORM, W. H. (eds.) (1962). *Man, Work, and Society; A Reader in the Sociology of Occupations*. New York: Basic Books. A valuable collection of readings.

ODAKA, K. (1963). 'Traditionalism, Democracy in Japanese Industry'. *Industrial Relations*, 3 (1): 95–103.

PALMER, G. L. (1960). 'Contrasts in Labor Market Behaviour in Northern Europe and the United States'. *Industrial and Labor Relations Review*, 13 (4): 519–532.

PARKER, S. R. (1965). 'Work and Non-Work in Three Occupations'. *Sociological Review*, 13 (1): 65–75. A study of bank employees, youth employment and child care officers which relates the content and meaning of work to the content and meaning of leisure.

PARKER, S. R. (ed.) (1965). *A Bibliography of Industrial Sociology (including the Sociology of Occupations)*. London: The Polytechnic Library.

PARKER, S. R.; BROWN, R. K.; CHILD, J.; SMITH, M. A. (1967). *The Sociology of Industry*. London: Allen and Unwin. The first British book of this nature, using British illustrative material wherever possible. Part 1 examines relationships between industrial and other social institutions; Part II the internal structure of industrial organizations; and Part III the sociology of occupations and the roles of work and non-work. There are annotated suggestions for further reading.

PATTEN, T. H. (1968). *The Foreman, Forgotten Man of Management*. New York: American Management Association.

PERLMAN, R. (ed.) (1965). *Wage Determination: Market or Power Forces?* Boston: D. C. Heath.

PERLMAN, S. (1928). *A Theory of the Labor Movement*. New York: Macmillan. An early classic of the American literature.

PLAMENATZ, J. (1963). *Man and Society,* Volume 2. London: Longmans Green. In the course of 140 pages devoted to Marx, examines his views on ideology.

PRANDY, K. (1965). *Professional Employees: A Study of Scientists and Engineers.* London: Faber and Faber. Scientists and engineers are examined in terms of satisfaction with earnings, status, promotion prospects, and use made of skill; in terms of class and status consciousness and ideology; and in terms of consequent attitudes towards collective action.

PUGH, D. S.; HICKSON, D. J.; HININGS, C. R.; MACDONALD, K. M.; TURNER, C.; LUPTON, T. (1963). 'A Conceptual Scheme for Organizational Analysis'. *Administrative Science Quarterly,* 8 (3): 289–315.

PURCELL, T. V. (1953). *The Worker Speaks His Mind on Company and Union.* Cambridge (Mass.): Harvard University Press.

PYM, D. (1968). 'Individual Growth and Strategies of Trust' in PYM (ed.) (1968), pp. 316–334.

PYM, D. (ed.) (1968). *Industrial Society: Social Sciences in Management.* Harmondsworth: Penguin.

RECK, D. (1968). 'Rules, Standards, and Rationality' in DUBIN (ed.) (1968), pp. 427–430. Draws attention to the relationship between control standards and rational decision-making.

RHENMAN, E. (1968). *Industrial Democracy and Industrial Management.* London: Tavistock.

RICE, A. K. (1963). *The Enterprise and its Environment.* London: Tavistock. A case study of Indian textile mills documenting success in matching 'task requirements' with 'human and social needs'.

RIESMAN, D. (1958). 'Work and Leisure in Post-Industrial Society' in LARRABEE and MEYERSOHN (1958).

RIESMAN, D.; BLOOMBERG, W. (1957). 'Work and Leisure: Fusion or Polarity?' in ARENSBERG (1957), pp. 69–85; NOSOW and FORM (1962), pp. 35–41. A discussion based on the assumption that we cannot look at leisure without inquiring about its relation to work. Is it escape, counterpoise, or possibly the managing partner?

RITTI, R. (1968). 'Work Goals of Scientists and Engineers'. *Industrial Relations* 7 (2): 118–131.

ROBERTS, B. C. (1956). *Trade Union Government and Administration in Great Britain.* London: Bell and Sons.

ROBERTS, G. (1967). *Demarcation Rules in Shipbuilding and Shiprepairing.* Cambridge: Cambridge University Press. Useful in exploring the origins and nature of demarcation rules in a specific industrial milieu, and the social mechanisms through which the affected parties have sought to achieve normative agreement on them.

ROBINSON, O. (1969). 'Representation of the White-Collar Worker: The Bank Staff Associations in Britain'. *British Journal of Industrial Relations,* VII (1): 19–41.

ROETHLISBERGER, F. J. (1942). *Management and Morale.* Cambridge (Mass.): Harvard University Press.

ROETHLISBERGER, F. J. (1945). 'The Foreman: Master and Victim of Double Talk'. *Harvard Business Review,* XXIII (3): 285–294. Also in DUBIN (1961), pp. 209–217.

ROETHLISBERGER, F. J.; DICKSON, W. J. (1939). *Management and the Worker.* Cambridge (Mass.): Harvard University Press. The detailed account of the Hawthorne investigations on which such a vast amount of theorizing, experimentation, personnel policy, and conventional wisdom came subsequently to be based.

ROLPH, C. H. (1962). *All Those in Favour? An Account of the High Court Action Against the Electrical Trades Union and its Officers for Ballot-Rigging in the Election of Union Officials.* London: Andre Deutsch.

ROSE, A. M. (ed.) (1962). *Human Behavior and Social Processes.* Boston: Houghton Mifflin.

ROSS, A. M. (1962). 'Prosperity and Labor Relations in Western Europe: Italy and France'. *Industrial and Labor Relations Review,* 16 (1): 63–85. Includes comments on recent developments in collective bargaining in these countries.

ROSS, A. M. (1966). 'Work and Leisure in the Round of Life' in HABER (1966).

ROSS, A. M.; HARTMAN, P. T. (1960). *Changing Patterns of Industrial Conflict.* New York:

Wiley & Sons. The authors use their own analytical framework for interpreting the twentieth-century experience of fifteen countries, seeking to explain national trends and international differences in the frequency and duration of industrial disputes. In the process they include data on the trade union structure and collective bargaining systems of the countries concerned.

ROSS, N. S. (1969). *Constructive Conflict*. Edinburgh: Oliver and Boyd.

ROSTOW, W. W. (1954). *The Dynamics of Soviet Society*. New York: Mentor Books.

ROSTOW, W. W. (1963). *The Stages of Economic Growth*. Cambridge: Cambridge University Press.

ROWTHORN, B. (1967). 'Unions and the Economy' in BLACKBURN and COCKBURN (1967), pp. 210–227.

ROY, D. F. (1954). 'Efficiency and "The Fix"; Informal Intergroup Relations in a Piecework Machine Shop'. *American Journal of Sociology*, LX (3): 255–266. Also in LITTERER (1969), Vol. 1, pp. 204–214. Describes work-group manipulations of a piecework system of payment.

ROYAL COMMISSION ON TRADE UNIONS AND EMPLOYERS' ASSOCIATIONS. (1967). Research Paper 4: *Productivity Bargaining: Restrictive Labour Practices*. London: H.M.S.O.

RUBNER, A. (1966). *The Ensnared Shareholder*. Harmondsworth: Penguin. The doyen of shareholders' rights argues that too many directorial boards fail in their duty by pursuing other objectives than profit maximization and by not distributing the largest possible dividend. In the course of his arguments he casts useful light on the nature of top management goals.

RUNCIMAN, W. G. (1966). *Relative Deprivation and Social Justice*. London: Routledge and Kegan Paul. Drawing upon the notions of relative deprivation and reference group, Runciman examines attitudes to social inequality in twentieth-century England. The book's relevance to the present essay lies in its demonstration of the dynamics of aspirations—though on a societal, not an organizational, level.

SAYLES, L. R. (1958). *Behavior of Industrial Work Groups*. New York: Wiley & Sons. A much-quoted study which argues that 'the way jobs are distributed and flow into one another and the nature of the division of labour' mould the types of work groups that evolve and their modes of conflict-behaviour.

SCHEIN, E. (1965). *Organizational Psychology*. Englewood Cliffs (N.J.): Prentice-Hall. A useful introductory survey containing a critical evaluation of the various assumptions made by management about men's orientations to work.

SCHNEIDER, E. V. (1957). *Industrial Sociology: The Social Relations of Industry and the Community*. New York: McGraw-Hill. A well-known introductory text, drawing mainly on American experience and sources.

SCHULTZ, G. P.; WEBER, A. (1960). 'Technological Change and Industrial Relations' in HENEMAN *et al.* (1960), pp. 190–221. Specially useful for a list of references on the impact of technological change on employees, organization structure, labour relations and local community.

SCOTT, M. B. (1965). 'The Social Sources of Alienation' in HOROWITZ (1965), pp. 239–252.

SCOTT, W. G. (1965). *The Management of Conflict: Appeal Systems in Organizations*. Homewood (Illinois): Irwin and the Dorsey Press. An interesting study of formal judicial systems created and operated unilaterally by management to give organizational members an avenue of appeal when they think they have been treated unjustly.

SCOTT, W. H.; BANKS, J. A.; HALSEY, A. H.; LUPTON, T. (1956). *Technical Change and Industrial Relations*. Liverpool: Liverpool University Press. A study of the relations between technical change and social structure in a large steel plant in Britain.

SCOTT, W. H.; MUMFORD, E.; MCGIVERING, I. C.; KIRKBY, J. M. (1963). *Coal and Conflict*. Liverpool: Liverpool University Press. A comparative investigation of four mines in the Lancashire coalfield. It describes the particular problems of the main occupational groups, and relates them to an assessment of morale, based on a wide variety of indices.

SEEMAN, M. (1959). 'On the Meaning of Alienation'. *American Sociological Review*, 24 (6): 783–791. Also in COSER and ROSENBERG (1966), pp. 525–538. A much-quoted article on which a considerable amount of theoretical and empirical work has been based.

SEEMAN, M. (1967). 'On the Personal Consequences of Alienation in Work'. *American Sociological Review*, 32 (2): 273–285.

SELZNICK, P. (1966). *TVA and the Grass Roots*. New York: Harper and Row. At one level, a sophisticated analysis of the TVA's methods and policies; on another, a fruitful exploration of the way men behave in a bureaucracy.

SHEPARD, J. M. (1970). 'Functional Specialization, Alienation, and Job Satisfaction'. *Industrial and Labor Relations Review*, 23 (2): 207–219.

SHIBUTANI, T. (1955). 'Reference Groups as Perspectives'. *American Journal of Sociology*, LX (6): 562–570. Also in HOLLANDER and HUNT (1967), pp. 74–83. An introduction to the concept of the reference group in its varying usages.

SHIBUTANI, T. (1962). 'Reference Groups and Social Control' in ROSE (1962), pp. 128–147.

SHILS, E. A. (1961). 'Georges Sorel: Introduction to the American Edition' in SOREL (1961), pp. 11–25

SHONFIELD, A. (1965). *Modern Capitalism*. London: Oxford University Press.

SHUCHMAN, A. (1957). *Codetermination: Labor's Middle Way in Germany*. Washington: Public Affairs Press.

SILVERMAN, D. (1968). 'Formal Organizations or Industrial Sociology: Towards a Social Action Analysis of Organizations'. *Sociology*, 2 (2): 221–238. A discussion of functionalist and action approaches to organizational analysis. Silverman opts for a social action analysis and suggests how such an analysis might proceed.

SIMMEL, G. (1955). *Conflict*. Glencoe (Illinois): The Free Press.

SIMON, H. A. (1964). 'On the Concept of Organizational Goal'. *Administrative Science Quarterly*, 9 (1): 1–22. Also in ANSOFF (1969), pp. 240–261; ETZIONI (1969), pp. 158–174. A valuable contribution to the complex debate on the nature of so-called organizational goals, how they emerge, and how they change.

SIMON, H. A. (1965). *Administrative Behaviour*. New York: Free Press. A classic text of organization theory which is centred around the concepts of decision-making and rationality. There are important chapters also on authority, communication, and criteria of efficiency.

SIMON, H. A.; SMITHBURG, D. W.; THOMPSON, V. A. (1950). *Public Administration*. New York: Alfred A. Knopf.

SLICHTER, S. H. (1941). *Union Policies and Industrial Management*. Washington D.C.: Brookings Institution. A classic of the earlier American industrial relations literature.

SLICHTER, S. H.; HEALY, J. J.; LIVERNASH, E. R. (1960). *The Impact of Collective Bargaining on Management*. Washington D.C.: Brookings Institution. Quite impossible to summarize, this is a massive and masterly survey of the whole range of issues which can arise between management, unions, and work groups. It serves as an invaluable source of data and ideas on all aspects of the social organization of work and the goals of work groups.

SOREL, G. (1961). *Reflections on Violence*. New York: Collier Books.

SOMERS, G. G.; CUSHMAN, E. L.; WEINBERG, N. (eds.) (1963). *Adjusting to Technological Change*. New York: Harper and Row. The impact of change on labour and management, and their responses, are viewed historically and in the more recent collective bargaining agreements. Industrial adjustments are related to community and government interests, and there is a chapter on the situation in Western Europe. A useful collection.

SPENCER, P.; SOFER, C. (1964). 'Organizational Change and its Management'. *Journal of Management Studies*, 1 (1): 128–142. A useful review of the organizational literature concerned with organizational change and flexibility.

SPIRO, H. J. (1958). *The Politics of German Codetermination*. Cambridge (Mass.): Harvard University Press.

STEIN, M.; VIDICH, A. (eds.) (1963). *Sociology on Trial*. Englewood Cliffs (N.J.): Prentice-Hall.

STRAUSS, G. (1963). 'Some Notes on Power-Equalization' in LEAVITT (1963), pp. 41–84. A useful critical survey of the 'personality-versus-organization' controversy.

STRAUSS, G. (1964). 'Professional or Employee-Oriented: Dilemma for Engineering Unions'. *Industrial and Labor Relations Review*, 17 (4): 519–533.

STURMTHAL, A. (ed.) (1957). *Contemporary Collective Bargaining in Seven Countries*. New York: Cornell University Press. Contributions from eight authors describe the structure and legal setting of collective bargaining in America, Britain, France, Germany, Italy, Norway and the Netherlands. The account now needs supplementing, of course, in the light of subsequent developments.

STURMTHAL, A. (ed.) (1966). *White-Collar Trade Unions*. Urbana (Illinois): University of Illinois Press. The past, present, and future of white-collar unionism in America, Britain, Japan, France, Germany, Austria, Sweden and Australia are analysed.

TAGLIACOZZO, D. L. (1956). 'Trade Union Government, Its Nature and its Problems: A Bibliographical Review, 1945–55'. *American Journal of Sociology*, LXI (6): 546–553.

TAGLIACOZZO, D. L.; SEIDMAN, J. (1956). 'A Typology of Rank-and-File Union Members'. *American Journal of Sociology*, LXI (6): 554–581.

TANNENBAUM, A. S. (1966). *Social Psychology of the Work Organization*. London: Tavistock. A useful introductory text.

TANNENBAUM, A. S. (1968). *Control in Organizations*. New York: McGraw-Hill. An important collection of research-based papers concerned with the processes of power and influence within organizations. The organizations explored include industrial and business firms, trade unions, voluntary associations and colleges. Contains many useful references.

TANNENBAUM, F. (1951). *A Philosophy of Labour*. New York: Alfred A. Knopf.

TAWNEY, R. H. (1938). *Religion and the Rise of Capitalism*. Harmondsworth: Penguin.

TAWNEY, R. H. (1961). *The Acquisitive Society*. London: Fontana. First published in 1921, this critique of the principles on which capitalist society rests is still relevant to current debate.

TAYLOR, G. W. (1961). 'Collective Bargaining in Transition' in WEBER (1961), pp. 343–358.

TAYLOR, G. W.; PIERSON, F. C. (eds.) (1957). *New Concepts in Wage Determination*. New York: McGraw-Hill.

THOMPSON, J. D. (1967). *Organizations in Action*. New York: McGraw-Hill. An important contribution to organization theory, concerned with the behaviour of organizations in their environment. Particularly useful in giving much stimulating insight into management goals. A dominant theme is uncertainty, where it arises, and how organizations seek to cope with it.

TILGHER, A. (1930). *Work: What it Has Meant to Men Through the Ages*. New York: Harcourt Brace.

TILGHER, A. (1962). 'Work Through the Ages': Extracts from the 1930 study in NOSOW and FORM (1962), pp. 11–24.

TOPHAM, T. (1967). 'New Types of Bargaining' in BLACKBURN and COCKBURN (1967), pp. 133–159.

TOURAINE, A. (1965). *Workers' Attitudes to Technical Change*. Paris: O.E.C.D. Full of very useful material on individual and trade union attitudes to technical, organizational, and social change. Change is seen as being judged in terms of the worker's total life experience—his social and economic environment, his commitments and aspirations, his view of employers and employment, and the value he puts on his working career. The theoretical framework informing the work is therefore admirably inclusive.

TRÉANTON, J-R.; REYNAUD, J-D. (1964). *Industrial Sociology 1951–62, A Trend Report and Bibliography*. (*Current Sociology*, Vol. XII, No. 2, 1963–64). Oxford: Blackwell. Ninety-one pages of annotated bibliography.

TRIST, E. L.; BAMFORTH, K. W. (1951). 'Some Social and Psychological Consequences of the Longwall Method of Coal Getting'. *Human Relations,* 4 (1): 3–38. Also in BURNS (1969), pp. 331–358; LITTERER (1969), Vol. 1, pp. 263–275. A standard early reference comparing the consequences for efficiency and job satisfaction of alternative methods of organizing coal-getting.

TRIST, E. L.; HIGGIN, G. W.; MURRAY, H.; POLLOCK, A. B. (1963). *Organizational Choice.* London: Tavistock. An important example of the Tavistock pursuit of a better 'fit' between task requirements and human and social needs. The pursuit was successful in this group of Durham coal-mines, showing that alternative modes of work organization can exist for the same technology, giving the possibility of organizational choice.

TURNER, A. N.; LAWRENCE, P. R. (1965). *Industrial Jobs and the Worker.* Cambridge (Mass.): Harvard University Press.

TURNER, H. A. (1957). 'Inflation and Wage Differentials in Great Britain' in DUNLOP (1957), pp. 123–135. Also in MCCORMICK and SMITH (1968), pp. 228–242.

TURNER, H. A. (1962). *Trade Union Growth, Structure and Policy.* London: Allen and Unwin.

TURNER, H. A. (1969). *Is Britain Really Strike-Prone?* Cambridge: Cambridge University Press.

TURNER, H. A.; CLACK, G.; ROBERTS, G. (1967). *Labour Relations in the Motor Industry.* London: Allen and Unwin. Concerned to explain the high incidence of disorder in some sections of Britain's car industry, the authors, using inter-company and international comparisons, examine and reject various explanations and put forward their own, which they claim has relevance beyond the motor industry.

VEBLEN, T. (1958). *The Theory of Business Enterprise.* New York: Mentor Books.

VENESS, T. (1962). *School Leavers.* London: Methuen. Explores the reasons for choosing a particular job, and sets up a typology of orientations which mould choice—'tradition' direction, 'inner' direction, and 'other' direction.

VITELES, M. S. (1954). *Motivation and Morale in Industry.* London: Staples Press.

VOLLMER, H. M.; MILLS, D. L. (1962). 'Nuclear Technology and the Professionalization of Labor'. *American Journal of Sociology,* LXVII (6): 690–696.

VROOM, V. H. (1964). *Work and Motivation.* New York: Wiley & Sons.

WALKER, C. R. (ed.) (1962). *Modern Technology and Civilization: An Introduction to Human Problems in the Machine Age.* New York: McGraw-Hill. A useful collection of readings.

WALKER, C. R.; GUEST, R. H. (1957). *The Man on the Assembly Line.* New Haven: Yale University Press. A classic study of the automobile worker.

WALTON, R. E.; MCKERSIE, R. B. (1965). *A Behavioural Theory of Labor Negotiations.* New York: McGraw-Hill. A powerful piece of theorizing, indispensable to students of management-labour relations.

WARD, J. W. (1964). 'The Ideal of Individualism and the Reality of Organization' in CHEIT (1964), pp. 37–76.

WEBB, S. and B. (1920). *Industrial Democracy.* London: Longmans Green. This classic of the Webbs is still an indispensable reference for anyone interested in trade union structure, government, functions, methods, and relations with other unions, the law, and society.

WEBBER, R. (ed.) (1969). *The Culture of Management: Text and Readings in Comparative Management.* Homewood (Illinois): Irwin and the Dorsey Press.

WEBER, A. (ed.) (1961). *The Structure of Collective Bargaining.* Glencoe (Illinois): The Free Press.

WEBER, M. (1930). *The Protestant Ethic and the Spirit of Capitalism.* London: Allen and Unwin.

WEBER, M. (1964). *The Theory of Social and Economic Organization.* New York: Free Press. The origins of much subsequent theorizing, teaching, and interpretation concerning the nature of bureaucracies, the social mechanisms that bind men within them, the nature and sources of authority, the functions of bureaucratic rules, and many other themes. Quite apart from his significance in the general development of sociology, Weber has often been claimed by organizational theorists as one of the founders of their discipline.

WEDDERBURN, K. W. (1965). *The Worker and the Law*. Harmondsworth: Penguin. The first full introduction to British labour law and its place in British industrial relations and society.

WEINSTEIN, P. A. (ed.) (1965). *Featherbedding and Technological Change*. Boston: D. C. Heath.

WEISS, R. S.; KAHN, R. L. (1960). 'Definitions of Work and Occupation'. *Social Problems*, 8 (2): 142–151. Explores the various meanings of work held by people in different occupations or work situations.

WEISS, R. S.; RIESMAN, D. (1966). 'Work and Automation: Problems and Prospects' in MERTON and NISBET (1966), pp. 553–618.

WELFORD, A. T.; ARGYLE, M.; GLASS, D. V.; MORRIS, J. N. (eds.) (1962). *Society: Problems and Methods of Study*. London: Routledge and Kegan Paul.

WHITE, H. (1961). 'Management Conflict and Sociometric Structure'. *American Journal of Sociology*, LXVII (2): 185–199. Analyses the organizational significance of chronic conflicts among departments of a manufacturing company regarding research and development.

WHITE, S. (1968). 'The Process of Occupational Choice'. *British Journal of Industrial Relations*, VI (2): 166–184. A useful survey of the literature dealing with sociological and psychological factors affecting occupational choice.

WHITEHILL, A. M.; TAKEZAWA, S. (1968). *The Other Worker: A Comparative Study of Industrial Relations in the United States and Japan*. Honolulu: East-West Center Press.

WHYBREW, E. G. (1968). *Overtime Working in Britain*. Research Paper 9, Royal Commission on Trade Unions and Employers' Associations. London: H.M.S.O. A study of the origins, functions, and methods of control of overtime working. Includes important data showing how workers' aspirations with respect to earnings result (a) in strong pressures being brought on lower managers to extend and maintain overtime and (b) time being wasted in order to create a need for it.

WHYTE, W. H. (1961). *The Organization Man*. Harmondsworth: Penguin. Necessary reading as the source of the concept of 'organization man' which has now become a cliché of popular discussion. Its central theme is the alleged shift away from the Protestant Ethic as the core of attitudes towards work and life generally, and towards a Social Ethic which legitimizes the pressures of the group and of society upon the individual.

WILENSKY, H. L. *et al.* (1962). 'A Symposium: Work and Leisure in Modern Society'. *Industrial Relations*, 1 (2): 1–45.

WILENSKY, H. L. (1966). 'Work as a Social Problem' in BECKER (1966).

WILLIAMS, L. K.; WHYTE, W. F.; GREEN, C. S. (1966). 'Do Cultural Differences Affect Workers' Attitudes?' *Industrial Relations*, 5 (3): 105–117.

WOLIN, S. (1960). *Politics and Vision*. Boston: Little, Brown & Co. Has relevance for the 'convergence theory' debate in that Chapters IX and X argue against the tendency to reduce all politics and government to forces arising from the socio-economic structure.

WOODWARD, J. (1965). *Industrial Organization: Theory and Practice*. London: Oxford University Press.

WOODWARD, J. (ed.) (1970). *Industrial Organization: Behaviour and Control*. London: Oxford University Press.

WOOTTON, B. (1955). *The Social Foundations of Wage Policy*. London: Allen and Unwin. Financial rewards are often seen as determining status and other forms of social valuation. Wootton explores the extent to which the reverse is true—that established social valuations determine financial rewards.

WORTHY, J. C. (1957). 'Management's Approach to Human Relations' in ARENSBERG (1957).

ZWEIG, F. (1951). *Productivity and Trade Unions*. Oxford: Blackwell. Contains a useful discussion of 'restrictive practices' and an inquiry into job rules inspired by union or work group in five major industries in Britain.

Subject Index